PENGUIN BOOKS
Brexit and Ireland

Tony Connelly has been reporting on Europe for RTÉ since 2001, firstly as Europe Correspondent, and more recently as Europe Editor. He lives in Brussels.

Brexit and Ireland

The Dangers, the Opportunities, and the
Inside Story of the Irish Response

TONY CONNELLY

PENGUIN BOOKS

PENGUIN BOOKS

UK | USA | Canada | Ireland | Australia
India | New Zealand | South Africa

Penguin Books is part of the Penguin Random House group of companies
whose addresses can be found at global.penguinrandomhouse.com.

First published by Penguin Ireland 2017
This edition published with a new final chapter in Penguin Books 2018

002

Copyright © Tony Connelly, 2017, 2018

The moral right of the author has been asserted

Printed and bound in Great Britain by Clays Ltd, Elcograf S.p.A.

A CIP catalogue record for this book is available from the British Library

ISBN: 978-0-241-98242-6

'A fatal space had opened, like that between a liner and the dock which is suddenly too wide to leap; everything is still present, visible, but it cannot be regained.'

— James Salter, *Light Years*

'I distrust anyone who foresees consequences and advocates remedies to avert them.'

— Lord Halifax, British Foreign Secretary (1938–40)

Contents

1. What Just Happened?   1
2. In the Land of Eternal Autumn   21
3. How Perishable is Ireland?   40
4. Is Kenny Available?   56
5. The New Zealand Grudge Match   83
6. The China Syndrome   101
7. Our Own Private Idaho   114
8. Is There Such a Thing as a British Fish?   130
9. Room 201   158
10. From Bjørnfjell to Svinesund   189
11. The Great Disruption   209
12. An Unpleasant Sheet of Water   233
13. Old Habits of Wariness   252
14. The Unity Play   283
15. Le Royaume Uni: Nul Points   303
16. A Red, White and Blue Brexit   321
17. The Bullet Point   345

Acknowledgements   383
Index   385

1. What Just Happened?

On the night of 23 June 2016, the mood in Number 10 was buoyant. Thirty-three million people had just voted in the referendum on whether the United Kingdom should remain in the European Union, or leave. Last-minute polling pointed to a narrow victory for Remain.

The drinks were flowing. In anticipation of some celebratory dancing, someone had curated a playlist around the theme of belonging. There was Rick Astley's 'Never Gonna Give You Up', the Human League's 'Don't You Want Me Baby?' and 'Don't Look Back in Anger' by Oasis. 'Should I Stay or Should I Go?' by the Clash, Will Young's 'Leave Right Now' and East 17's 'Stay Another Day' were added to the mix. After months of gruelling preparation, who would deny hard-working civil servants some musical irony?

This was not, it should be noted, Number 10 *Downing Street*. This Number 10 was the bar on the ground floor of the UK's embassy complex in Brussels. Officially called the UK Representation to the European Union, but most commonly referred to as UKRep, it has since 2009 occupied a formidable Art Deco building just off the Schuman roundabout in the so-called European quarter. Diagonally across the roundabout is the hulking cruciform of the European Commission – the seat of the hated EU bureaucracy, according to Brexit lore. Beyond, a parade of restaurants, cafés and bars refreshes a daily swarm of officials, lobbyists, journalists and politicians. In the Funky Monkey, an Irish watering hole, journalists, lobbyists and EU officials had gathered for a party of their own. UK Rep staff had also been invited, but most felt uncomfortable about drinking in the presence of journalists while an existential referendum was in the balance.

One senior British member of the European Commission did drop in. 'People were nervous and chatting away,' he recalls. 'The general view from the hacks, which they were getting from their desks in London, was: watch out for Sunderland. If Newcastle and Sunderland are close, then it's very bad news for the Remain campaign. If they are lost, then it's all over.'

Outside, there was an eerie mood of expectation and foreboding. There had been a heavy thunderstorm all evening. 'It was a night of huge rainstorms,' recalls the British Commission official. 'There was a weird orange sky. It was all very apocalyptic. It was something like a bad production of Shakespeare.'

UK Rep has around 170 staff, including 100 policy experts. They are all British civil servants, seconded to Brussels or hired locally. The Ambassador himself, Sir Ivan Rogers, opened the bar. Number 10 is more sixth-form café than gentlemen's club. But Rogers and his number two, Shan Morgan, were determined to get the drinks in early. The polls would close at 10 p.m. British time. A hard core would stay all night.

One thousand kilometres to the west, another, more sober operation was under way in Government Buildings on Merrion Street in Dublin. This was not an Irish referendum, but it might as well have been. Officials from virtually every government department had been tasked with drawing up detailed explorations of how a Leave vote might affect

Ireland. The first task, whatever the result, was to communicate a clear Irish response.

As voters were going to the polls in the UK, most of the Irish team had tried to get home early. The plan was to get some sleep and reconvene at Government Buildings at 3 a.m. A camaraderie among the core officials had built up over time, and they wanted to share the experience of referendum night. Two rooms had been kitted out just below the landmark dome on the top floor of the government complex. Room 301 is the smaller, discreet, oak-panelled room that had been reserved for conference calls or any impromptu meetings that might be needed between senior officials, decision-makers and principal officers. Room 308, a larger, yellow-hued and more functional room, was the main hub for staff to work and to watch the results. Tables had been removed and sofas were commandeered from throughout the building. Large screens beamed Sky News and the BBC; a Twitter wall was mounted so that officials could assess reaction across social media. An IT unit was on call from 3 a.m. in case of technical glitches. There was tea and coffee in the kitchen next door; unlike at Number 10, there was no alcohol. A quick ring around earlier in the day had established where pizza might be sourced from 3 a.m.

There had been intense preparations in Dublin in the final weeks of the referendum campaign. There was one fundamental imperative: if Britain voted to leave the EU, the Irish state would have to show its citizens and the world that it could withstand the immediate impact and that, no matter what, Ireland would be remaining in the EU. From 7 June, officials had determined where ministers would be, built web pages, prepared press notes, and briefed media advisers and Irish embassies abroad. A stakeholders group, involving bodies like ICTU, IBEC and the European Movement Ireland, and that had been meeting for several months, was contacted in the final week to ensure that messaging would be streamlined. The 12-strong Cabinet Subcommittee on the EU, chaired by the Taoiseach, Enda Kenny, and comprising 11 senior ministers, would have to sign off on the preparations and finalize speeches. On Monday, three days before the vote, the switchboard was warned to expect 'an increased number of calls'. Callers were to be directed to an online 'consumer friendly' fact sheet on what would happen next.

On the eve of the vote, the main referendum team met in Room 308. They included Rory Montgomery, a former Irish Ambassador to the EU and now the Second Secretary General in the Department of Foreign Affairs, and at least 12 other officials from the departments of the Taoiseach and Foreign Affairs. They had war-gamed three scenarios: a clear Leave result at 5 a.m.; a clear Remain result; and an unclear result. Each scenario required five essential elements: a schedule of what would happen on the day; how to manage the media response; what press releases would be issued by government departments and agencies and when; what documents would be circulated; and how the government should engage with 'stakeholders' at home and abroad.

The document for the Leave scenario was *much* thicker than that for Remain. There was an hour-by-hour schedule, beginning with stock-market reactions. There would be a holding statement from the government ready to go at 6 a.m. By 7 a.m. Irish officials in London, Belfast, Brussels and Edinburgh would hold video conferences just as the Frankfurt stock market was opening. At 7.15 a.m. the Taoiseach would phone EU leaders and leaders of the opposition ('if necessary'). An emergency Cabinet meeting would take place shortly afterwards. A WhatsApp text-message group was set up comprising the communications operatives from each government department and from state agencies, and any other officials who needed to be in the loop.

If you were looking for a time and place when Brexit anxiety first hit Ireland, you might start in the Colmcille Heritage Centre, on Church Hill, in Letterkenny. The date was 23 February 2013. It was the second day of the Colmcille Winter School, the annual gathering of politicians, writers, thinkers and researchers. The theme of the three-day conference was 'Will the Euro/The Single European Currency Survive?' The pre-dinner speaker was Dr Edgar Morgenroth, specialist in transport and infrastructure at the Economic and Social Research Institute (ESRI) in Dublin.

Morgenroth had done his PhD at Keele University in the mid 1990s. 'I came across well-educated people there,' he recalls. 'They were clever, but had some strange views about the EU. You couldn't argue with them. They were not amenable to facts.'

While Morgenroth was working on his speech, another speech was being prepared in London. David Cameron, the British Prime Minister, had first raised the prospect of a referendum on EU membership in 2010, when he declared that voters had been 'cheated' out of a vote on the Lisbon Treaty. In the May general election that year, 148 new Tory MPs were elected, many of them eurosceptics. The UK Independence Party (UKIP) had been growing in popularity, and Cameron was desperate to head off the threat. He pulled Conservative MEPs out of the European People's Party, the centre-right grouping in the European Parliament. He promised a referendum if any new powers were transferred to

Brussels. He vetoed the EU Fiscal Compact (the rest of the EU simply converted it to an intergovernmental treaty sitting just outside the EU's formal structures). He opted out of huge swathes of EU laws governing cooperation in the police and criminal justice spheres. He promised to cut the numbers of EU citizens moving to the UK and to reduce their access to benefits. Each concession only emboldened the eurosceptics.

Finally, Cameron decided to seize the initiative once and for all. On 23 January 2013 he delivered a speech at the Bloomberg offices in London. It was actually quite pro-EU: he announced five principles to guide a deep-rooted reform of the Union to make it, in his view, fit for purpose in the twenty-first century. But it was his promise (or threat) to hold an in–out referendum on EU membership that grabbed the headlines. Cameron presented the vote in the following terms. The eurozone crisis would mean the EU being transformed beyond all recognition. It desperately needed to become more flexible and economically dynamic. There was a clamour for powers to flow back to member states and national parliaments. A treaty change that dealt with all these issues would provide Britain with a once-and-for-all opportunity. 'It is time for the British people to have their say,' he told the audience. 'It is time to settle this European question in British politics. I say to the British people: this will be your decision.'

Edgar Morgenroth watched with interest, and considered the implications for Ireland. Before Cameron's speech, he had put the chance of a British withdrawal from the EU at 5 per cent. After the speech he increased it to 30 per cent.

The day after Cameron's speech, Rory Montgomery,

Ireland's Permanent Representative to the EU in Brussels, met his British counterpart, Jon Cunliffe, at a breakfast of ambassadors. Ireland had just assumed the rotating presidency of the European Union, so Montgomery was in the chair. He went through the speech with Cunliffe, and got the impression that British diplomats were not too concerned. A general election was two years away, and Cameron was not expected to win an overall majority; the pro-EU Liberal Democrats would surely kick an in–out referendum into touch in any new coalition.

Morgenroth's own speech, a month later, was politely received. It outlined with a remarkable degree of prescience the contours of the Irish Brexit debate: agri-food and fisheries would be affected, small- and medium-sized enterprises (SMEs) exporting to the UK would be hit, supply chains in both directions would be vulnerable, customs checks would push up costs. The final slide concluded: the border with Northern Ireland would become a 'real' border again. This could have serious implications for the peace process: it would strengthen dissident republicans.

A year and a half later, in the summer of 2014, a team headed by Geraldine Byrne Nason, the Second Secretary General in the Department of the Taoiseach, produced a 10-page catalogue of the issues that might affect Ireland, should Britain leave the EU. It was an attempt to be as comprehensive as possible, but it was all very hypothetical. The British general election was still nine months away. The document was shared with government departments. No alarm bells were ringing.

Two months before the election, Tom Scholar, Cameron's chief EU adviser, travelled to Dublin for a meeting with Montgomery, by then back in Ireland and running the EU

Affairs Division inside the Taoiseach's Department. For four hours they went through the ins and outs of Cameron's Europe policy. If Cameron were to win the election, what might the various stages be as Britain moved towards a possible referendum? Montgomery spoke ruefully about Ireland's recent referendum experiences (the Nice and Lisbon treaties rejected by voters, then approved when the polls were rerun). He went through what had worked and what hadn't worked during the campaigns.

As the talks concluded, the focus was not on the UK leaving the EU, but on what kind of deal Cameron might get from the rest of the EU on a new relationship, and how he would sell that to the British voter.

In the general election on 7 May 2015, Cameron defied the polls and won a decisive overall majority. While UKIP hadn't won a seat, it took an impressive 12.6 per cent of the vote. Cameron would have to hang tough on Europe to keep UKIP at bay; meanwhile, he would have to start probing the EU to see what concessions he might win. Declan Kelleher, Montgomery's successor in Brussels as Ireland's EU Ambassador, held a number of discussions with Sir Ivan Rogers, who had taken over from Jon Cunliffe. In London, Dan Mulhall, who had arrived as Ireland's Ambassador to the UK, was discovering that the British–EU conundrum would start to dominate each working day.

At this stage Dublin was still trying to get a sense of what Cameron might be thinking, and what the EU might be prepared to offer. But the spectre of Britain leaving the EU now felt more palpable. The EU's reputation was being battered, first by the Greeks nearly tumbling out of the euro in July, and then by the horrific refugee crisis that unfolded later in the summer. On 9 November 2015 Enda Kenny delivered a keynote speech to the Confederation of British Industry in London, urging Britain to remain in a reformed EU. Briefing documents supplied by the embassy to the audience spelled out the deep interdependency of the British and Irish economies, and the potential impact of a British withdrawal on the Northern peace process.

Around the time of Kenny's CBI speech, Cameron wrote to his EU counterparts about the possibility of reducing EU migration to the UK. There was immediate resistance, not just from the German Chancellor, Angela Merkel, but also from Cameron's own officials, who knew that blocking EU citizens from living and working in the UK breached the EU's fundamental rules on freedom of movement. 'Cameron didn't go as far in his demands on migration as he would have wished,' recalls a senior Irish diplomat closely involved in the negotiations. 'It didn't help him later on.'

As 2015 drew to a close, EU officials were assessing which member states were more sympathetic to London's position, even drawing up a league table of British-friendly member states in order to assess how the negotiations might go. Denmark was awarded a bronze medal; the Dutch won silver.

But the gold medal went to Ireland.

This was not entirely surprising. Ireland and the UK were extremely close on key issues involving the single market and taxation. Ireland, indeed, had its own particular demand. It was first raised during a meeting between the Foreign Secretary, Philip Hammond, and Ireland's Minister for Foreign Affairs, Charlie Flanagan, at a meeting in Iveagh House in December 2015. Cameron wanted the UK to have the power to impose social-welfare restrictions on EU citizens working in the UK. Dublin was anxious that those restrictions would *not* apply to Irish citizens. Cameron gave Kenny strong assurances that they wouldn't, but Dublin had to handle it delicately. The other 26 member states, whose citizens would be explicitly hit by these restrictions, might not take too kindly to the Irish getting a special deal.

On the night of 19 February 2016, all 28 EU leaders gathered in Brussels for a special summit meeting. They agreed a deal that Cameron could bring back in triumph to London and then sell to the voters. The UK would be granted an 'emergency brake' restricting EU migrants from claiming in-work benefits that could run for up to seven years. Child-benefit payments for children living outside the UK would be indexed to the cost of living for all new arrivals to the UK, extending to all workers from 1 January 2020. There were other concessions on Britain's relationship with the eurozone, and an explicit opt-out on any treaty references to 'ever-closer union'.

The next day Cameron held an emergency Cabinet meeting, the first on a Saturday since the Falklands War. The Cabinet endorsed the deal. The Brexit referendum would be held on 23 June. Cameron declared he would fight 'heart and soul' for Britain to remain in the EU.

Any optimism that Cameron had won a decisive deal quickly evaporated. The agreement was mocked in the tabloid press. The Tory eurosceptic hardliner Jacob Rees-Mogg, MP, called it 'very thin gruel'. Within hours Michael Gove, one of Cameron's closest allies, jumped ship. He joined fellow Cabinet ministers Iain Duncan Smith, John Whittingdale, Chris Grayling, Theresa Villiers and Priti Patel on the Leave side.

The referendum campaign was officially up and running.

Almost immediately, Ireland's Ambassador, Dan Mulhall, suggested to Dublin that the government should get involved.

Mulhall enthusiastically led the charge, making dozens of speeches, appearing on numerous broadcast channels, blogging, writing op-eds, and tweeting on a daily basis. Ireland had a simple message: for the sake of Irish–British relations, and for the sake of stability in Northern Ireland, it would be better if Britain remained in the EU.

The embassy focused its firepower on the Irish community. Mulhall sent newsletters to every Irish organization and wrote opinion pieces for the two main Irish papers in Britain, the *Irish Post* and the *Irish World*, going as far as he could go, stopping just short of asking people to vote Remain.

But there was a problem. The Irish community in Britain is not homogeneous. Mulhall spoke to several groups of recently arrived immigrants: younger, well qualified, aware of the issues. Almost all of these people would vote Remain. Tens of thousands of other Irish people were associated with Irish clubs and community centres, read the *Post* and the *World*, and were focused on the Irish issues that Dublin was desperate to highlight. But, equally, there was a hidden cohort of Irish in the UK, many of them settled there for decades, who were less receptive to the official Irish message.

'Half the Irish community is over 65,' says one senior Irish official. 'That demographic voted very strongly to leave. One would have to assume that people who had lived here for 30, 40, 50 years had been subject to the same influences as their neighbours, who were British.' Another senior Irish figure said of the Irish campaign, 'I don't know if it made a blind bit of difference. You would have had Paddy from Mayo, living in Birmingham for 30 years, next door to Johnny from Birmingham. They were probably likely to think much the same way.'

Worse, there was growing unease at the highest levels in government that complacency was setting in at Downing Street. The referendum was never formally on the agenda of any meetings between Kenny and Cameron, but it was always discussed. The standard line from Cameron had been that fear of the economic damage would secure the Remain vote, just as fear of Labour's economic policies had supposedly clinched the May 2015 general election.

'There was always this kind of harking back to the 2015 surprise victory,' says a senior official in the Department of the Taoiseach. 'They saw that as an unbeatable strategy. If people are scared enough on the economic consequences of something, they won't vote for it. If the Tories could frighten people about Labour and Miliband on the economy, then they could do the same thing on Brexit.'

Philip Hammond had travelled to Dublin for a bilateral meeting as Foreign Secretary with his counterpart Charlie Flanagan. The trip included a breakfast at the British Embassy with fourteen invited guests, including members of the opposition. One of them was the Fianna Fáil leader Micheál Martin, who had been in charge of running the second campaign to get the Lisbon Treaty referendum passed in Ireland. That project had been enormous: it involved negotiating protocols at EU level that would reassure Irish voters. Before securing the protocols, exhaustive research had to be done on what had gone wrong. The research, Martin recalls, 'taught us a lot about how you pitch a message'. The formula was: 'We've heard you, we've listened to you, we've done the changes because of your message.'

Martin realized that the British had done none of this for the British EU referendum.

'Philip Hammond outlined the British strategy post the

Bloomberg speech,' he recalls. 'I remember saying to myself this was very naive. They seemed to have a view that there would just be a row with Brussels [ahead of the February negotiation]. It was important there was the *perception* of [a] row. "We'll emerge with the package, we'll put it to a referendum and we'll win." The thing wasn't thought through. The deal [from the other member states] they got was very poor.'

By the time the campaign was under way, it was rather delicate for Kenny to be giving advice to Cameron. According to one senior official: 'The Taoiseach on a few occasions did respond, not in a dire-warning kind of way, but as friendly advice. He told Cameron, "Yes, but referendums are different to general elections. People don't fear the consequences of referenda in the same way they fear the consequences of a general election. We have some experience of this kind of thing. On referenda people are voting on everything. It's a free kick at a government. If it's voting about you as Prime Minister they'll take that very seriously, but they don't always take referenda very seriously, or think about the consequences."'

The message from Kenny to Cameron was, in essence: You'll really need to work hard on this one.

Meanwhile, as the referendum campaign rollicked along in an increasingly poisonous atmosphere, it was often difficult for the Irish Ambassador to divine the intentions of Irish voters. Some of the questions from the audience at events in Irish clubs made him wonder if they were more inclined towards the Leave arguments.

That worry was shared by Dara Murphy, Ireland's Minister for European Affairs, and one of six ministers to canvass in the UK for a Remain vote. On 13 June, 10 days before the vote, Murphy travelled to the Haringey Cultural Centre in

Tottenham to address an audience of mostly Irish-connected voters. He was joined on stage by David Lammy, the local MP and a rising star in the Labour Party. At this stage, polling suggested that Labour voters in urban centres were not falling into the Remain camp as readily as expected.

'It was a big crowd and we both spoke,' recalls Murphy. 'The audience should have been pretty pro-Remain. But there was a very strong sense that this wasn't going particularly well. There was a line of questioning that was most disconcerting. It was nothing to do with the EU. It was about social exclusion, access to the workforce for their children. I came away feeling quite pessimistic.'

Staff in the Irish Embassy had been gathering as much intelligence on voter intentions as possible, plugging into a grid of public and private polling, think tanks, political parties and media organizations. Professor John Curtice from Strathclyde University, one of Britain's leading polling experts, came to the embassy twice for lunch. Staff processed everything they were getting, and in turn reported sophisticated analysis back to Dublin. As referendum day approached, that analysis was getting darker. At a gathering one evening of embassy staff and an Irish government minister, a straw poll was held.

Of the eight people present around the table, seven of them predicted a Leave victory.

The potential for Irish citizens to vote Leave was graphically on display at a GAA match between the Taoiseach's own Mayo team and London in the suburb of Ruislip on 29 May. With Kenny attending the match in order to urge the Irish in Britain to vote Remain, one man, wearing a Mayo jersey, rained on the entire parade by telling RTÉ News he was voting Leave because 'our work has been taken up by thousands and thousands of [migrants] crossing over into Britain'.

On 16 June, a week before polling day, the campaign was upended by a brutal and tragic event. At 12.53 p.m., the Labour MP Jo Cox was stabbed and shot to death on the street in Birstall, Yorkshire, where she was about to hold a constituency meeting. Cox, a passionate supporter of the EU and the refugee cause, was murdered by a 52-year-old English nationalist called Thomas Mair. He had links to neo-Nazi websites in the US. He shouted 'Britain first!' as he carried out his savage attack on Cox.

In the aftermath, there was a widespread belief that the toxic messaging from the Leave campaign, fixated as it had been on immigration, might be staunched. Polls suggested that public outrage had put a dent in the Leave momentum.

On the evening of 23 June, referendum day, Dara Murphy was travelling to Luxembourg for a meeting of European Affairs ministers, known as the General Affairs Council (GAC). The meeting had been shifted to the day after the vote in the hope, or expectation, that ministers could quietly celebrate a Remain victory. After years of exasperation over Britain's place in the EU, the issue would be settled.

At 9.45 p.m. UK time, Murphy received a phone call from David Lidington, his British opposite number. Polls were due to close in 15 minutes.

'At that stage they were quite optimistic,' Murphy recalls. 'He wanted to know could we meet for breakfast. He said things were going okay, were going well. That was the general mood, people were getting their own general reports and wisps of what was happening.'

Murphy called the Taoiseach to tell him of the vibe he was

picking up. Kenny had spent the previous two days hosting the US Vice-President, Joe Biden, in Mayo, an act of state-craft that included a round of golf at Castlebar Golf Club on the day of the vote. The Taoiseach kept in touch by phone with Mark Kennelly, his Chief of Staff, Martin Fraser, the Secretary General to the government, and Feargal Purcell, the Government Press Secretary. He arrived back in Dublin just after receiving Dara Murphy's update. At around 11.30 p.m. Kenny's Press Officer, Jack O'Donnell, offered to text him on any breaking news throughout the night as the count unfolded. The assumption was that the Taoiseach would be getting some sleep.

Murphy continued on to Luxembourg with two officials. They checked in to the Novotel in the Kirchberg district of the Grand Duchy, a windswept plateau studded with tower-ing EU buildings, hotels, office blocks and a vast shopping centre. Numerous EU delegations had gathered in the Novotel bar to watch the results trickling in on Sky News. There were grounds for optimism, not just from Lidington's phone call. A YouGov poll released as polls closed at 10 p.m. predicted a Remain victory by 52 per cent to 48 per cent. Nigel Farage, the UKIP leader, told Sky News by phone that he thought the Remain side was going to 'edge it'. Boris Johnson, MP, the former Mayor of London and a prominent Leave campaigner, appeared to have conceded.

But that was before the thunderbolts from the north-east of England. At 1 a.m. Luxembourg time, the Newcastle result flashed up on Sky News. Newcastle had been expected to vote heavily in favour of Remain; but Remain prevailed only by a whisker. The real shock came from Sunderland, which had been expected to go Remain by an eight-point margin. It actually voted Leave by *22 points*.

One of the Irish officials had spent weeks analysing how the result might go, with a spreadsheet covering every constituency. When Newcastle and Sunderland broke, he turned to Murphy, realizing that most of his work on the spreadsheet had gone to waste.

'The UK will be leaving the European Union,' he said.

At that moment, Dan Mulhall was due to appear on a panel discussion at an all-night gathering in the London School of Economics. At 8 p.m. he had gone to Villandry, a smart restaurant in Great Portland Street, for a dinner organized by Roland Rudd, the Treasurer of Britain Stronger in Europe, the pro-Remain group, and the brother of Amber Rudd, a pro-Remain Tory MP. The dinner was held as a thank-you for those who had bankrolled the campaign. It was a discreet but sumptuous occasion, with 150-odd guests, separate from the main 'watch event' for the Remain side, which was at the Royal Festival Hall. The head of BT, the Chief Executive of Eurostar, and senior bankers were all in attendance. So was Jim Messina, President Obama's chief polling expert and the man whose social-media strategy had helped to win the election for the Conservatives in 2015. Peter Mandelson, the Labour grandee and former EU Trade Commissioner, was also present. TV screens had been mounted so that the guests could watch referendum coverage.

Mulhall bumped into the Chancellor of the Exchequer, George Osborne. Osborne told him that private polling suggested a Remain vote, but that it was very close. Mulhall texted to staff back in Dublin that things were looking okay. But Osborne may have been putting on a brave face. According to a key Remain source who attended the event, Osborne 'had a face like a sheet'. Mandelson, too, was worried. He had been travelling around the country and the message he was picking up was not positive.

In Dublin, meanwhile, members of the Irish government's referendum team, who had been at home since late afternoon, were watching the coverage. When Newcastle and Sunderland came in, most realized that it would be a long night without sleep. They began arriving at Government Buildings and Room 308 ahead of the 3 a.m. rendezvous.

One senior official checked his Paddy Power online betting account to discover to his amazement there were *still* decent odds on a Remain victory. But it felt hollow. 'The newer members of the team kept watching, still saying, "Hey! That one's just come in!"' recalls one official. 'The more seasoned ones just looked at each other and went, "This is it: game over."'

The pizza that had been ordered grew cold on the tables.

In Luxembourg, Dara Murphy's Private Secretary called. She had just received a message: 'The British have cancelled the meeting in the morning.' The Irish delegation in the Novotel watched the news coming in for another hour. 'It was obvious this wasn't going to be even *that* close in relative terms,' says Murphy.

Two further messages came in during the night. The meeting between the Irish and British delegations would take place, but a couple of hours later than scheduled. It would not be a celebratory breakfast.

Ivan Rogers was born in Bournemouth and educated at a grammar school, entering the civil service in 1992. Having served as a Private Secretary to the former Chancellor, Kenneth Clarke, he was seconded to the Cabinet of Sir Leon Brittan, the UK's EU Trade and External Affairs

Commissioner, and later became the Principal Private Secretary to Tony Blair. He left Number 10 to work in the City of London for both Barclays and Citigroup, returning to Downing Street in 2012 as Cameron's Adviser for Europe and Global Issues. In 2013 he was back in Brussels, this time as Permanent Representative, where he struck up a firm friendship with Declan Kelleher, his Irish counterpart, who himself had just arrived from Ireland's embassy in China. By the time of the Brexit referendum, he had been 'Sir Ivan' for less than half a year, the title having been bestowed on him in the 2016 New Year's Honours.

Rogers was always of a disposition that was realistic, verging on the gloomy. It was a character trait that would later lose him his job. In the months leading up to the referendum, he was significantly more pessimistic than anyone else in Cameron's circle, and regarded the Remain camp as being overly confident.

One prominent figure shared Rogers's fears. Ten days before the vote, Gordon Brown travelled to Brussels. He had breakfast with Rogers in his residence before meeting Jean-Claude Juncker, the President of the European Commission. Brown was certain Remain was going to lose, and he said so to Rogers. Things were 'very bad' in northern England among working-class voters. The Cameron government was saying nothing *positive* about staying in Europe. Gordon Brown was convinced that it was going wrong, and potentially by a significant margin. Rogers was startled, but generally agreed with Brown's analysis.

Brown conveyed the same message to Juncker and his Chief of Staff, Martin Selmayr. Juncker wasn't surprised. The President of the Commission had suspected for some time that the referendum would be lost.

Now, as Rogers watched the slow death of Britain's membership of the European Union unfold on his TV screen in Brussels, the Taoiseach was in his residence in Dublin, unable to tear himself away from the coverage. He ended up getting little sleep, exchanging text messages throughout the night with Jack O'Donnell as the constituencies rolled in.

At 4.50 a.m. O'Donnell sent one final text message to the effect that the BBC was predicting a Leave victory and that a Cabinet meeting would now be needed at 7.30 a.m. The Taoiseach replied that the Cabinet Secretariat would make the suitable arrangements.

Most indicators had suggested that Ireland had recovered for the most part from the disaster of the property crash and the effects of the EU–IMF bailout. Economic recovery depended on both Ireland and the UK being in the EU single market. Now, we were like the 20-something driver who, with just one or two penalty points, had upgraded to a sleeker model, only to be suddenly blindsided by a souped-up Bentley, driven by a drunk driver with no insurance. When we crawled from the wreckage to catch the number plate, we discovered it belonged to our next-door neighbour.

2. In the Land of Eternal Autumn

Gerry O'Reilly spent most of Thursday, 23 June 2016, on the phone to his currency adviser in Dublin. When not on the phone, he was listening to experts on radio and television. 'They were all saying, "Ah, sure this won't happen at all." Everybody thought there would be a Remain vote.'

O'Reilly was calling from his mushroom farm in Westmeath. As is the case for most Irish mushroom growers, the vast bulk of O'Reilly's exports go to the UK. The contracts are negotiated in sterling and, as the revenue comes in, the bank converts it to euro. The stronger the British pound, the better it is for exporters like O'Reilly; by the same token, a significant weakening in sterling could be catastrophic. On the day of the referendum, sterling was hovering at around 74p to the euro. It was assumed that a Leave vote would weaken sterling, and a Remain vote would strengthen it.

'Everybody figured, ah, well tomorrow this could be 72p again, or 71p,' he recalls. As the evening wore on and voting continued in the UK, O'Reilly called the bank again. The exchange rate at which the money is converted can be hedged forward by weeks, months or even a year. They told him not to panic. They would be open all night. Since mushroom growers have small profit margins, currency hedging is a critical part of the business. Hedging forward means locking in a particular exchange rate over the medium or long term to avoid a damaging fluctuation. Since the referendum result would trigger a sharp rise or fall, hedging at the right time and at the right level was crucial.

Then the Sunderland vote came in.

'I phoned again after midnight, and they said, "Sunderland has voted, and they've decided to leave." There was a certain shock at that stage. But they said, "Look, there's another 300 [constituencies] to come in." I remember thinking about it. I just didn't believe it .,. . why would they leave? I sold a little bit of my money forward on that particular night for two or three weeks, figuring by tomorrow morning we'd be okay.'

The next morning things were not okay.

'Sterling was up nearly at 86p to the euro. That was almost 20 per cent gone off my total sales figure.'

Gerry O'Reilly was by no means the worst affected. Within several months, five Irish mushroom producers would go to the wall as a result of the drop in sterling, including one in Tipperary, with the loss of 70 jobs.

In Room 308, keyboards rattled with frantic emails. Printers whirred. Faces in Irish embassies across Europe appeared on video-conferencing screens. Phone calls were made to ministers, the chief executives of Irish state agencies, and other key stakeholders.

One of the latter was Danny McCoy, the Chief Executive of IBEC. He had gone to bed the night before 'uber-confident' there would be a Remain vote, even after having witnessed the Sunderland result. When he checked his phone at 5 a.m., he was in a state of disbelief. His first thought was that IBEC had prepared two news releases, so he had to make sure the right one was sent to news desks. There was another heart-stopping complication: IBEC had paid for an ad campaign urging British voters to vote Remain. They had erected billboards inside Dublin Airport with the message 'Don't Go!' for the benefit of British visitors. 'Thank You!' billboards had been prepared in anticipation of a Remain vote. McCoy frantically called his office to ensure the billboards did not go up. 'I can't think of any [other] day where I was ringing people at six in the morning knowing they were up.'

The government communications plan for a Leave vote had to go live immediately. At 6.25 a.m. an email was sent to government press officers, copying Kenny's Secretary General, Martin Fraser, with a holding news release. This would be the state's first official response. The Irish government, it said, 'notes the outcome of the UK EU referendum this morning. The result clearly has very significant implications for Ireland . . .' Three minutes later, the holding statement was circulated to the Department of Foreign Affairs, to Ireland's network of embassies and to Cabinet ministers.

Although the communications plan, which would include the key statement by Kenny, had been finessed in the days leading up to the vote, officials had to allow statements elsewhere to go first, with the Irish response being tweaked where necessary. The Irish Permanent Representative in Brussels alerted Dublin to a joint statement from the presidents of the Commission, Parliament, Council and the Dutch Prime Minister (the Netherlands held the rotating presidency). 'We knew the choreography of what was about to take place,' recalls one staffer. 'We also knew we needed to be flexible. The Irish couldn't be storming out with their response.'

That also meant waiting for the official response from Downing Street. Some senior officials in Room 308 had wondered if David Cameron would tough it out. There had been an assumption that the Tory leadership question would not be resolved until the autumn, a belief supported by statements from Boris Johnson and Michael Gove, the most prominent Brexiteers.

At around 8.15 a.m. Cameron emerged with his wife, Samantha, from Number 10. Room 308 suddenly went quiet. The emergency Cabinet meeting was just over, and Charlie Flanagan, the Minister for Foreign Affairs, was slumped on one of the sofas, looking up at the screen. Feargal Purcell, the Government Press Secretary, stood nearby. 'We watched Cameron make the speech,' recalls one official. The moment Cameron uttered the words 'above all this will require strong, determined and committed leadership', there was a collective expulsion of breath around the room. 'Anyone who has ever drafted a speech and heard that line went, "Ohh . . ." We knew exactly where that was going.'

David Cameron was resigning after six years as Prime Minister. His gambit to stop his backbenchers 'banging on about Europe' had backfired spectacularly.

Cameron's key civil servant on Europe, Sir Ivan Rogers, had left his Brussels apartment at 6 a.m. to drive to the UK Permanent Representation. He'd had 30 minutes' sleep. When he arrived at UK Rep, some endurance drinkers were still there. There had been tears, anger and disbelief. It was not just disappointment at an outcome they had worked hard to avoid. These were civil servants who had spent their professional lives working on EU policy. They were largely supportive of the EU project, or at least they did not accept the tabloid depiction of 'Brussels'. Many had settled in Brussels, raised families there. Now, some feared for their livelihoods.

Rogers met his top team, and phoned Number 10 and the Foreign and Commonwealth Office. Cameron had never told Rogers he would quit if he lost the vote, but Rogers had assumed he would. Article 50 of the EU Treaty, which governs the mechanism by which a member state may leave the Union, would have to be triggered, and he felt that Cameron no longer had the legitimacy to do this.

Rogers called all the staff together. According to those present, he did his best to rally the troops. UK Rep remained absolutely central to what was now going to happen: there would be a negotiation based on Article 50, and officials should 'stick with it'. Britain would have to enter the most serious, complex negotiations the country had ever undertaken, and the shell-shocked officials in front of him – the people with the *expertise* – would be absolutely depended upon if Britain were to conclude a successful deal.

The speech was a hard sell. According to one embassy official, the sense of anger and shock was just so overwhelming. A senior diplomat told staff they had to accept they were part of that educated 'elite' that angry voters, who were struggling to make ends meet, had rejected. To many, the label didn't seem real or fair.

Rogers's Deputy, Shan Morgan, was due to appear at a committee meeting of fellow EU ambassadors that morning. One diplomat recalls: 'It took place in a completely weird atmosphere because, of course, everyone was mesmerized by the British outcome.' Morgan arrived late. 'There were lots of group hugs, words of sympathy. People were completely stunned. She was stunned.'

Within a week, the Foreign Office was to send two professional in-house counsellors to Brussels to carry out group-therapy sessions at UK Rep. The idea was that staff would vent, pour out their feelings of rage, frustration, help-lessness. One staff member suspected that the caring approach was really intended to prevent officials venting to the media instead.

The two counsellors who came over from London had travelled over only two months before. On that occasion, they were counselling UK Rep staff in the immediate after-math of the Brussels terror attacks.

Back in Dublin, the Taoiseach's statement was adjusted to include a tribute to his departing British counterpart. When Kenny faced the media in the government press room, he was standing alone between an Irish flag and an EU flag.

'For a Leave vote the audience was global,' says one offi-cial. 'So the image was: "We're staying in, folks."' In the final draft of the statement, Kenny said he was 'very sorry' the Leave vote had prevailed, but he appealed for calm. He said the negotiations for Britain to leave the EU were unlikely to begin for a couple of months. 'We must take this breathing space . . . and use it wisely,' he said.

Beyond the press room there was anything but a sense of calm. The FTSE 100 was in freefall and would plunge more than 8 per cent in its biggest opening slump since the finan-cial crisis, wiping £120 billion off the value of the 100 biggest UK companies. The pound fell to lows not seen since 1985, falling 11 per cent against the dollar and 6.3 per cent against the euro. Mark Carney, the Governor of the Bank of Eng-land, called for calm and warned of 'volatility'. Irish banks exposed to the UK represented around 21 per cent of total Irish banking assets. Shares in the Irish stock market were 9 per cent lower.

At 10.42 a.m. the Taoiseach's Department issued a series

of tweets from the Irish Central Bank, attempting to reassure the markets. The Central Bank was 'closely monitoring' the impact on the banking sector. Pointing out that the ECB was ready for 'all contingencies', the Central Bank said it was 'satisfied that measures are in place to address any issues which may arise'. On cue, government departments issued their Leave statements. IDA Ireland and Enterprise Ireland sent letters to every client. Bord Bia announced workshops for food exporters for the following week.

Within Ireland's diplomatic service, the hard, brutal fact of the Leave victory was hard to take in. One Brussels-based diplomat recalls: 'People were quite stunned. The more everybody thought about it, the more the appalling vista opened up. People hadn't really thought about it in depth at that point. Anyone who dealt in that area, you could see huge complications opening up. People were saying, this is going to take a *generation* to sort out, it's so complex.'

The contours of that complexity had been steadily mapped out by civil servants in the months leading up to the referendum. Once Brexit became a theoretical danger, changes were made. Inside the Department of the Taoiseach, the Economic, International Affairs and Northern Ireland Division, in existence since 2011, was broken up. The British–Irish and Northern Ireland parts were taken over by Dermot Curran, a senior official from the Department of Jobs, Enterprise and Innovation, to focus on the all-island and Ireland–Britain aspects of Brexit. Assistant Secretary John Callinan took charge of the Economic and International Division, with a greater focus on the EU side. Officials from all government departments, including key parts of the Department of Foreign Affairs, amalgamated into a fully blown interdepartmental group.

The emerging Contingency Plan was about preparing for all the scenarios that might arise ('the good, the bad and the ugly', as one official put it), trying to anticipate what they might look like, but not really expecting them to actually happen. 'At that stage [late 2015] we were going a bit deeper into potential consequences. But it wasn't about remedies and solutions.'

On 10 and 11 November 2015, 15 Irish bishops from North and South visited the European institutions in Brussels, meeting the First Vice-President of the European Commission, Frans Timmermans, Ireland's Commissioner, Phil Hogan, a number of Irish MEPs, and staff from the Irish Permanent Representation and the Northern Ireland Executive Office. One meeting was with Jonathan Faull, the most senior British official in the Commission and the head of the Commission's Brexit Task Force.

'I was wheeled in to talk to them about Brexit,' Faull recalls. 'What was supposed to be a half-hour discussion turned into an hour and a half. It was fascinating, particularly with the bishops from the border areas. They said basically there was now a young generation in Ireland thinking that the border isn't significant any more, that you go from one place to another very freely. They described how some parishes even straddle the border. As I began to set out what Brexit might mean, you could see they were visibly shocked by the implications.'

Officials began with the obvious aspects of impact, and tried to structure the work flow. Each department was given a risk register. Officials were tasked with supplying information along the immediate, medium and longer terms so that the potential risks could be assessed in a streamlined fashion. There was no shortage of overlap and cross-referencing with other departments, but no one could assume that someone else was doing the spadework.

One senior official from the Department of Jobs, Enterprise and Innovation recalls the sheer scale of what they had to figure out: 'We had everything from labour migration, work permits, expert control duties, military goods, trade, the World Trade Organization, foreign direct investment, the IDA, exports, Enterprise Ireland, InterTradeIreland, chemicals, health and safety, mergers and acquisitions, competition policy, innovation, [the EU research programme] Horizon 2020, the COSME programme [for SMEs]. Even just name checking what we were covering took about 20 or 30 pages. There wasn't an officer or an agency that wasn't impacted.'

The methods used were based on OECD best practice, essentially the same tools that went into creating the state's annual National Risk Register (NRR). But there was a striking difference: no one knew how deep the impact of the Brexit meteor would be. What *was* certain was that, like any meteor strike, there would be very few upsides. 'You were anticipating areas of impact,' recalls a senior official. 'From the get-go they weren't areas of impact that were positive. They were potentially threatening.'

Diplomats like to refer to 'the landing zone': the place where negotiations will finally end up, to the satisfaction – more or less – of all the parties involved. Because Cameron's government hadn't articulated what they would do if that vote was Leave, Irish officials were operating in a vacuum. 'We had *no* landing zone,' recalls one exasperated official. 'We didn't even know where the Brits would *think* of ending up.'

The work continued up until the final week of campaigning, with departmental inputs being stitched together in the final few days. At the last minute the Department of Foreign Affairs had to assess if it was ready for a spike in passport queries and citizenship applications.

While the exhaustive research was going on, the political message was sharpening. On Friday, 13 May, Enda Kenny had spoken at a Bloomberg event in the Gibson Hotel in Dublin. He said our ambition should not be to preserve what we have, but to *build* upon it, to break down barriers, not to *erect* them. 'We have become close,' he declared of Ireland's bond with the UK. 'We should stay close. And we should stay together in Europe.'

As dawn broke on 24 June, Britain hadn't listened.

The government's Contingency Plan, which ran to 130 pages, was kept confidential, as it would essentially form the basis of the Irish government's negotiating strategy when Article 50 was triggered. But a condensed version of the Plan had been prepared for release to the media while the Taoiseach delivered his statement. The top priority was that the state would ensure financial stability via the Irish Central Bank and the ECB. Everything would be done to preserve the peace process, the Good Friday Agreement and the Common Travel Area. Ireland would be remaining in the EU. Ireland Inc. would be protected, companies that exported would be strengthened, new investment opportunities would be targeted, new markets for Irish goods would be sought out, tariffs and customs controls would be avoided if at all possible, energy supplies would be safeguarded, European PEACE and Interreg funds would be continued for the time being, as would cross-border health services.

On closer inspection, the condensed Contingency Plan was rich in the vaguely aspirational. The words 'analysis', 'revise', 'ensure', 'monitor', 'assess', 'identify', 'prioritize' cropped up an awful lot. In the *Irish Independent*, Kevin Doyle noted that the document was 'not exactly the type of reassurance that would let you "Keep calm and carry on". People might have hoped for something a bit more tangible as the stock markets and sterling crashed.'

In Luxembourg, European affairs ministers gathered for their scheduled meeting in a sombre mood. The British minister David Lidington, a prominent Remainer, was called upon to speak first. 'He was very brave but exceptionally disappointed,' recalls Ireland's minister, Dara Murphy. 'He thanked everyone for their support. He expressed his own disappointment. But even at that stage he said, "The people have spoken."'

Some of the ministers wanted Britain to trigger Article 50 immediately, but the message from Kenny to Murphy that morning by phone had been that the British needed time. Murphy, who was third to speak, conveyed this to the other member states. 'That was the tensest meeting I've ever attended,' he recalls.

The six foreign ministers of the founding member states raced to Berlin to call on Britain to trigger Article 50 immediately. That met a frosty response from Chancellor Angela Merkel, who said there was no hurry.

The imperative for Ireland, as the day unfolded, was to remind the outside world that it would be remaining in the European Union. The other message that officials in Room 308 were trying to get out was that Britain wasn't leaving the EU *that day*.

Local radio stations buzzed with callers asking questions that no one could really answer. What would this mean for Ireland's trade? What about Northern Ireland? Would the border come back? Customs posts? The North had voted to remain in the EU – could it? The 30,000 people who cross the border every day to work – would they have to show passports? Sterling was plunging; exporters would feel the effects within days, because their goods were more expensive in the most important market. A frantic tech worker wondered if he could be stopped crossing a notional new border because he was carrying 'intellectual property'.

It quickly became clear that the delicate constitutional settlement that had underpinned relations between the island of Ireland and the United Kingdom was shifting underfoot. Martin McGuinness, the Deputy First Minister of Northern Ireland, called almost immediately for a referendum on a United Ireland. The First Minister, DUP leader Arlene Foster, described the call as opportunistic, saying there was 'no way' a majority would vote in favour in any case.

Economic prospects also looked wobbly. Irish share prices fell more heavily than UK ones. The *Irish Times* quoted sources saying that the Minister for Finance, Michael Noonan, had warned Cabinet colleagues of the severity of the consequences for the public finances if there was a post-Brexit slump.

The Taoiseach travelled to Brussels for a summit of EU leaders. It was a strange gathering. The agenda, which had been fixed for some time, was supposed to be about the migration crisis, but Britain's imminent departure was all the international media was focused on.

Ordinarily, much of the work at these European Council meetings is pre-cooked by diplomats, officials and ministers from the member states, and much of the tweaking and haggling over the final text is done by the so-called sherpas – the officials representing each EU leader, who meet several days ahead of the event. On this occasion, the sherpa meeting took place on Sunday, 26 June. The British sherpa was excluded. Enda Kenny's sherpa was John Callinan, Head of the Economic and International Policy Division in the Department of the Taoiseach. He was joined by Declan Kelleher, Ireland's Permanent Representative in Brussels (both men unable to watch the European Championships match between France and the Republic of Ireland that was taking place in Lyon at the same time). The sherpas agreed a short text that would focus on the UK's rights and obligations as it prepared to leave the EU.

On Tuesday, 28 June, one week after the referendum, all 28 leaders gathered in Brussels. After the meeting on migration, David Cameron held his last summit news conference. He told reporters that the tone of the meeting had been one of 'sadness and regret'. He himself regretted the outcome of the referendum, but did not regret holding it. 'It was the right thing to do,' he told reporters. He also said that immigration had been a key factor in the Leave victory, and this was something the EU should reflect on. There was a you-win-some-you-lose-some tone to his statement; one observer described Cameron as having the demeanour of someone who had lost a rugby match.

The next day, the other 27 leaders met for an informal summit. For the first time since 1973, a British Prime Minister had been excluded from the room. Ireland's position on how the EU should proceed was a subject of interest. Dublin was known to be close to London on many European issues; Enda Kenny had been the Prime Minister's most passionate advocate when Cameron was trying to get a decent deal back in February. Among other leaders, though, there was an impulse to make the UK's exit deal sufficiently puni-tive so as to discourage other member states from following them out of the club. The text the sherpas had agreed on the Sunday was only slightly tweaked during the meeting of the 27, with one exception. Chancellor Merkel made it clear in the room that there should be a specific line regarding the four freedoms – free movement of goods, services, capital and people – included in the final communiqué. If Britain wanted access to the single market, they would have to accept all four freedoms – including free movement of EU work-ers, a clear red line for Brexiteers. 'Nobody stood up and said, "No, we don't support the four freedoms,"' says one senior Irish official.

According to one source, later appointed as one of the EU's senior negotiators, there was no wobbling on the Irish side at the summit. 'The freedom of movement line was agreed by Kenny, and repeated in his press conference afterwards. This was very significant. It wasn't [Slovak Prime Minister Robert] Fico or [former Polish President Jarosław] Kaczyński saying it. It was Kenny. Kenny gave it more weight.'

The Brexit result triggered a spate of bloodletting within the Conservative Party. Boris Johnson had been expected to stand for the leadership, but pulled out at the last minute when he learned that his ally, Michael Gove, was about to launch his own bid. Stephen Crabb, the Work and Pensions Secretary, dropped out of the race due to lack of support and within days was embroiled in a 'sexting' scandal. With the leader of the Labour Party, Jeremy Corbyn, clinging to office after a dismal referendum campaign and the financial mar-kets in free fall, the country appeared in amateurish disarray. The *Economist*'s front cover showed a pair of Union Jack underpants halfway up a flagpole, under the headline 'Anarchy in the UK'.

The antics at Westminster were viewed with increasing alarm in the rest of Europe, and in Dublin. None of the arguments about what *kind* of Brexit the UK had voted for had yet taken shape. 'It was quite striking that the British had not prepared in any way for the eventuality of Brexit,' recalls one Irish minister. 'We knew this, and we knew the reason why. We knew they weren't preparing because, of course, they didn't want to be seen to be preparing for an outcome they were campaigning not to have.'

UK Rep issued a statement that Britain would continue to play its role as a full member state and would take a 'constructive' approach to negotiations on any new EU laws and regulations. But if Britain was the swing vote on a policy that would kick in *after* they left, then they would abstain.

The problem was that under the EU's weighted voting system, an abstention was equivalent to a No vote. The first big issue to come up after Brexit was a proposal to further reduce mobile-phone roaming charges for citizens travelling to other member states. There was a group of countries that wanted the wholesale caps that determine the charges to be as low as possible. Britain was part of that bloc (as was Ireland), and the British Ambassador's vote became the determining one. 'If the Brits had stayed where they were, we would all have ended up with lower caps,' recalls the diplomat. 'Ultimately, the British abstention meant higher roaming charges for everyone.'

The Taoiseach was facing his own problems in the first fortnight after the Brexit vote. In media interviews on Sunday, 3 July, Dara Murphy and the Minister for Health, Simon Harris, both raised the idea of an all-island forum on Brexit involving all political parties, interest groups, citizens and stakeholders who had something to offer, or to learn. The problem was that the idea had not been first floated with First Minister Arlene Foster, whose party had campaigned vigorously for a Leave vote. The next day in Dublin, at a hastily scheduled meeting of the North South Ministerial Council, Kenny was given a humiliating public slapdown by Foster. After the meeting, Foster said: 'I believe that there are more than enough mechanisms by which we can discuss these issues on a North–South basis. Frankly, I don't believe there are any mechanisms needed because we can lift the phone to each other on a daily basis if that were so needed.' The implication was that the phone hadn't been lifted.

Recalling the events, Murphy accepts that the issue was badly handled, but feels that the idea was sound. 'We had a responsibility under the Good Friday Agreement. It became obvious that we'd have to get as much input from all of our own bodies and interested parties around the country, and that this should be extended to include the whole island. The Taoiseach felt it was vital that we extend it to cover the whole island, in a way that was voluntary and open. If [the DUP] wished to attend, fine. If they didn't, that was also fine.'

There was an anxious mood in the country. Because of the fall of sterling, farmers were getting 30 cents per kilo less from meat factories for carcass beef. The Irish Farmers' Association (IFA) warned that this was below the cost of production. Businesses operating near the border had historically lived with currency fluctuations, but this was different. 'We had two problems,' said John Foy, the Manager of a large SuperValu store in Cootehill. 'One was the bottom falling out of sterling and the other was the media – particularly one popular phone-in programme – which practically invited people to get in the car and head for a supermarket in the North.'

Ireland is big in mushrooms. But it wasn't always that way.

Harvesting mushrooms is notoriously labour-intensive. There is no quick, mechanical fix: they have to be picked by hand. In the early 1980s, Britain was producing 110,000 tonnes of mushrooms a year. Today, that figure has slumped to 46,000 tonnes. A big part of the reason is that while Britain boomed in the eighties, fewer and fewer people were interested in that kind of work. This was not a problem in Ireland, where the economy was weak. And the Irish industry made use of this advantage in another way. British mushrooms were presented to supermarkets unwashed and unsorted. As Gerry O'Reilly, who is the Chairman of the IFA's mushroom sector, recalls, the Irish industry came to specialize in a more labour-intensive – and ultimately profitable – presentation, 'all beautifully sized and heads facing up, all white and clean. The English said, "We're not going to do that." But with their lovely presentation, the supermarkets said they loved the Irish mushrooms, and they took them.'

As British producers went into decline, Irish producers began to boom. Production went from virtually zero to 90,000 tonnes a year: 70,000 in the Republic, 20,000 in the North. Irish producers then bought up the declining mushroom farms in the UK: today, 65 per cent of the UK mushroom sector is Irish-owned. Meanwhile, seven days a week, 50 articulated trucks loaded with mushrooms on 26 pallets would head for Irish ports, to deliver their delicate, hard-won, heads-up produce to British supermarket chains. Ireland is now the largest producer of mushrooms in the world per capita. 'We grow enough mushrooms for

32 million people,' says Gerry O'Reilly. 'We grow over 9 per cent of all the mushrooms grown in Europe – all from 53 Irish farms. All down little country roads.'

O'Reilly's farm produces 50 tonnes of mushrooms per week, and all of it goes to the UK. Mushrooms are typically a low-margin crop: you have to grow an awful lot of them to make a profit. A typical farm in Ireland would have cost €30,000 to set up in the 1980s; today it costs around €2 million. Growers need to create an entirely artificial climate – approximating a land of perpetual autumn – by means of high-powered fans, air-conditioning and computerized metering to measure the CO_2, the temperature and the humification inside huge, black polythene-covered tunnels.

Labour consumes 42 per cent of all costs. In Ireland, the labour is provided almost exclusively by Poles, Romanians, Bulgarians, Lithuanians and Latvians. 'They all work and live in the area, use the local schools, shop in the supermarkets, drink in the pubs,' says O'Reilly. 'They're good for the community.'

After the referendum and the drop in sterling, Gerry discussed the crisis with his wife, Mary. 'We were asking ourselves, will we manage or not? Because you see your friends – and these are people I know and we farmed with – they were going out of business. They were saying, "We can't stick this, we can't stay." We were appealing to the government looking for help, a holiday period on PRSI payments – my farm alone would send in €100,000 a year in PRSI . . .'

Luckily they had enjoyed a good beginning of the year because sterling had been extremely strong, so they were in the black when Brexit struck. 'But then two weeks on, three weeks, five weeks . . . we were saying we're not going to make it, it's getting worse and worse. Any bit of funds you had at the early half of the year were disappearing.'

The IFA lobbied the government in September, three months after the referendum, not to increase excise rates on agricultural diesel and other road fuels. There was a demand for a €2 million grant to help the sector find efficiencies. In the event, the publicity surrounding the mushroom farmers' plight proved useful. Irish producers, including Gerry, were able to approach Tesco, Sainsbury's and Safeway, telling them, 'Look, this is prime-time stuff in Ireland. It's not cry wolf, it's serious. And they believed us. And in fairness they raised the prices just before Christmas to match the new exchange rate.'

But the short-term fix is one thing. Long term, Brexit poses huge problems. The concern is not that the UK, outside the single market and the customs union, would suddenly revive its own industry. O'Reilly thinks it would be impossible, as they would have to rely heavily on foreign labour – an unlikely resource post-Brexit. Rather, the problem is that mushrooms are highly perishable. Any delays due to customs checks, paperwork for tariffs, country of origin, VAT payments and so on could be fatal. 'Mushrooms growing on my farm can leave at 6 o'clock in the evening,' explains O'Reilly, 'and they're in the shops tomorrow morning in Manchester, Liverpool, all across England. If we're going to have lorries stopped and checked, and customs on each side, all of that is going to be a delay for a fresh, perishable product.'

Irish mushroom producers were the first fallen foot soldiers in the opening skirmishes of Brexit. Their plight was a harsh warning to the vast agri-food sector. Brexit was peeling back the lid on food production, and Ireland was suddenly feeling perishable.

3. How Perishable is Ireland?

A report for the European Parliament in March 2017 showed that Ireland was the country most exposed to the economic effects of Brexit – by far. Germany exports 2.8 per cent of its GDP to the UK; Ireland exports 6.9 per cent. Beef exports to the UK alone are worth around €2.5 billion annually. Some regions are particularly exposed: in Cavan and Monaghan, one in five jobs depends on foods exports to the UK. Britain is not self-sufficient in food, so it relies on Ireland to make up the shortfall; Ireland is not self-sufficient in energy, so it relies on the UK to provide the bulk of its energy needs. Like the parody of an old-fashioned notion of marriage, Ireland feeds the UK, and the UK keeps Ireland warm at night.

The essential problem is this. Since Ireland and the UK joined the EEC together in 1973, all trade between both countries has come to be governed by shared membership of the single market and customs union. There are no barriers to that trade. Exports and imports flow back and forth across the Irish Sea, and back and forth over the land border. Britain has said it wants to leave the single market but still access it, or to have the closest possible trading relationship with it. Norway is not a member of the EU, but it is a member of the European Economic Area, an organization that brings together the EU and the European Free Trade Association (EFTA). That means it is regarded as part of the EU single market and as such enjoys full free-trade access and participates in areas such as research and development, education, social policy, the environment, consumer protection, tourism and culture (though it does not participate in the Common Agricultural Policy (CAP)). In return, Norway must accept the four freedoms (free movement of people, goods, capital and services); it must pay into the EU budget; and it must accept the body of EU law without having a seat at the table. These are things that the UK has so far refused to countenance.

Similarly, the UK has said it wants to leave the EU customs union yet still develop some kind of associate membership with it. The EU customs union means EU member states can trade goods and services with each other tariff-free. The EU has separate customs-union arrangements with three non-member states – Turkey, Andorra and San Marino – which provide preferential trading access, but these arrangements are much more limited in scope than full membership of the customs union.

If the UK leaves the single market and the customs union, a new trade agreement could take a long time to hammer out. The most recent EU trade agreement is the one with Canada. It took seven years to negotiate, and was famously held up when the tiny regional parliament of Wallonia in Belgium refused to ratify it. If it proves impossible to agree an EU–UK trade deal within the two-year departure period, the UK will have to revert to trade rules laid down at World Trade Organization (WTO) level. Under this rather grim scenario, there would be massive disruption in trade flows. Goods going in either direction would face tariffs. Some goods could become so much more expensive that customers would go elsewhere.

The problem doesn't end there. Within the single market, all the goods produced in one country and sold in another must comply with the same rules and standards. That means, for example, that the French lawnmower sector can't lobby against British lawnmowers just because they don't comply with some obscure French blade-cutting tradition. When it comes to food and agricultural products, the issue is particularly acute. The trade in food can be devastated if there is an animal-health scandal. There has been no shortage of these in Europe: BSE, foot and mouth, dioxins in pig meat and cheese, horsemeat turning up in beef burgers, bird flu and so on. Over time, the regulations governing livestock and other food products (the so-called sanitary and phyto-sanitary rules) have become deeper and more complex, governing the way animals are raised, slaughtered, processed, labelled and transported across EU borders.

Post-Brexit, any food that is produced in Northern Ireland and sent across the border into the Irish Republic will have to be checked by the Irish Department of Agriculture, Food and the Marine, since the UK would be under an entirely different standards and regulations regime. Equally, the UK would have its own food standards and Irish exporters would have to comply with those. Of course, common sense would suggest the UK should simply adopt the same food and hygiene standards with which it has complied as an EU member. But if Britain signs new trade agreements with other parts of the globe, it would likely have to relax its own standards to facilitate food imports, say, from Brazil or Argentina.

In 2015 alone, Ireland exported €39 billion in goods and services to the UK, 17 per cent of total Irish exports. (Only the USA, at 22 per cent, accounts for more Irish exports.) Even more dramatically, Ireland relies on the UK for 32.2 per cent of our imports. Many of these goods are not just the consumer stalwarts that line our supermarket shelves. They are also 'intermediate' goods, i.e. the parts or ingredients needed to produce stuff that Irish companies go on to export.

Ireland's pharmaceutical and chemicals sector is highly profitable, so it ought to be able to weather a reduction in its exports to Britain. But it accounts for over 60 per cent of the corporate tax take per employee in the entire manufacturing sector. The food and drink sector has a lower turnover, and lower profit margins, but it employs more people relative to its financial footprint. And because profit margins are low, those companies are much more vulnerable to any restrictions in trade, any slowdown in the UK economy or any fall in the exchange rate.

Much of the discussion of exports post-Brexit has focused on goods, but Ireland is arguably even more exposed in the services sector. In 2015 we exported €23.5 billion in services to the UK, compared with only €15.5 billion in goods. IT or computer services are the most valuable, accounting for around €7 billion each year and a 30 per cent share of the total value of services exports. Services are also big employers. The transport, tourism, communications, business, repairs and processing sectors are worth a combined €73 billion in gross added value to the Irish economy, and, in 2014, employed 989,000 people.

The regional vulnerability is striking. The 2015 ESRI report points out that Kilkenny, Laois, Waterford, Tipperary, Roscommon, Cavan and Monaghan would be hit hard because they rely heavily on the Brexit-sensitive sectors of agriculture, forestry and fishing. The most sensitive sector of all, food and drink, is particularly important to Kilkenny, Longford, Cavan and Monaghan. Textiles are important in Donegal and Wicklow, while basic and fabricated metals are key in Offaly, Limerick, Waterford and Monaghan.

Chemicals and pharmaceuticals are the significant industries in South Dublin, Wicklow, Cork, Waterford and Roscommon. It is not hard to see just how politically toxic Brexit could become at the regional level.

And what are the implications of Brexit for North–South trade?

The North is much more heavily dependent on the South as an export market than the South is on the North. In 1974, some 9.3 per cent of exports from the South went to the North. By 2014, it had declined to 1.8 per cent. By contrast, according to figures supplied by the Northern Ireland Statistics and Research Agency, up to 37.9 per cent of the North's services exports went to the South in 2013, and 25 per cent of manufacturing exports followed suit in 2014. The North is thus particularly vulnerable to the changes Brexit is likely to bring. It has a small population, and an economy that has historically been skewed in favour of the public sector. That means it struggles to hold on to talented young people once they leave for university, and in some sectors of the economy the labour provided by Eastern Europeans will most likely no longer be available. The North needs to import a large amount of meat and dairy products, according to evidence provided to the House of Lords by the food lobby group NIFDA. This is likely to mean higher prices for consumers. The farming sector, for its part, is bound to be in for a post-Brexit shock. A total of 87 per cent of farm income is derived from the single farm payment under the EU's Common Agricultural Policy. That tap will be turned off once Britain leaves. The Treasury has said it will continue to support the sector after 2020, but few observers believe they will match the vast CAP subsidies.

Ireland's fishing fleet depends on access to UK waters

under the EU's Common Fisheries Policy (CFP). Might the UK close those waters post-Brexit?

Ireland has become much more dependent on the UK for energy. There are gas and electricity interconnectors, and there's a single electricity market on the island of Ireland. Brexit will have implications for how that interdependence is governed, both in terms of the rules underpinning it and the investment decisions taken by the UK in the future. Also, how will Brexit hit cross-border education, security cooperation, health services, pension and social-welfare entitlements?

Of graver importance, the peace process in Northern Ireland is no longer guaranteed to continue its stable trajectory: a fundamental element of the Good Friday Agreement is the de facto evaporation of the land border, and the flow of people, goods, services, ideas, culture and students back and forth. The EU provides a stabilizing third wheel in what had previously been, to quote the former Taoiseach John Bruton, an 'unequal bilateral' relationship. Irish and British ministers have built relaxed and productive rapports over the years when they meet at Council of Ministers meetings in Brussels or Luxembourg. Issues that are tricky on the island can be approached in a more relaxed format in Brussels; likewise, Irish and UK ministers can get a common understanding on EU policies via the British-Irish Council.

The EU has spent billions on shoring up the peace process and nurturing cross-community, cross-border links. The money has been perceived by loyalists and nationalists alike as *neutral*, and therefore acceptable. Suddenly, with Brexit, one of those rare issues that had once united communities now threatened to divide them.

*

These, then, were among the worries that Ireland was facing as Brexit became a reality in the summer of 2016.

The election of Theresa May, the Home Secretary, as leader of the Conservative Party on 11 July ended the destabilizing vacuum in British politics. Dublin felt that this was the best outcome. According to one senior diplomat, 'Theresa May was far and away the most adult of the bunch.'

But the sense of respite did not last long. May had campaigned for Britain to remain in the EU, if somewhat half-heartedly. Now, any hopes she would import her Remain instincts into Number 10 were quickly dashed. She promoted a number of high-profile Leave campaigners to high office, most notably Boris Johnson, who became Foreign Secretary. 'Brexit does mean Brexit,' she said in her first reported remarks as Prime Minister, 'and we are going to make a success of it.'

One of May's first acts was to create two new government departments that would show Brexit was for real. The Department for International Trade, headed by the long-standing eurosceptic Dr Liam Fox, would seek new trade agreements around the globe. This was an unambiguous signal the UK would be leaving the EU customs union. The Department for Exiting the European Union, or DexEU, as it quickly became known, would, meanwhile, take on the giant administrative burden of extracting Britain from the EU. 'I remember receiving correspondence with the new letterhead from DexEU,' recalls Dara Murphy, Ireland's Minister for European Affairs. 'To see it on a letterhead was quite stark, the fact that they had already established a department quite early in the process to do this.'

The way the new department was structured was also an indication of how polarized Whitehall was becoming in the wake of the Leave victory. According to one senior British diplomat, DexEU would be deliberately controlled in a partisan manner, both in its structure and in the personnel involved. Had DexEU been simply attached to the Foreign and Commonwealth Office (FCO) or the existing Cabinet Office, it would have maintained a certain neutrality. But there was little room in the toxic miasma swirling around Brexit for neutrality. It was clear Theresa May wanted a much more ideological department to manage Britain's withdrawal. She chose David Davis, MP, a former Tory leadership candidate and prominent Leave campaigner, to head the new department.

Sir Ivan Rogers, who was overseeing the shock transition from the vantage point of UKRep, had asked Theresa May if he was still needed in Brussels. The answer from her, and from the Cabinet Secretary, Sir Jeremy Heywood, was very much a yes. Sir Ivan was the *éminence grise*, the person who understood it all, who had the networks and the knowledge. He could transfer intelligence back to the centre, help set up the new DexEU department, and inform the Prime Minister's new sherpa, the senior adviser who would report directly to her on all matters Brexit. The sherpa would now be Olly Robbins, the new Permanent Secretary of DexEU. Robbins had taken over from Rogers as Tony Blair's Principal Private Secretary and had continued serving under Gordon Brown when Brown replaced Blair as Prime Minister. Robbins later moved to the Home Office as Second Permanent Secretary (yet another key official that May brought with her from the Home Office). Critically, Robbins had developed a close working relationship with John Callinan when he was in charge of British–Irish relations in the Taoiseach's Department.

The mechanism for leaving the EU had, appropriately enough, been drafted by a former British diplomat, John Kerr. Article 50 of the Lisbon Treaty was conceived just after 10 new countries had joined the EU in 2004; at the time it was felt that, if any country was going to leave, it might be one of the new ones. The text of Article 50 has five paragraphs. Any country could leave: it would simply have to inform the European Council, which would then take charge of a divorce negotiation lasting two years. EU law would cease to apply on the day withdrawal took place, and the departing country would be excluded from any EU discussions about the issue while the negotiations were under way.

In essence, Article 50 gives all of the negotiating leverage to the EU, not the departing member state. But which part of the EU? Almost immediately, during the first meeting of the EU27 on 29 June, there was a dispute over who would be in control.

The EU is made up of several institutions. The European Commission is the executive arm, charged with developing EU policy, safeguarding the rights of EU citizens, ensuring EU law is implemented and looking after the general European 'interest'. The European Council represents the heads of government (the Council of the European Union, somewhat confusingly, is where ministers from each country come to negotiate). The European Parliament is the directly elected assembly that is supposed to provide a third layer of democratic accountability.

The European Council was quickest out of the traps. On 26 June, Jeppe Tranholm-Mikkelsen, the Council Secretary General, appointed Didier Seeuws, a former Belgian diplomat, to head a Council Task Force on Brexit. This caused something of a flap within the European Commission, which had assumed *it* would be in charge of the negotiations. At the EU summit two days later, Commission President Jean-Claude Juncker addressed the leaders of the remaining 27 member states. He said he didn't want to get into a 'typical Brussels turf war', but then produced a six-page legal opinion as to why the Commission should be in charge.

The scrap between the Commission and Council over who would be negotiating Brexit was parked. But the uncertainty was unsettling for the Irish government. The potential scale of the damage Brexit might do was well understood. But just how bad would depend on a host of unknowns. Even with the Tory leadership issue settled, Dublin didn't know for sure whether Britain would go for a hard Brexit (leave the single market and the customs union) or a soft Brexit (stay in both); nor did it know when the process would start. It didn't know if the future trading relationship would be negotiated *alongside* the divorce, or only afterwards.

In the first week of July, a senior Irish official, who would later be instrumental in the negotiations, gave a sense of the precarious position Ireland was in. 'We will need to take one step back from the UK. We need to be ruthless and clear. This will be a negotiation between the EU and the UK. Other member states are affected as well as Ireland. We'll have a special case in relation to the North, but we're just one voice – we'll have to make a strong and clear voice.'

The official was under no illusions about the weakness of the British negotiating hand, and the risks that posed for Ireland. 'Britain will start by saying they want everything they have at the moment, i.e. they'll start at the top and force the EU to start taking things away. In other words, make them the bad guys. The UK can't end up with what they have now.

They'll have to lose their rights, their access, their powers. But they're canny. They'll get a good deal. They will need a hard slap, though, on one big issue. We'll need to make sure it doesn't affect us. That's the space we'll need to watch.

'You'll see a shift in language from the Brits towards Ireland. We're on the other side from them. Associating ourselves too much with them will unnerve the public, the idea that we're in the same boat as the Brits. We have a child together, the North. They remain the most important trading partner. They will try to pull us out of the EU. They'll make it hard for us to stay in. That would solve the North issue and weaken the EU. The UK is in a weak position and they'll have to play every card they have. And we're a card. Expect people to start talking about it. It will weaken Ireland's position. Who's to blame for the mess? The Brits will start to shift the blame, saying it's the EU's fault. If they start to win the propaganda war, the EU will start to look unattractive to Ireland.'

On 26 July 2016, Enda Kenny arrived in Downing Street for his first encounter with Theresa May. The new Prime Minister was very much an unknown quantity. She had made two visits to the Irish Embassy in London: once, on 20 January 2016, as the guest speaker at the annual Journalists' Charity event; and two years previously, in order to sign a visa agreement alongside Tánaiste Frances Fitzgerald.

One senior diplomat said that during the January visit, Theresa May had stayed at the embassy for a couple of hours. 'It was charming,' he recalls. 'It was a very nice evening. She was less frosty and warmer than I had anticipated. She has an image of being rather austere, but was quite good fun and quite amusing. Her speech was well crafted and delivered.'

But now she was Prime Minister, and in charge of a British foreign policy that could do serious damage to Ireland's national interests. Irish officials understood May had to navigate the treacherous waters of the Conservative Party, in thrall, as it suddenly was, to its eurosceptic wing. They could appreciate the logic of appointing Boris Johnson, Liam Fox and David Davis in order to prove her Brexit credentials. Other Irish officials had known the Prime Minister from her Home Office days, having encountered her during meetings in Brussels. 'She was a very stable, sober, thoughtful person,' recalls one senior civil servant.

May and Kenny held a 15-minute meeting on the first floor of Number 10. They then joined officials from both sides for lunch in the dining room. The first change was culinary: in David Cameron's time there were always three courses for lunch. Theresa May offered two. For dessert, the assembled guests ate pavlova, while the Prime Minister had a small bowl of fruit. May was accompanied by Fiona Hill, her Joint Chief of Staff and former Media Adviser in the Home Office, and Mark Sedwill, a former British diplomat and at that time Permanent Secretary at the Home Office. May frequently deferred to her officials. She also confessed that, despite having spent several years attending justice ministers' meetings in Brussels, she had only just learned to her surprise that when attending leaders' summits as Prime Minister she would be 'on her own' in the room, and not accompanied by officials.

'She was very, very cautious,' recalls one Irish official present. 'The Taoiseach explained our concerns, but it was very much a getting-to-know-you meeting. There had been a very easy relationship between the Taoiseach and Cameron. This was more formal.'

The Prime Minister revealed no hints of her thinking on the single market or customs union. 'She was extremely cautious. It was all about taking her time and analysing,' says the official. 'She didn't go into much detail, but she responded to the Taoiseach, saying she was aware of the importance of the issue.'

Another Irish official was encouraged. 'It was good, businesslike,' he recalls. 'Very clearly, from the word go they were saying all the right things. They were talking up their determination to avoid damaging the peace process, keeping open the border, not returning to the borders of the past. They were talking up the Common Travel Area and their commitment to that and the status of the Irish community in Britain. All the things we wanted to hear, they were saying.'

At a joint media briefing after the lunch, the Prime Minister said she was determined to maintain 'the closest possible relationship' between the two countries, despite Brexit. There was a 'strong will' to preserve free travel across the border (she suggested this could involve the use of data on passengers arriving from outside the British Isles). She insisted the referendum would not undermine the peace process: 'It is in all our interests to work together to safeguard our national security, and the outcome of the referendum will not undermine it. We are both fully committed to working together in support of the Northern Ireland Executive to build a better, stronger, safer future for the people of Northern Ireland.'

In separate remarks to reporters, the Taoiseach was more explicit: 'I do not favour, and would not agree to, a hard border with a whole range of customs posts, and neither does the Prime Minister. There will be no hard border from

Dundalk to Derry in the context of it being a European border, and by that I mean customs posts every mile along the road.'

Those who had followed May's (limited) utterances during the referendum campaign would have recalled that she had been much more candid then about the implications for the Irish land border. 'It is inconceivable,' she had said, 'that a vote for Brexit would not have a negative impact on the North–South border, bringing cost and disruption to trade and to people's lives.'

After the meeting, a senior EU negotiator contacted a number of British officials to ask them how there could be no hard border in Ireland if the UK were to leave the customs union. According to the negotiator, the officials said: 'We don't know. We don't have an answer.'

By the time August came around, Ireland was still metabolizing the new reality. There would be a new, 12-strong Brexit Cabinet Committee involving the Taoiseach, the Tánaiste and the ministers of all the big government portfolios. John Callinan was appointed to head up an integrated Task Force within the Department of the Taoiseach, which would coordinate the overall response to Brexit. Assistant Secretary Eamonn Molloy was moved up to take control of British–Irish–Northern Ireland issues. The EU Affairs Division was repatriated to Foreign Affairs and headed by Rory Montgomery. There was now a clear division of labour: the Taoiseach's Department would drive Brexit policy; the Department of Foreign Affairs would implement it via outreach to other capitals and EU institutions. The Minister for Foreign Affairs, Charlie Flanagan, duly set off to meet the other EU foreign ministers. There were plans for new postings to the London, Brussels, Berlin and Paris embassies. Extra legal and trade staff were brought in. The interdepartmental committee on Brexit was scaled up. There were management subcommittees and working groups dealing with any and all Brexit implications.

There were signals, at least, that Ireland's plight was not being overlooked. On 15 and 16 July, many thousands of miles away from the Irish border, delegates gathered in the Mongolian capital Ulaanbaatar for the 11th Asia–Europe Summit. Unprompted, German Chancellor Angela Merkel warned Asian and EU leaders that Northern Ireland would be one of the factors that would have to be dealt with. (According to one diplomatic source, she delivered the same message to a conference of German ambassadors in Berlin at the end of August.)

But before summer's end, there would be a major development that would place a very harsh spotlight on Ireland's relationship with the European Union. On 31 August, the European Commission announced that Apple had benefited from an illegal sweetheart tax deal with the Irish government to the tune of €13 billion. It followed a two-year investigation of Apple's tax affairs in Ireland, in particular into two so-called tax rulings allegedly negotiated between the Revenue Commissioners and the US multinational. According to the EU Competition Commissioner, these arrangements allowed Apple to pay an effective corporate-tax rate of 1 per cent on its European profits in 2003, and only 0.005 per cent in 2014. The decision prompted a viscerally harsh response from the government, perhaps the most robust invective ever directed at Brussels from an Irish administration. Enda Kenny declared: 'I make no apology whatsoever for the decision to appeal this. This is about us as a sovereign nation. This is about the rights of a small nation. I'm not sure if the European Commission wants to ingratiate themselves with more powerful countries than ours.'

The Minister for Finance, Michael Noonan, described the decision as a 'bridgehead' upon which there might be further attacks on Ireland's corporate-tax policies, a source of resentment that could be traced to Nicolas Sarkozy's row with Kenny during his first EU summit in 2011. 'There is a lot of envy across Europe about how successful we are in putting the HQs of so many companies into Ireland,' Noonan said.

Inevitably, the Apple eruption filtered into the wider Brexit debate at home and abroad. Speaking to *Today FM* from Strasbourg, UKIP leader Nigel Farage described the judgement as 'extraordinary'. He said: 'I think Ireland, in the next few years, perhaps short few years, is going to have to have the same debate about its relationship with the European Union, about its right to its own government.'

4. Is Kenny Available?

In July, an official in the Department of the Taoiseach received a curious email. It came from the diary secretary of David Davis, the Secretary of State for DexEU – aka 'Minister for Brexit'. The email read: 'The Secretary of State has told me he wants to meet Kenny. Please let us know if Kenny is available.' A senior diplomat immediately wrote to a British official further up the Whitehall food chain. 'The message was sent [back],' recalls the diplomat, '(a), the Taoiseach is not Davis's interlocutor and (b), you don't refer to the Prime Minister of a country by his *surname*.'

David Davis grew up in a council flat in South London, raised by a single mother. Once an SAS reservist, he exuded a blend of street-fighting grit and breezy confidence throughout what was, until Brexit, a somewhat chequered career in Conservative politics. Theresa May revived that career by appointing him Minister for Brexit after she became Prime Minister.

Davis's first scheduled visit to Dublin was on 8 September. Ahead of the trip, he wrote sunnily in the *Irish Times* of Britain's 'new' partnership with the EU. 'And,' he wrote, 'there will be no closer relationship, friendship and alliance than the one that exists between the UK and Ireland. [My engagements in Dublin] will be amongst my earliest meetings in my new role ... and I am certain they will lay the foundations for an even more successful, warm and purposeful working relationship.'

According to one Irish minister, in the weeks leading up to the meeting, the turf wars between Boris Johnson, Liam Fox and Davis over who was running Brexit had become so intense that they were jockeying to see who could pull the highest rank on overseas trips. For the visit to Dublin, the higher the rank on the Irish side, the more authority it would confer on Davis – hence the email seeking an audience with 'Kenny'. 'Were we aware that this was part of the issue? Absolutely,' recalls the minister. 'There was a battle as to who would be the boss: would it be Boris, Davis, Fox? They were trying to reach out to the Taoiseach, to the Tánaiste. But the Taoiseach meets Theresa May.'

By the time the British delegation arrived in Dublin, Irish ministers and officials had become exasperated. Utterances from the triumvirate of Brexit ministers on the key issues had been contradictory. London was talking up full access to the EU single market, but insisting there would no longer be free movement of EU citizens. 'We were getting really frustrated with them, every time one of their ministers contradicted [another],' recalls the minister. 'Worse than the jockeying was the fact that they had different messages. That was of no use to us. We were trying to establish what exactly they wanted.'

Dublin figured the best option was to have one overall meeting with everyone present: ministers and officials. That meant on one side David Davis and Robin Walker, MP, the Parliamentary Under-Secretary of State at DexEU, who had responsibility for Ireland; and on the Irish side Charlie Flanagan, the Minister for Foreign Affairs, Frances Fitzgerald, the Tánaiste and Minister for Justice, and Dara Murphy, the Minister for European Affairs. 'We felt it would be much better from our point of view if we all got into the same room at the same time,' says one senior source who was present. 'That meant we could give one line, and receive one line.'

Another official recalls: 'The British have a style of having many meetings in order to press certain buttons. With Frances Fitzgerald they would have pressed a security button, and focus on Home Office-style issues dealing with immigration, but also security. We'd like to see it as one piece. That's why we had one meeting. Individual meetings allow them to pick people off.'

On one level, the encounter went well, although the room in Iveagh House was somewhat crowded. The British side was 'constructive' on the Common Travel Area and the Northern Ireland question. They also seemed to be very keen on maintaining security cooperation with Ireland. Davis was asked about the European Arrest Warrant (EAW), a key EU instrument that allows suspects in one member state to be arrested and extradited at the behest of another (it will remain, until Brexit, the only legal method of extraditing suspects from one side of the Irish border to the other). He replied that he had campaigned for Britain to opt out of the EAW, but that Theresa May had already decided she wanted the UK to keep it.

But when it came to other sensitive topics, the mood changed. Davis began resorting to what were essentially Brexit campaign slogans when the questions became difficult. 'What was striking was a bullish confidence,' recalls another senior Irish official. 'He was still at the point where he was dismissing difficulties with "It will be fine, don't worry", "It's still early in the day", "Brexit means Brexit", "We want an orderly departure", etc.'

Things got worse when the British side accused the EU of

wanting to punish the UK for leaving. The mood darkened and the discussion became heated. 'They were saying,' recalls another senior source, '"We will not be punished. It would not be in the interests of Europe. We will not accept it." It was pointed out back to them that if there was any negative impact, *they* had brought it on themselves. There *will* be a downside for the UK, *and* Ireland. It's just about trying to keep it as minimal as possible. They were surprised at the response they got from us. It was the first really cold delivery from us that we're in the [EU]27. The EU position was that we wanted it to be the best possible relationship, but that any attempt to divide and conquer member states would not work with Ireland.'

The meeting ended with no statement from the British side.

That night, 500 guests settled down to the British–Irish Chamber of Commerce dinner. The Chamber normally invites British politicians to the dinner, and it just so happened that the hastily arranged Davis visit coincided with the event, so he was invited to attend. Davis ended up sitting next to the Taoiseach, who had been booked for many months as the keynote speaker. The Brexit minister noticeably declined to take the microphone to contribute to the discussion, which would normally be an option for high-level British guests. However strong the urge to grab the Brexit mantle, Davis, it seemed, was reluctant to opine on the burning issue of the day.

'It's so centralized in London,' observed one Irish diplomat, 'that only Theresa May speaks.'

On Friday, 11 February 2000, an EU Commissioner travelled to Belfast to meet political leaders. The new Northern

Ireland Executive was up and running, but in a fragile state. The Commissioner had come to try to solve a problem over EU funds for the new administration, held up because of the lack of a North–South element to one part of the money. In a surreal twist, the Commissioner turned up on the very day the Stormont Assembly was on the brink of collapse because of the impasse over IRA-weapons decommissioning.

The night before, the Northern Ireland Secretary, Peter Mandelson, had passed legislation to suspend the Executive. Throughout that Friday there were frantic moves involving all parties, including the British and Irish governments, to stop the suspension going ahead. In the midst of the chaos, the leaders of the Northern political parties still had to make time to meet the senior EU official. The DUP had a policy of not talking to Sinn Féin, so the meetings had to be done separately. The Commissioner did, however, talk to the First Minister, David Trimble, and the Deputy First Minister, Seamus Mallon, together. Conscious of the alternative title of the Belfast Agreement, the Commissioner tried to ease the tension with a joke: 'I suppose this is *Bad* Friday?'

The Commissioner was Michel Barnier. At the time, he was in charge of the EU's regional affairs portfolio. 'He couldn't understand why he had to meet DUP and Sinn Féin representatives *separately*,' recalls a senior EU official who was present. 'He said, "I'm just repeating the same thing all day with different people. Can't we have this discussion together?"'

Over time, Michel Barnier would shed his incredulity and develop an intuitive feel for the complexities of Northern Ireland and the sensitivities of tribal enemies. Between 1999 and 2004, Barnier would oversee the spending of €531 million in EU funding for Northern Ireland under the PEACE II programme, as well as tens of millions of euro in regional and structural payments.

In August 2016, having served as both French foreign and agriculture minister, and then as the EU Internal Market Commissioner, Barnier would be making one last big return to Brussels. This time he would be taking on one of the most formidable roles of his career: Chief Negotiator on Brexit. And, once again, the antagonisms of Northern Ireland would be something he would have to deal with.

The issue of who would become the EU negotiator was a keenly watched parlour game all summer. The European Council had appointed the Belgian diplomat Didier Seeuws as its lead official on Brexit just three days after the referendum, stealing a march on the Commission. Although the Council would be taking overall ownership of the Brexit divorce, the European Commission would have to be heavily involved in the day-to-day nitty-gritty of the negotiations.

According to several former Commission figures, once the Council had appointed Seeuws, the Commission wanted a heavyweight political figure. One choice was Frans Timmermans, the deeply Anglophile and multilingual Dutch Commissioner. But it was Michel Barnier who was approached. He had been working with the Commission on developing EU defence policy and was close to President Juncker. He also had experience in negotiating with the British during his reform of financial services as Internal Market Commissioner (in 2010 the *Daily Telegraph* wondered if he was 'the most dangerous man in Europe').

'It was a smart choice,' says one senior former Commission official. 'He is serious, hard-working, French, and tied into the Franco-German elite view of Europe. He has experience of the UK with the financial-services stuff. He was initially considered a huge threat but turned out to be okay, a safe pair of hands, usually good at assembling a good team around him.'

The British tabloids focused their attention on the fact that Barnier was French and (supposedly) federalist, and therefore not to be trusted (the *Daily Express* called him a 'Brit-bashing EU-mad French politician'). According to one senior Commission official: 'We would need somebody who is known, who would be accepted on the EU side, who has a reputation if we're to be able to negotiate with the British. *Anybody* French would have invoked the same reaction. We need someone who is clearly on the side of the 27, not too soft on the British, but who at the same time is able to negotiate with them.'

Phil Hogan, Ireland's EU Commissioner, believes Ireland has been fortunate in having someone who knows Northern Ireland intimately as the Chief Negotiator. 'You don't learn that overnight. You have to feel it, and hear it on a regular basis before you get the nuance of what the political dimension is to the fragility of the peace.'

Furthermore, Barnier has a long ministerial CV that gives him a political feel for the most acute issues for Ireland: he has variously been an agriculture minister, a fisheries minister and a regional affairs Commissioner. But Brexit is unlike anything the EU has done before. It will throw up tensions and dynamics that are entirely unpredictable. When the EU negotiates a major treaty, whether it's a trade agreement or a new country joining, the Commission is the main negotiator because it has the expertise. But this is an accession process in *reverse*. 'It's the most serious negotiation we'll ever have done,' says one EU official. 'It will be different from the agreements between the EU and Ukraine or Georgia or Turkey. In those negotiations there is always a sense of fairness: once the criteria for the third country is set out, you don't move the goalposts. This is different. It's a divorce. It's divisive.'

It was also a divorce in which both parties were still under the same roof. There were fears bordering on paranoia that Britain would try to undermine the EU's position from within by trying to pick off one country at a time. Diktats flowed from the 13th floor of the Commission's headquarters that Brexit could *not* be discussed until Britain triggered Article 50. From an early stage, the mantra went out: no negotiation before notification. Officials spoke of being in fear for their jobs if they briefed reporters on anything Brexit-related. The Commission deployed encryption software known as SECEM to ensure that any Brexit documents would be traceable in the event of emailing or printing. Even the normal interaction between interest groups and the Commission has been affected. One senior official in the Irish Farmers' Association recalls trying to get some insights during regular meetings with the Commission's agriculture directorate: 'If Brexit came up they said, "Sorry, we can't discuss it." There was a clear instruction that they couldn't. You were free to ask a question, but they just wouldn't answer it.'

It was not just officials who were under pressure not to get into anything that smacked of pre-negotiation. One senior Commission figure believes the paranoia about British tactics was not misplaced. 'The Brits were trying to get concessions from different people,' she says. 'They were trying to get the Eastern European states to agree some kind of bilateral deal or understanding that would safeguard the interests of all British citizens in their member states, and vice versa. But they were rebuffed. The Brits were *furious* that there was a solid wall on "no negotiation".'

Of all member states, Ireland was most vulnerable to British pressure at pre-negotiation. Irish officials were watching their backs. Everyone knew that Ireland would be worst affected by Brexit, so there were sideways glances to ensure there was no under-the-counter bilateralism.

'We have actually been extremely correct in how we've approached things and at pains to say this,' insists a senior Irish diplomat. 'Other member states would ask the question or raise an eyebrow. But our discussions with the British have been exclusively about our own issues. We haven't sought to broaden the discussion into a wider speculation about how the [EU–UK] negotiations might be organized.'

At the political level, the British government was still participating in the regular Council meetings in Brussels and Luxembourg. One Irish minister recalls: 'I had to tell my British counterpart three times, "No, I can't discuss that with you." Three times, in the *same* meeting!'

Sir Ivan Rogers was having 'intense' contacts throughout the autumn with his Irish opposite number, Declan Kelleher, with whom he was on close terms. In general, whether it was meeting other ambassadors or senior EU officials, Rogers was reduced to arranging furtive coffees around the European quarter to get a sense of what the EU was thinking.

One senior British diplomat recalls: 'I kept on saying to the Commission side, and the Council side, "Look, I understand you want no negotiation without notification, and you don't want any pre-negotiations, and you're desperately worried that we Brits will pick apart your solidarity, etc., etc. But, in the end, guys, it's a mistake not to have some pre-discussions in some quiet fashion, because you've got to work out what the art of the possible is." I do think we'll all regret this afterwards. Most negotiations I've ever worked on have a lot of pre-cooking and pre-discussion and a lot of pitch-rolling where the two sides start to understand each other better.'

But the EU27 wasn't interested.

On 16 September, they gathered in Bratislava to plot the future direction of the European Union, minus Britain. The focus was on deepening defence and security cooperation, including with NATO. Enda Kenny was already having to balance Ireland's need to stay close to the British with loyalty to the other 26 member states. He told reporters in Bratislava: 'The Europeans understand that the contribution they've made to the peace process in Ireland has resulted in the border that used to be there – one of the most heavily militarized borders for many years – being moved. In that sense what we want to do is maintain our cooperation with our European colleagues and, at the same time, maintain our contact and close relationships with the United Kingdom.'

The Irish government would have its first encounter with Michel Barnier in Dublin over three weeks later, on 12 October. Throughout September, Barnier had been getting to grips with his new role. He set up his own team within the Commission, which was given the somewhat elaborate title of Task Force for the Preparation and Conduct of the Negotiations with the United Kingdom under Article 50. It was quickly shortened by staff to the snappier TF50. The Task Force would grow to around 30, drawing in expertise from the vast directorates-general as the preparations got under way.

Already, the broad parameters of the Brexit negotiations were taking shape. Like every nasty divorce, one of the first issues would be over money. Britain was on the hook for billions of euro in commitments, programmes and pledges contained in the EU budget that ran for many years into the future. According to a number of calculations, this could amount to between €40 billion and €60 billion. As *Financial Times* journalist Alex Barker wrote in a paper for the Centre for European Reform, there were 'pension pledges, infrastructure spending plans, the decommissioning of nuclear sites, even assets like satellites and the Berlaymont Building – all these must be divvied up in a settlement if Brexit is to be anything but a hard, unmanaged, unfriendly exit.'

This was not just of academic interest to Dublin. Through the so-called Balance of Payments facility and the European Financial Stabilisation Mechanism, the EU had extended loans to Ireland that included one for €22.5 billion. The government was also conscious that Ireland had benefited from billions in EU funds over the years, and now Eastern European countries needed reassurance that money pledged to *them* would be honoured. But putting a €60 billion exit bill in lights was, according to one Irish minister, 'injudicious'. A scrap over money would hold up the negotiating process. Ireland wanted the divorce done as quickly as possible, so that talks about trade could begin.

Whereas David Davis and his accompanying minister held one meeting with three Irish ministers, Michel Barnier was afforded the courtesy, if that was the right word, of *four* separate encounters: with the Taoiseach, with Charlie Flanagan, with Frances Fitzgerald and with Dara Murphy. Barnier had similar messages for each, but his knowledge of Ireland was described as 'encouraging'. He spoke fondly about the

€13 million Peace Bridge in Derry, part funded by Brussels, and urged the government to make a strong case to the other 26 member states based on the risks of Brexit to the peace process.

There was scope for technical discussions. Barnier was accompanied by three TF50 officials: Sabine Weyand, Stéphanie Riso and Georg Riekeles. Weyand, the Deputy Chief Negotiator, is a German official plucked from the Commission's powerful trade directorate-general, and thought to be favoured by Chancellor Merkel. She has been portrayed as both the brains and the brawn of TF50. One Irish diplomat describes her as follows: 'From Alsace, extremely smart and sharp, can smell if the stuff isn't up to snuff. Extremely efficient and effective as a coordinator. A good strategic sense.'

Stéphanie Riso was familiar to Ireland from her days as Deputy Head of Cabinet for Olli Rehn, the Commissioner during the EU–IMF bailout.

Barnier's meeting with Dara Murphy took place during a long lunch on the top floor of Government Buildings. Ireland's key Brexit negotiators, John Callinan and Rory Montgomery, were present, as were officials Elizabeth McCullough and Conor Gouldsbury. Discussing the Common Travel Area, Murphy recalls, 'We were all struck that he had a very detailed knowledge of it already. We had been prepared to give him information around the Good Friday Agreement. But he was already aware of it.'

Educating EU institutions and 26 capitals about the nuances of the Good Friday Agreement would be a major challenge. The peace agreement was a highly elaborate constitutional balancing act that did not lend itself to straightforward explanation. In September 2016, a senior Irish figure circulated a confidential 'non-paper' to the key Brexit negotiators on the EU side as part of what has been described as a 'pedagogical' process. The negotiators included Barnier, Didier Seeuws and Jeppe Tranholm-Mikkelsen, the Secretary General of the European Council. The three-page document described Northern Ireland as 'one of the EU's greatest successes ... [whose] transition from violent conflict to peace and political stability stands as a positive example to other regions facing similar problems.' Those gains 'must be a priority' during the Brexit negotiations.

The paper also emphasized the European dimension to a British–Irish problem, one reflected in 'an island with an invisible border, common trading standards and a sense of pooled sovereignty including a shared European identity [which] provides crucial reassurance to the nationalist community in Northern Ireland'. It drew attention to the 'physical border crossings and checkpoints [which were] powerful symbols of division and are primarily associated with the 30 years of violence in Northern Ireland'. Any reintroduction of a hard border would have 'a devastating impact on Northern Ireland and in particular on the thousands of people whose daily existence is a cross-border one'.

Furthermore, the Good Friday Agreement was 'based on the assumption of [the] continuation of EU membership by both the UK and Ireland' and the explicit recognition of its validity would 'need to involve the European Union'. Nationalists who dreamed of a United Ireland needed to be reassured that 'new obstacles to this option are [not] put in place by the fact that Ireland will remain in the EU while the UK does not.' In fact, a shared European identity had been a 'significant' factor in nationalists accepting the terms of the Good Friday Agreement and 'in unionists exploring the Irish element to their identity'.

The document set out the bilateral trading links between Ireland and the UK ('more than €1.2 billion per week') and the potential hit on the economy. For every 1 per cent GDP decrease in the UK economy, Ireland would suffer a 0.3 per cent decline. In language certain to press buttons in Brussels, the 'non-paper' concluded: 'The economic impact of Brexit could also have a negative impact on sovereign borrowing costs with potential knock on budgetary impacts.'

If Ireland and Europe were confused by the messages from, and disarray inside, the British system in August and September, there was brutal clarity on Sunday, 2 October.

The location was Birmingham, and the occasion was the Tory Party Conference. It was Theresa May's first as Leader and Prime Minister, and the first Conservative gathering since the Brexit vote.

May took to the stage and delivered a speech ringing with nationalist vigour and studded with hard-Brexit signposts. 'We have more Nobel Laureates than any country outside America,' she declared. 'We have the best intelligence services in the world, a military that can project its power around the globe, and friendships, partnerships and alliances in every continent . . . The referendum result was clear. It was legitimate. It was the biggest vote for change this country has ever known. Brexit means Brexit – and we're going to make a success of it.' There would be no spelling out what Britain wanted in terms of the single market or customs union, but the clues were pretty powerful. 'We are going to be a fully independent, sovereign country – a country that is no longer part of a political union with supranational institutions that can override national parliaments and courts. And that means we are going, once more, to have the freedom to make our own decisions on a whole host of different matters, from how we label our food to the way in which we choose to control immigration.'

At a stroke, Theresa May was ruling out any future role for the European Court of Justice or the free movement of people. That, in effect, ruled out membership of the single market. The Brexit faithful lapped it up.

Irish officials had not been warned in advance. But they were geographically closer than Theresa May perhaps realized. While the Conservatives were decamping to Birmingham, a large contingent of Irish civil servants was simultaneously travelling from Dublin to London. The group was made up of every senior government official across every department. They were in London to meet their opposite numbers in Whitehall. It was an annual meeting, established under a 2011 bilateral agreement between David Cameron and Enda Kenny; but the timing was no coincidence: the UK civil servants were, in the words of one member of the Irish team, 'off the leash for a short time'.

The meeting was held in the Foreign and Commonwealth Office on King Charles Street, close to Buckingham Palace. It attracted zero media attention, but it was not entirely surreptitious. On this occasion, the Irish side was to be represented by the Taoiseach's most senior civil servant, Martin Fraser, with Theresa May's Cabinet Secretary, Sir Jeremy Heywood, representing the British side. Irish Ambassador Dan Mulhall joined the meeting late, having travelled back by train from Birmingham.

There were perhaps around 50 officials and diplomats in the three bright, palatial rooms of the FCO's Locarno Suite. Originally designed by George Gilbert Scott for diplomatic dinners and conferences, and completed in 1868, the suite was named after the signing in 1925 of the Locarno Treaties, which were supposed to close the book on the First World War and settle the future relationship between the victorious powers and a defeated Germany.

The rhetoric from Birmingham was burning the ears of the participants in the Locarno Suite. British officials did their best to reassure their Irish counterparts that Theresa May's speech was simply playing to the gallery. 'There was a fair bit of real-time interpretation being done,' says one Irish official. 'They were trying to downplay some of the rhetoric being heard around Europe, including in Dublin, that was quite hostile and provocative and extreme. They were asking people to make allowances for the fact that she was at her party conference. But it was a little bit naive to think that it wouldn't be heard elsewhere.'

Another Irish diplomat viewed the Birmingham speech as at least giving some clarity. There still lingered what he termed a 'diehard optimism' that Theresa May hadn't actually, up to that point, meant what she'd said: 'The British were saying, "Ah, here, this is a political speech, don't take every word literally." My own view at the time was, once you've said something in public, it's hard to *unsay* it. In a way it confirmed her objective, which was to win the support of the Brexit side of the Tory Party, and the media.'

There was also an unspoken understanding that many of the senior officials on the British side were disappointed at the outcome of the referendum. 'It's fair to say that on the other side, most of the people in the room wouldn't have been happy with the [Brexit] situation,' recalls one Irish secretary general. 'So there was a degree of remorse and regret on their side, and equally on our side.'

Martin Fraser and Sir Jeremy Heywood made opening

speeches, before follow-up introductions by John Callinan and his opposite number, Olly Robbins, the Permanent Secretary in DexEU and Theresa May's sherpa. The assembly then broke off into separate groups. At one point there was a subset of exclusively Brexit-related discussions that lasted for two hours. One of these had *10* senior civil servants on each side.

There were five key Brexit areas under discussion: the peace process; the border; the Common Travel Area; police and security cooperation; and bilateral trade. But identifying the issues was about as far as all the highly qualified, high-level officials could get. 'You couldn't *not* talk about these things,' recalls one senior Irish official. 'But in practice you couldn't say an awful lot about them. Calling them out and recognizing them was the biggest issue, to be blunt.'

'The customs union idea, we knew, was going to be huge,' says one Irish official, 'but we didn't know where it was going to land. There was a lot of talk of them potentially staying *in* the customs union.' The two-day summit concluded with a greater understanding of the gravity of the impact of Brexit on relations between Ireland and the UK, and between North and South. The gathering helped to deepen the bond between Olly Robbins and John Callinan, the two key negotiators.

In the evening, officials repaired to the Red Lion on Westminster Street to unwind after the intensity of the discussions.

'There was a shared determination to deal with these issues creatively and effectively to reflect the unique circumstances on the island,' says one Irish diplomat. 'There was a determination not to let things sit.'

Irish officials were anxious about any perception among

the other 26 member states, or the EU institutions, that Ireland was engaging in covert negotiations. Dublin was in constant contact with the European Commission and the Council, so there was nothing being hidden. Suspicions along these lines were raised by Michel Barnier when he arrived in Dublin a few days later. 'It was a point he made quite bluntly,' says one Irish diplomat. 'He came saying, "The Commission is your negotiator, work out your position with us." He wasn't saying exactly, "Don't meet the British," rather "Stay within the proper channels."'

It was excruciating at times. 'We had to repeatedly dance on the head of a pin,' says one senior Irish negotiator. 'This no-negotiation mantra – we fully accepted that and the logic was impossible to argue with. But we had an existing work programme [with the British]. Brexit ran right across it. There was no way of avoiding it.'

Officials had to make it clear they needed to stay within certain boundaries. 'In the beginning it was something we had to labour with the British. A couple of rounds of that and it was clear what the boundaries were. We would have been perceived [by the other 26 member states] as being very close to the Brits on a number of issues, so there was always a perception that somehow we'd be, if not a proxy for them, too *sympathetic* in the negotiation process.'

That problem was acknowledged by senior British diplomats. 'There was a sense,' admits one British ambassador, 'that Ireland was the weakest link. There's always been that worry. You've got the distrust thing: are they secretly having deep discussions, deep negotiations or pre-negotiations with the Brits? It's a massive issue for the Irish establishment as to how you handle this. How do you demonstrate that you're firmly part of the 27 and won't break rank, but nevertheless how do you convince the other 26 that this is a much more existential issue for the Irish, and for your economy and society, than it is for them?'

There was always the suspicion, despite the bonhomie, that a solution for Ireland might be exploited by Britain in other areas. Avoiding a hard border was a case in point. 'The [European] Commission were wary of one thing,' says another senior Irish diplomat. 'If we came up with a bespoke solution for the Irish border, there was a fear that the Brits might then seize on it and say, "Well, you've agreed it in Ireland, now you're going to have to agree to it in Dover–Calais", or wherever else they had a problem.'

Following Theresa May's conference speech in early October, the Irish civil service realized it was looking at a hard Brexit. The pressure was on. Charlie Flanagan urged all ministers to engage more intensively with their Northern counterparts. He spoke of negotiating a special status for Northern Ireland. The Export Trade Council, headed up by six ministers, announced it was intensifying the search for markets beyond the UK. The Minister for Agriculture, Michael Creed, travelled to China, while the Minister of State for Food, Andrew Doyle, visited South Korea. A North South Ministerial Council meeting was scheduled for 18 November. In the Dáil, Sinn Féin's Mary Lou McDonald accused the Taoiseach of being flat-footed on Brexit, claiming that a one-day conference was all the government had done.

With political pressure building, the focus switched to the All-Island Civic Dialogue scheduled for 2 November. Throughout September and October, officials worked intensively to create a platform to allow interested parties to air their grievances and start looking for solutions. 'There was a huge amount of preparation,' says one key official involved. 'It was being built from scratch. The choreography of it was important. The idea was to build a list of people that was representative across the 32 counties.'

While all the political parties in the North had been invited, the DUP remained publicly opposed. 'There was no expectation that they would attend or respond, and they didn't,' recalls the official. 'There was no follow-up with them, and there was no wish to push them further. The Ulster Unionist Party was personally supportive, but it was too difficult politically for them to appear. There *were* unionist individuals present: the Ulster Farmers' Union, business leaders and so on. So we were reasonably satisfied that there was a cross-party presence.'

The meeting took place in the Royal Hospital Kilmainham and was hosted by Enda Kenny and Charlie Flanagan. Some 250 politicians, civil servants, business people, trade union figures and community representatives turned up, including 75 from the North. There was an opening address by the Taoiseach, followed by two party-political plenary sessions, then panel discussions on the North–South and British–Irish implications. Martin McGuinness, the Deputy First Minister, painted the starkest picture of all. 'I've been involved in some of the most historic and important negotiations that this island has seen in 100 years,' he told the audience, 'more particularly the Good Friday Agreement and the St Andrews Agreement. What we are facing into now, in my opinion, is just as big as that – maybe even bigger.'

The idea was that between November and January 2017 the process would continue via so-called sectoral dialogues, in areas such as transport, tourism, agriculture, fisheries, human rights and energy. These were held mostly outside Dublin, often close to the border. A second big forum would be held in February. That one would go deeper into the more sensitive areas.

The November meeting received lukewarm coverage in the press, which focused on the Taoiseach's unscripted remarks, before the forum got under way, that the EU–UK negotiations would get 'vicious' and that Theresa May could trigger Article 50 as early as December. The *Irish Independent* was particularly biting. An editorial complained: 'Rather than spending the time preparing Ireland's position on the pending negotiations, the Government decided it was best for "civic society" to sit in a room and have a collective counselling session about Brexit.'

Amid the general climate of scepticism and anxiety, the government was constrained on several fronts. The detailed, and yet limited, explorations of the Locarno Suite meetings between British and Irish officials were best left discreet and not hailed as evidence of hard work. In public, the UK seemed by turns to be confused, or flippant, or heading towards a hard Brexit. The EU was still officially in 'no-notification, no-negotiation mode', and was keeping an eye on any furtive discussions between Dublin and London civil servants.

There was, however, some hope from an unexpected quarter: the British House of Lords.

'We were conscious throughout the referendum campaign,' recalls Lord Jay of Ewelme, a former career diplomat, 'that far too little attention had been paid to the potential implications for Ireland, North and South. That was a worry to us.'

After the referendum, a number of peers on the House of Lords Select Committee on the European Union began arranging expert hearings. The first report produced concerned the impact on Ireland. 'We did [Ireland] first because it had been ignored,' says Lord Jay. 'It was extremely important that at least we in Parliament, we in the House of Lords, should make clear to the [British] government that they needed to take it seriously, and much more seriously than they had done so up till then.'

The Lords Select Committee was pushing against the time-honoured institutional neglect of Northern Ireland by the British body politic. 'It was probably a reflection of what so often has been the case in Britain,' Lord Jay reflects. 'Northern Ireland has seemed, in a funny kind of a way, so distant and so difficult and so complicated that it tends to be seen rather apart from the other political implications affecting Britain.'

The Chairman of the Committee, Lord Boswell of Aynho, recalls: 'We were slightly concerned that what you might call the official level was saying, "No return to the borders of the past, that's unthinkable." But there was no sort of dissemination of that view into the wider body of public opinion or debate.'

The hearings were conducted from September to November. The Committee wanted to produce a report quickly, but the difficulty was finding the time to fit in all the hearings, where to conduct them, and convincing experts who weren't available, or who were only available late in the day. It helped that one particular House of Commons clerk was also clerk to the British–Irish Parliamentary Assembly, and that the Lords had enjoyed regular contacts with the Oireachtas. It also helped that three of the Committee members, including Lord Boswell, were former agriculture ministers who had a relatively good experience of Irish agriculture issues at EU level.

All told, the Committee took evidence from 42 stake-holders. They included professors of history, politics and immigration law, as well as politicians from Britain and both sides of the border, business leaders, union groups, commu-nity and cross-border organizations, the farming and tourism lobbies, the Police Service of Northern Ireland, Ambassador Mulhall and many others. They were questioned in detailed and often sympathetic hearings in London, Dublin and Belfast. They painted a broad canvas of implications and anxieties. One particularly important session was the joint appearance of John Bruton and Bertie Ahern, two former Taoisigh who had never shared a platform before.

'It became very clear,' recalls Lord Boswell, 'when we had the double-header of Bertie Ahern and John Bruton. It was tremendously interesting. [We realized] this is as big a prob-lem for the island of Ireland, on both sides of the border, as it is for the UK.'

Both Bruton and Ahern delivered detailed evidence about the issues Dublin had already mapped out: the Good Friday Agreement, the Common Travel Area, the agri-food trade, the complexities of the British–Irish relationship. The evi-dence was as compelling, and frank, as it was colourful. John Bruton told the Lords that if they were ever to buy a sand-wich at a service station in the UK, the bread had probably come from England, the butter from the Republic and the filling from the North. The loss of mutual EU membership would be felt more intensely in Ireland than in Britain, 'but we had no say in the matter'. There had been, within both communities in Northern Ireland, 'a sense of isolation, in terms of being disregarded or [being] in a permanent minor-ity.' This, he pointed out, lay behind 'some of the very aggressive tactics that were adopted by republicans, and indeed, at times, by loyalists.' That sense of isolation was at risk of returning, post-Brexit.

Bertie Ahern reminded the Committee that at one point there were 40,000 people on the security payroll in Northern Ireland. He acknowledged that the new arrangements would have to be negotiated between the UK and the EU, but, he added, 'There is the small matter of an international agreement – the Good Friday Agreement – which says different.'

The Lords produced an 80-page report and published it simultaneously in Dublin and London on 11 December. It recommended that both governments quickly negotiate a bilateral agreement in parallel with the Article 50 negotiations. Such a deal would 'guarantee open land borders and sea boundaries, support cross-border trade, and preserve EU funding for cross-border projects'. If Britain and Europe neglected the impact on Ireland, the report said, Brexit could undermine the peace process and the improved relations between the islands.

'Both the UK and Irish governments desperately want to avoid a return to hard borders,' Lord Boswell said at the launch. 'But the Republic of Ireland will remain in the EU, and any agreement to allow an open border to remain will have to be agreed by all the other EU member states.'

All the pinch points were included in the report. An open border would be 'impossible' if Britain left the customs union, so innovative solutions would have to be found. This could be through technology, or by replicating the Norway–Sweden border (Norway is outside the customs union, while Sweden is inside). The EU could even, the report suggested, agree to a bilateral UK–Irish deal on trade and customs. The authors admitted that this would be 'unprecedented'.

The Lords were at pains to stress that the other EU member states, and the European institutions, would have to be 'kept abreast' of any bilateral negotiations. Deference, or even politeness, on that score, however, turned out to be gossamer thin. In the face of a growing determination by the other 26 member states that there could be absolutely no negotiation, bilateral or otherwise, until the UK triggered Article 50, there was a rueful realization on Ireland's part that it simply could not pre-cook something with the British, and then ask the other member states to sign off on it. It would have been, to put it mildly, very *tempting* for Dublin to do this. The anguished cry of beef farmers, dairy producers, fishermen and exporters was that the status quo with the UK be maintained.

But Brexit had broken the status quo, and Ireland had declared for the EU27.

The rejection of the report's central findings was as swift as it was brutal. Although he acknowledged the Committee's work, Michael Noonan, the Minister for Finance, said Ireland and Britain could not do deals 'on the side'. Enda Kenny, at an EU summit in Brussels four days later, said bluntly that a bilateral deal was 'not available in the context of Ireland being a member of the European Union negotiating team'. Dara Murphy, accompanying the Taoiseach to the summit, described the idea as 'nonsensical'.

This response was a considerable disappointment to the Lords. 'Deliberately or not,' says Lord Jay of Ewelme, 'there was a misunderstanding. The Irish government's position is a very awkward one. They have to negotiate, you know, discuss things with us, as indeed as is happening behind the scenes (it's quite clear there are very intense discussions going on even now between Dublin and London). But at the same time the Irish government is part of the EU27. What we said in the report, and what we believed – and I *still* believe – is that only the Irish government and the British government really understand the potential implications. And it makes a huge amount of sense for those two governments, taking into account also the views from Belfast, to decide among themselves what is the best way of responding to Brexit. Of course, the discussions would have to include the rest of the EU, so that they would not be surprised by what was being discussed or going to be agreed. Otherwise they weren't going to be able to endorse it.'

In fact, coinciding with the Lords Select Committee report was a growing belief, among those in Europe with a keen stake in how Ireland coped with Brexit, that Dublin was barking up the wrong tree. Throughout the autumn, a number of Irish officials in Brussels had been fretting that the government had been placing too much emphasis on the bilateral relationship with London, and not enough on the rest of Europe. One diplomat explains: 'Part of the concern was that the immediate focus in Dublin was very much on the border in Northern Ireland and the Common Travel Area . . . We kept on saying to them from Brussels, this is not going to be a negotiation between London and Dublin, this is going to be a negotiation between the EU and Britain. And it's going to be done through Brussels.'

Another Irish diplomat, however, took the opposite view: 'Clearly we had to talk to the British. The fact is, a lot of the 26 weren't interested at that stage. Minister [Charlie] Flanagan had 70 meetings between June and [February]. He met every single foreign minister, and a number of them multiple times. So I don't think we can be accused of not having talked to our partners. They must be sick of seeing us at this stage. Our set of issues [is] unique to us. They're not really of interest to *them*.'

On 9 January, Phil Hogan, Ireland's Commissioner for Agriculture in Brussels, published an op-ed in the *Irish Times*. In an unmistakable, and sharply worded, message to the Irish government, Hogan said that Dublin's strategy had to change.

'Brexit will happen,' he wrote, 'and we now need to take a very strategic and far-sighted review of our relationships with both the UK and the rest of our European partners. There will be a new dynamic in European affairs, and Ireland needs to be absolutely prepared to influence, shape and lead that dynamic and change.

'If we don't step up to the plate in managing this fundamental shift in our relationship with our European neighbours, then others will shape the environment for us.

'It is also important that our political relationship with the United Kingdom matures to reflect the changed political and legal circumstances.'

In other words, Ireland would have to step away from the UK, and turn more closely towards the Continental embrace. It would be a 'fundamental error' if Dublin placed an 'excessive reliance' on its bilateral relationship with the UK as a way to protect its strategic interests.

'It was coming to my attention,' recalls Hogan from his seventh-floor office in the Berlaymont Building in Brussels, 'that the Irish authorities were concentrating too much of their time looking to the relationship between Ireland and the UK. My article was an attempt at a wake-up call to this new reality. There are two issues' – the peace process and trade – 'that have to be negotiated. But the recognition of those two issues has to be in Brussels, not in London.'

5. The New Zealand Grudge Match

Any external observer of the recent economic history of Ireland could not have avoided a particular narrative: the economic boom had come about because Ireland was an open, flexible, skilled, low-tax, English-speaking economy right at the gates of the single market, prolific at securing hi-tech, highly skilled, world-beating multinationals. They had fuelled the boom, and the recovery.

But the sector that would come to dominate the Brexit debate had nothing to do with Big Tech or Big Pharma or the Double Irish. That sector was food.

The food produced in Ireland, whether animal or vegetable, by-product or finished product, will go to the very heart of how the nation will cope with, or recover from, Brexit. Food – whether living, free-range, slaughtered, processed, powdered, mass-produced into individually wrapped slices, converted into microwaveable dinners, scooped up from the sea, frozen and shipped to tables around the planet – will be at the centre of the worst problems Ireland faces when Britain formally leaves and works out its new relationship with the EU.

What we harvest in one part of the island and then send across the border to be slaughtered, processed, skinned, marinated, churned, powdered, milled, grated – all of this will be caught up in the consequences of Brexit. Responding to a survey of food-supply chains in four border counties, one Monaghan food producer mentioned a local haulage company that operated on a cross-border basis. On checking, the authors of the report discovered the company's trucks were transporting food from Monaghan over the border into Armagh and Down, back over the border again into Louth and down to Dublin Port. From there the food was shipped to Great Britain, processed and then sent *back* by lorry again to a distributor in the West of Ireland. This entire paradigm of economic activity was now under threat.

On the night of the Brexit referendum, the BBC signal found its way to a quiet farmhouse near the village of Ballacolla in County Laois. Jer Bergin and his wife, Margaret, stayed up till 1.30 a.m., and went to bed thinking that the UK would be remaining in the European Union. Outside, the dew settled on 150 acres of pasture and tillage. In the distance, Jer Bergin might have heard the rush of traffic on the M8 motorway from Dublin to Cork. But at 6 a.m. the sound that would rouse him from his sleep was an RTÉ News alert on his phone. He checked. Britain had just voted to leave the European Union.

'Almost immediately,' he recalls, 'the confidence was sucked out of the beef trade.'

The Bergins keep around 200 cattle. Jer Bergin has been farming on the south Laois land since he left agricultural college in 1984, but the farm has been in the family for generations. 'It's a pure farming area. There's nothing else here,' he says. He has witnessed dramatic changes in the beef sector over the years, but nothing prepared him for the shock of Brexit. 'Throughout that day, it was a major point of conversation with other farmers. "Sure, they'd never do it," was the attitude. "They'd never be that stupid."'

In the days after Brexit, incomes fell. 'We had a bit of confidence going back a few months,' recalls Bergin. 'Prices had been heading the right way. But immediately sterling was devalued and that was used to drop prices. When I was selling cattle in the second half of the year they were worth 20 cents to 25 cents per kilo less than they should have been. You're getting into €100 per head of cattle. That's when your margin gets hit.'

Beef has the potential to be far and away the biggest single Irish casualty of Brexit. That is because of the mind-boggling amount of beef we export to the UK – 270,000 tonnes in 2016 – and because of the amount of money that trade is worth: at least €2.5 billion annually. According to a March 2017 IFA Position Paper, exports to the UK represent 50 per cent of Irish beef production.

Over the past 60 years, Ireland's beef industry has evolved from the bucolic, spit-on-the-palm charm of village cattle marts and boats groaning with live animals to a hi-tech, high-value-added machine. The machine has embedded itself in the British market: it has colonized the shelves of the major supermarket chains and inveigled its way into the taste buds and psychology of British consumers. 'The product is very much accepted,' says Cormac Healy, Senior Executive Director of Meat Industry Ireland. 'It's almost seen as British. Or Irish. What's the difference?'

The producers who convert the thousands of head of cattle into shelf-ready cuts are wealthy and influential. The entire sector is enmeshed at a human and political level with the UK agriculture lobby. Every part of the supply chain – from farming organizations, including the British National Union of Farmers, to the British government itself (even its most fervent Brexiteers) – is shouting one loud demand: that the status quo continue. Meeting that immovable object is the irresistible force of the EU26, who will not accept that the status quo should continue, because they will not accept that Britain should be allowed to have the best of both worlds: trading freely with the EU while dispensing with the obligations of membership.

'We're firmly on the European side,' says Kevin Kinsella, Director of Livestock with the IFA. 'That's the camp we're in. But, on the other hand, we have all these relationships built up with the UK: the retail sector, the food sector, the farming sector. We're not about to let that disappear over-night just because we're in the other camp.'

In Ballacolla, County Laois, Jer Bergin concurs. 'There isn't another market out there that has the same preferences, that likes what we do, that we can do well in, with the right breeds, the right system, the easy market to access. I keep hearing commentators say we must find alternative markets. There *are* no alternative markets. Not to the level of what we do. You can't. There is no replacement for the UK market. It's worth fighting for, and it's worth holding on to.'

For centuries, Ireland exported live cattle and sheep by boat to Britain. The physical market in Dublin, formally estab-lished in 1863 by Dublin Corporation, reached its peak in the late 1950s, when in one year alone a quarter of a million head of cattle were exported from Stoneybatter. In 1960, a record 425,000 sheep were sold at the same market.

Declan O'Brien, who specializes in the history of the trade at the University of Limerick, described the scene in the *Farming Independent* in January 2016. 'At its peak in the 1950s the Dublin Cattle Market, located on Prussia Street in Stoneybatter (nicknamed 'Cowtown'), was the largest weekly livestock sale in Europe. Of the one million cattle, sheep and pigs exported "on the hoof" annually from Dublin, almost all were bought at the market before being driven to boats moored along the North Wall.

'At a time when the country's economy depended on agriculture, and the cattle trade in particular, Dublin's market was akin to the national "stock exchange" – effectively setting prices at fairs and markets throughout the country and processing the final sales of animals destined for export.'

The market was held each Wednesday and attracted buyers from Dublin's abattoirs but also from British livestock traders acting for slaughterhouses and farmers in the north of England and Scotland. 'Sales masters' would have agents buying cattle at fairs or direct from farmers across the South, Midlands and West, before moving them by train or road to be 'finished' (i.e. given a final change of diet to give the meat certain characteristics before slaughter) in Kildare, Meath or Dublin, or sold immediately at the market. Afterwards, the slow-moving bovines were driven to nearby abattoirs, or down to the North Wall Docks to be live exported.

'Although butchers and processors took a significant proportion of the sheep and heifers, exporters were the premium buyers and they set the tone of the trade, as well as adding a certain international panache to proceedings,' wrote O'Brien. 'Many of the exporters were English buyers who would arrive the evening before the market by boat and stay overnight in local bed and breakfasts or the nearby City Arms Hotel. Some even joined the "jet set" as the 1960s progressed, flying in and out on the day of the sale. Either way, the goal was to assemble their lots of 300 or more cattle before breakfast. They would then settle their account, arrange for the stocks' shipping and head for the airport or boat.' Many of the cattle bound for the UK were store cattle, 'unfinished' at one and a half to two years of age. They would live out the rest of their short lives on the grassland farms of Yorkshire before being slaughtered for the retail trade.

With the advent of the co-op system and greater market transparency in the 1960s, some operators saw the benefit of processing meat in Ireland. The rise of the mart system put an end to the country fairs, and in turn the Dublin Cattle Market, which finally closed down in 1973.

Five months earlier, Ireland had joined the EEC. Suddenly there were grant supports and guaranteed prices. Beef-processing factories shot up, availing themselves of European structural funds. 'Before that you had all these small little abattoirs, where you had the butcher next door,' recalls Kevin Kinsella. 'Suddenly these big factories came along, capable of processing large numbers of animals. You were looking at guys taking in the animals, slaughtering them and leaving them in carcasses. They weren't cutting and slicing like they do now. They'd freeze them, so you were exporting frozen bone-end sides or quarters to England.'

Irish beef output was growing considerably, but the boom was not just in Ireland. The EEC had at an early stage prioritized food security. This was because of the great agriculture recessions in the 1930s and the disruptions to the food supply during the war. Financial supports would be used to protect farmers (the same was true in the UK and the US). Technical innovation, more investment, the shift from smaller to bigger farms, the reduction of risk – all of these contributed to higher yields. A European Commission report in 1980 found that, while the number of dairy cows in the EEC had remained static at 25 million since 1960, the average dairy yield had increased by over 33 per cent by 1979. European farmers were producing more food than their populations could eat. The higher revenue was going on processing, higher quality and fancier packaging rather than on producing more food, but farmers were reluctant to leave the land, and governments were reluctant to ease off on production – hence the growth of butter, beef and wheat 'mountains', and wine 'lakes'.

By the 1980s, the EEC's support policy revolved around buying beef for 'intervention' (i.e. cold-storing it until it could be sold later at a better price). When the beef was exported to markets outside the EEC, farmers were given further subsidies through export refunds. In time, the Common Agricultural Policy became the target of increasing displeasure. Environmental organizations accused the EEC of dumping beef on foreign markets in order to suppress local production.

The risk-sheltered international markets were enormously profitable, yet notoriously prone to allegations of corruption. In the 1980s, the buyers were in North Africa, the Middle East and Russia. They bought hundreds of thousands of tonnes of Irish beef at reduced prices. 'Some years we'd have in excess of 200,000 head of live cattle going between Libya and Egypt,' says Kinsella. 'Almost half of the value of the cattle was coming in the form of an export refund.'

In 1991, the Granada Television *World in Action* programme spoiled the party. The report alleged rampant abuse of export-subsidy schemes through the wholesale use of falsified documents, bogus stamps, the illegal labelling of carcasses, the switching of meat destined for intervention with inferior product, the falsification of weights on packages of beef, meat being designated as slaughtered on a date when it wasn't, the reboxing of meat purchased from the Intervention Agency and so on. The focus was Anglo-Irish Beef Producers (AIBP), owned by Larry Goodman. Goodman had created a vast empire of processing plants. He was attracting huge grants from the Industrial Development Authority to export hundreds of thousands of tonnes of beef to Libya, Iran, Iraq, Egypt and Morocco. The TV exposé, and subsequent claims in the Dáil, alleged an unhealthy relationship between Goodman and the then Taoiseach, Charles Haughey, over the promotion of his empire and over access to millions of pounds in export subsidies. A tribunal of enquiry was established in May 1991 and reported in August 1994, and the entire affair convulsed Irish politics for several years. Larry Goodman claimed the report had 'rebutted' allegations of institutionalized fraud, political favouritism and corruption. Fintan O'Toole wrote in the *Irish Times*: 'The report reveals that very substantial abuses of the EU intervention system occurred in Irish meat plants. Yet, when some of these abuses were raised in the Dáil, those who did so were accused by Mr Charles Haughey, of "trying to sabotage the entire beef industry in this country".'

In 1995, the European Commission sought IR£75 million in fines in relation to the practices uncovered in Ireland's beef factories.

It was an Irish EU Commissioner, Ray MacSharry, who put an end to the export-refund scheme. In 1992, he launched a series of reforms to the Common Agricultural Policy. Export refunds would be phased out, and the intervention price was reduced by 15 per cent over three years. To compensate for the loss in earnings, farmers would be supported directly through the so-called 'cheque in the post'. The payment was 'decoupled' from the amount of beef produced; instead it was based on the amount of land a farmer had and the number of livestock kept.

One effect was to encourage farmers to look for new markets, ones not featherbedded by subsidies. 'I cannot emphasize too strongly,' MacSharry warned farmers at a meeting in UCD in 1992, 'the urgency of putting in place a strategy now that will ensure that the beef industry reduces sharply its dependence on intervention and establishes a place on real markets.'

Farmers were furious and predicted the demise of agriculture; an effigy of MacSharry was tossed off the bridge in Athlone into the River Shannon. But, over time, the reforms were accepted and the effect was dramatic. In 1992, 245,000 tonnes of beef were put into storage in Ireland, accounting for nearly 735,000 animals. By January 1994, this had fallen to 7,381.

But what really transformed Ireland's beef industry was a statement by a British minister on 20 March 1996. On that day, the Secretary of State for Health, Stephen Dorrell, told the House of Commons that scientists had identified a 'previously unrecognized and consistent disease pattern' after investigating the deaths of 10 young people suffering from Creutzfeldt-Jakob disease (CJD), the human form of bovine spongiform encephalopathy (BSE), or mad cow disease. The 'most likely' cause of death was eating certain types of offal, before they had been banned from cattle feed in 1989.

Overnight, European beef was shut out of international markets.

Prior to the BSE crisis, Ireland was selling between 80,000 and 90,000 tonnes of beef to the UK. Britain's – and Europe's – BSE problem was suddenly Ireland's opportunity. Dystopian images of bovine pyres piled high with smouldering animals were beamed across the world. Irish producers had been peddling their wares in France, Italy, Scandinavia and the more recent EU member states Spain and Portugal. Now, next door, there was a vast new market for untainted Irish beef. Irish producers, recovering from the trauma of the Beef Tribunal, began building relationships with British supermarket chains and retailers. Some invested in cross-Channel processing facilities to get closer access to consumers; others targeted global giants like McDonald's. Today, one in five burgers sold in all McDonald's outlets in Europe originates in the Dawn Meats plant in Grannagh, County Waterford.

The Foot and Mouth disease outbreak in Britain in 2001 further consolidated the Irish beef presence in the UK. 'It was a real opportunity to get in,' recalls Kinsella. 'We made real, significant inroads into the retail sector, the Tescos, the Sainsburys, the Asdas.' By the mid 2000s, the big three meat processors in Ireland – Larry Goodman's ABP (as it's now called), Dawn Meats and Kepak – all had operations in the UK. Irish processors were now shipping chilled, shelf-ready cuts instead of frozen sides of beef. 'Twenty years ago it was in full carcass or quarter form, deboned over there in the UK and broken out into individual cuts,' says Cormac Healy of Meat Industry Ireland. 'Now our trade is really in cuts, putting as much value here in terms of the processing we do at this end.'

New technology has meant that these chilled cuts are landing on UK supermarket shelves on a just-in-time basis. In some cases retail packaging happens even closer to the British consumer. ABP employs 725 people at a packing plant in Hordley, Shropshire, and a further 732 in Shrewsbury. They take in vacuum-packed cuts from Ireland, and cut them into steaks at precisely the same weight, right down to the gram. Other meat companies have similar arrangements. British customers get their Irish beef as fresh as possible.

On the eve of the Brexit vote, Irish beef was as well established in the psyche of the British consumer as could be imagined. The reasons were as much to do with biology as with geography and history. Irish beef is grass-fed and comes from animals that are kept outdoors. So-called steer cattle, i.e. bulls that have been castrated, yield meat that has the taste, texture and colour that British consumers expect in their Sunday roasts. The gold standard of British food is the Red Tractor label; of all the other European producers, only Ireland's Origin Green label comes close in terms of the perceptions of British consumers.

Beef exports to the UK rose from 100,000 tonnes in the late 1990s to 270,000 tonnes in 2016. The price paid for beef is consistently higher in the UK than elsewhere in Europe. According to Defra, the UK's department of agriculture, the UK is only 65 per cent self-sufficient in beef, and Ireland accounts for 70 per cent of what Britain imports.

One contributor to that vast supply of beef is Jer Bergin. He sells his cattle to Kepak, having had to comply with the Bord Bia quality assurance scheme, including audits every 18 months. The product becomes part of Kepak's fully integrated, consumer-ready, delivered-for-retail system. Very little is wasted in beef production. Virtually every part of the animal and all the by-products are sold to dozens of markets around the world, but the vast majority of the animal in Ireland's case will go to the UK.

Before beef farmers like Bergin could contemplate what Brexit would mean in the long term, they had to deal with the short-term shock of the fall in sterling in the days after the vote. Early fears of the pound reaching parity with the euro proved unwarranted, but there is still long-term uncertainty because of the length of time it could take for the implications of Brexit to play out.

In some quarters, there has been resentment over how the fall in sterling worked its way into the system. 'When you have exchange-rate movement,' points out Eddie Punch, the General Secretary of the Irish Cattle and Sheep Farmers' Association (ICSA), 'either the exporter takes a hit in the price they get, or the importer has to pay a bit more. The

inevitable consequence in the long term is food price inflation in the UK. But in the short term what you got was meat
factories here cutting prices to Irish farmers. It was a source
of annoyance to us. The easiest thing to do is to try to buy
your beef cheaper off the farmers, because they're generally
in a weak position, because of the perfect competition
between thousands of farmers, versus only three meat factories. It's easier to talk down the beef price to your supplier
than to talk up the price to your supermarket customer.'

In other words, part of Ireland's dependency on the UK
market has already been felt: British retailers refuse to pay a
higher price to Irish processors, who in turn refuse to pay a
higher price to Irish farmers.

But the long-term problems are more worrying. The hard-
won access Ireland enjoys is at risk on several levels. The UK is
the highest-paying market. Its consumers and retailers are
among the most sophisticated in the world. But if Britain is
outside the customs union, it could in theory agree trade deals
with countries like Brazil and Argentina to bring in cheap beef.
It would also impose tariffs on Irish beef. Both of those changes
would further depress the prices Irish farmers currently get.

At present, Ireland exports just under 50 per cent of its beef
to the EU. Italy is the next most valuable market, and Irish
producers have made some good inroads, co-opting Italian
TV chefs to extol the aspects of upbringing, taste, texture, fat
content and colour that are unfamiliar to Italian consumers.
Irish beef is also sold in Germany, with large consignments
going via centralized cut-and-slice operations in Belgium.

The scope for a massive expansion that would offset a significant loss to the UK market is limited. An animal might
be killed on a Tuesday in Ireland, hung, cut, processed and
put on to a truck on Friday morning, brought to the

Continent by Monday and dropped at the distribution centre by the middle of the week. It would be aged at least 14 days before it reaches the shelves, meaning there are only a couple of weeks of shelf life after that. As the distances get longer, the shelf life declines.

The other problem is the way Irish beef looks and tastes. Continental bull beef (i.e. uncastrated) is pale, lean, and has an entirely different taste from beef from Irish steers. A senior IFA source ponders the post-Brexit dilemma: 'You're trying to get a buyer to buy more of something that tastes and looks different. In Germany, a restaurant chain with huge volumes did a blind taste test with their customers. They came back to the Irish processor and said, "Your beef won, but I can't sell it. I have loyal customers, but they're not going to buy it. They're not going to buy it because it looks different."'

For now, there is uncertainty, even a sense of paralysis, as players watch for how the negotiations will play out. Some observers are instinctively pessimistic. The IFA has focused on the importance of the UK market for Irish beef by scale and value, and the danger of displacing a huge amount of meat into what is already a mature and saturated beef market in the EU. EU beef production is between 7.5 million and 8 million tonnes annually and the amount European consumers eat has remained stable, at around 7.3 million tonnes, so there is not much room for manoeuvre. The sector in Ireland employs 100,000 farmers and 20,000 in processing, marts, transport and distribution. An IFA position paper presented to the European Commission concluded: 'At farm level, it is a low-income sector, with average farm incomes ranging from €10,000 to €15,000 depending on the enterprise type. Analysis by Teagasc has identified that 40 per cent of farms in the cattle sector are economically vulnerable.'

Professor Alan Matthews, a highly respected expert on agriculture and trade, told the Joint Oireachtas Committee on Agriculture: 'Brexit is going to be a big negative shock. We will hear calls for assistance, both from smaller food firms and farmers. My advice is that this is a permanent shock. This is not something which is likely to reverse itself in the near future.'

In East Wicklow, on a lowland farm, James Hill has been raising sheep with his father and brother for 37 years. Sheep farmers are just as exposed and fearful over Brexit as beef farmers, but they feel they have less clout. The fundamentals are the same: the sudden sterling shock, the worry about tariffs, access, a different animal-hygiene regime. But they face a more complex and entirely unpredictable dilemma. The problem relates to a country far across the planet. Ireland may have finally beaten the All Blacks in Chicago in November 2016, but sheep farmers face a very different grudge match with New Zealand.

Hill has a flock of 400 sheep grazing a small patch of rented hillside. The animals are slaughtered in Ireland and exported in portions to various EU markets. The offal goes to third countries, the skins and hides go to China. As in the beef trade, more and more processing is being done before the meat leaves Ireland. 'Traditionally we killed sheep, hung them on rails, put them in fridges, sent them to France and they went to cutting halls in France or Belgium, and they were knocked down into supermarket-sized packs. There's huge emphasis now on a ready-prepared, labelled and packed product.'

Twenty years ago Hill had over 1,000 sheep, but over time the lack of available labour and persistently low profit margins have forced him to reduce the flock size. In 1996, the

Teagasc farm-management survey indicated a gross profit margin of €53 per head in sheep production. 'It's virtually unchanged today,' says Hill. 'In terms of the net margin, because of the increase in fixed costs, you're down to single digits, maybe €9 per sheep.'

Ireland is 360 per cent self-sufficient in sheep meat, meaning we have to export a huge amount. Currently we sell 21 per cent of sheep meat production to the UK, so there will be potentially a significant hit from Brexit. But the key destination is the lucrative French market, where we sell 35 per cent.

So where does New Zealand come in?

One of the perpetual dilemmas for Britain when trying to figure out if it wanted to join the EEC was the impact the move would have on Commonwealth countries that had enjoyed generous trade access to the UK market. In 1961, when Britain first applied, half of New Zealand's agriculture exports, including 86 per cent of its lamb, went to the UK. The meat industry had actually been developed to service the British market. A first shipment of 842 cases of canned meat arrived in 1870, to be followed by the first consignment of frozen carcasses a decade later. Farm sizes in New Zealand increased, and breeds were developed that yielded both wool and meat.

When the UK finally did join, a deal was done whereby New Zealand sheep meat enjoyed preferential market access to the EEC from 1973 to 1977. After that, exports were subject to a tariff of 20 per cent. In 1980, New Zealand agreed to limit exports to 245,000 tonnes, and in return the tariff was dropped to 10 per cent. By the end of the 1980s, the quota was further reduced to 205,000 tonnes in return for a zero tariff.

Today, thanks to the original understanding dating back to 1973, New Zealand enjoys preferential trade access for 225,000 tonnes of lamb (it was formalized in an agreement with the EU in 1994). In 2016, New Zealand exported 172,500 tonnes of that quota, with half sold into the UK market (the IFA says that on average each year around 100,000 tonnes goes to the UK). Once the UK leaves the EU, what happens to that 100,000 tonnes? A New Zealand government source says the WTO rules are clear and that the quota is something the EU signed up to. As part of the 1994 quota agreement, the EU also sells produce into the New Zealand market. 'If all 225,000 tonnes is allocated to Europe, excluding the UK,' says Kevin Kinsella, 'it would crash the European market. That's putting an extra 100,000 tonnes on top of a mature, saturated market.'

Meanwhile, in the new Brexit landscape, the British government could enter a brand-new bilateral trade agreement with New Zealand, allowing tens of thousands of tonnes of New Zealand lamb into Britain.

'In effect,' says James Hill, 'the New Zealanders have an each-way bet.'

There would be the added complication of Britain's own exports. While the UK is relatively small in beef and dairy, it is big in lamb. It has 28 per cent of the EU flock and produces 313,000 tonnes of sheep meat each year. Some 100,000 tonnes of that is exported, the vast majority of which goes to the EU. It's unclear what the overall outcome of the New Zealand quota issue will be. The IFA admits it's possible that the impact of 100,000 tonnes of extra New Zealand lamb on the European market could be cancelled out by the fact that Britain's 100,000 tonnes might face tariff restrictions. 'But bear in mind seasonality,' says Kevin Kinsella, the IFA's Director of Livestock. 'The main UK production is in the summer and autumn. The main New Zealand season is in winter and spring, when their imports are at their highest standards.' In other words, seasonal factors may still mean a saturated market in the EU, to the detriment of Irish sheep farmers.

The geographical remoteness of the Southern Hemisphere is of little consolation in the age of advanced food technology. New Zealand traditionally exported frozen lamb, but now it's not necessary to freeze it. 'When it was frozen,' explains Kinsella, 'it ended up in food-service outlets, in the restaurant business. They'd pull out five legs two days before they needed them and then thawed them. Now they have the technology to land perfectly good-looking racks and legs in Sainsbury, Tesco, Asda. It looks like any fresh lamb, because it's chilled product. That's what is competing against Irish lamb.'

The New Zealand government disputes the idea that Irish lamb producers will take a hit. The country hasn't filled its 225,000 tonne EU quota of lamb since 2009, and the amount exported has declined steadily since then. The sheep population in New Zealand has also declined by 48 per cent since 1990. 'EU consumers aren't eating as much lamb as they used to,' says the New Zealand source. 'And they're not the only player in town. We're selling into other markets.'

Changing supply chains and capacity issues at meat plants and abattoirs has meant a steady flow of beef crossing the Irish land border in both directions. Some of the big processors have joint ownership North and South. Animals might be slaughtered in the Republic and deboned in a cutting plant in Northern Ireland. The Minister for Agriculture, Michael Creed, told the Seanad that in 2015 a total of 55,000 cattle went north for breeding or slaughter. Meanwhile, some 400,000 lambs from the North were processed in the South thanks to a significant reduction in processing capacity on the Northern side in recent years. Conversely, half a million pigs cross in the other direction to be slaughtered and processed in Northern Ireland. Some of the product would go on to Great Britain, and some would go back to the South. These movements are generally down to an economics that is made simple by mutual membership of the single market, and a border made transparent by the Good Friday Agreement. But the simple has become complex overnight, thanks to Brexit.

'How will the EU measure the quality and quantity of those products and animals crossing the border?' asks Kevin Kinsella. 'We've got to figure that out.'

There is a strict, highly complex, EU-monitoring regime that governs farm animals as they make their way along the supply chain. 'We have completely changed the way we farm over the past 10 to 15 years in response to these policy changes,' says Jer Bergin, the farmer from County Laois. 'The consumer demands the standards, the labelling: we have jumped through those hoops.'

If an Irish meat factory has been inspected by the Irish authorities according to EU hygiene rules, and approved to sell its products in the Irish market, it can also sell those products in the British and French markets without any further checks, as it is assumed that it will meet the relevant EU standards.

'That will no longer be the case after Brexit,' Professor Alan Matthews has told the Joint Oireachtas Committee on Agriculture. 'The British authorities may decide to change when they leave. They will have exactly the same regulations in place that we have. However, over time, these regulations may evolve and change. In any case, the British authorities will wish to ensure *our* processing plants meet *their* standards.'

6. The China Syndrome

One night in the late 1970s, a British Army unit was dropped by helicopter into a field near the border with the Irish Republic to begin a nocturnal patrol of the fields, boreens, rivers and ditches that made up the perilous frontier. Suddenly, the unit came face to face with an Irish Army patrol going about the same business.

There was an awkward armed stand-off in the darkness. Words were exchanged. Who was on whose territory?

'The British officer disputed the fact that he was in the wrong place,' recalls Gabriel D'Arcy, the Lieutenant leading the Irish patrol, 'and he was trying to tell me that *I* was in the wrong location. I said, "Look, I'm sorry, I'm quite certain *I'm* in the right location."'

Eventually, one of the British contingent checked the coordinates and realized they were, in fact, in County Monaghan, and not in County Armagh. 'They got the chopper back as soon as possible and got out of there,' recalls Gabriel D'Arcy. 'Those sorts of things happened every day.'

D'Arcy went on to become a captain in the Irish Defence Forces before retiring from the army in 1989. Originally from Ballinamore in County Leitrim, he was based in Dublin during his four-year border deployment, spending three to four months at a time in Castleblayney. By virtue of his shifts patrolling the countryside, manning checkpoints, and escorting cash transits, he came to understand the border's physical and economic topography. 'There was no economy,' he recalls. 'There was nothing going on. South Armagh? There was plenty of *illegal* activity, but there was little or no incentive to invest. There was nothing going on economically until the peace process and they started demilitarizing.'

Today, Gabriel D'Arcy surveys the boreens, ditches and rivers from his perch as Chief Executive of a giant dairy company. As head of LacPatrick, he understands the carefully woven supply chains that have bound together a matrix of farming communities, suppliers, processors, drivers and sales staff, all operating across an increasingly irrelevant Irish border.

'We've got people that work here in Monaghan and live in Armagh,' he reflects. 'We've got people in Artigarvan who live in Donegal. They don't recognize the border. They know it's a different administration and a different currency, but that's it.'

LacPatrick is the result of a merger between two of the oldest milk co-ops in Ireland: Town of Monaghan, founded in 1901, and Ballyrashane, on the Antrim coast, founded in 1898. The group today has a combined annual turnover of €360 million and a workforce of 300. Every year it buys 600 million litres of milk from 1,050 farmers on both sides of the border. LacPatrick has a contract to supply the global nutrition and healthcare giant Abbott with 160 million litres of milk, which is turned into infant formula at Abbott's Cootehill plant in County Cavan. The formula is then sold to China and the Middle East.

Brexit poses a direct threat to this arrangement. Most of the milk that LacPatrick processes for Abbott comes from Northern Ireland, D'Arcy says. 'It's UK milk. It's been brought into a Republic of Ireland factory, processed here and then brought to our key infant-formula customer, and they make infant formula with the key raw material . . . That factory is entirely predicated on formula going to China and the Middle East, and it's covered by an EU trade agreement. So, you can see the complexity here. That agreement requires that the powder is based on *EU* milk. Post-Brexit, any milk from Northern Ireland is out.'

There's little flexibility on this. 'Unfortunately, the regulatory regime is critical for China, because it's very sensitive about infant formula,' he says. 'They've had a number of scares and scandals over the years. They're very pedantic. They have approved EU milk as a key ingredient. They have not approved UK milk. That could take years.'

The same applies for the millions of litres of Northern Irish milk that LacPatrick processes into powdered milk for export to West Africa. This trade is governed by an EU agreement with the Economic Community of West African States (ECOWAS), stretching all the way from Mauritania to Angola. Only EU-approved products can be sold under that arrangement. 'While everybody is focused on the UK–EU talks,' says D'Arcy, 'one of my big concerns is: who's thinking about what needs to be a UK–ECOWAS agreement? Who is finalizing that? Who is on top of this?'

For years, millions of litres of milk have been sloshing about in tankers heading north and south across the Irish border. This was possible because both sides of the border were governed by the same EU rules. This point was made by the Irish Co-operative Organisation Society (ICOS), one of the first agri lobbies to beat a path to the door of the European Commission's Brexit Task Force in Brussels.

In its submission, ICOS pointed out that the four main co-ops – Glanbia, Lakeland Dairies, LacPatrick and Aurivo – between them process 600 million litres of milk, which cross the border from north to south. Of this, 120 million litres are sold as 'liquid milk', accounting for one quarter of the Republic of Ireland's entire pool of drinking milk. The submission pointed out that products containing Northern Irish milk would not be acceptable either in the single market or for international trade because of its 'non-EU' status. 'We need recognition of "status of Irish milk", in order to allow for the continuation of the trade of milk across the border,' the submission concluded. In other words, ICOS was suggesting that all milk produced on the island of Ireland be designated 'Irish' milk, even if 600 million litres of it originates in Northern Ireland, hence the UK.

How did this state of affairs come about?

Under the Anglo-Irish Free Trade Agreement, which came into effect on 1 July 1966, Britain abolished all import duties on Irish goods. Ireland, meanwhile, undertook to cut import duties on all British goods by increments until all duties had disappeared by 1975. UK dairy companies began investing in Ireland. In Killashandra in County Cavan, there was a creamery on one side of the road and a British-owned drying facility on the other side, with a pipe running in between.

On 1 January 1973, Britain and Ireland joined the EEC and the Anglo-Irish Free Trade Agreement became null and void. The prices Irish farmers were paid for milk immediately rose, and there was a rapid increase in production. 'Milk became the profitable sector,' says Nicholas Simms, a former member of the Irish Dairy Board. 'The only one where full-time farmers could make a living.'

The Milk Marketing Board persisted in Northern Ireland until Margaret Thatcher abolished it. The dairy industry there had to re-create, from scratch, new supply chains and production structures. A new super co-op called United Dairy Farmers (UDF) was established. It would purchase every drop of milk produced by Northern suppliers each month, and then the co-ops were invited to bid – whether for 1,000 litres or 10 million litres – at the market rate.

The co-ops south of the border, such as Lakeland, Town of Monaghan and Donegal Creameries, were investing in processing plants. With their greater capacity, one option was to source Northern milk to process in the new facilities. But the UDF was hoovering up all the milk in the North. So the Southern companies decided to go directly to the Northern farmers. Eventually UDF stopped running their auctions, and more and more Northern suppliers sent their milk over the border to be processed.

One reason for this was that from the mid 1990s, milk-quota regulations in the UK changed. Until then, each constituent part of the UK had its own quota. Following deregulation, there was a single UK quota, so that Northern Irish dairy farmers could purchase quota from English suppliers and increase their production significantly. With all that extra production, Northern farmers needed somewhere to process the milk, and to sell it. Within 10 years, Northern farmers were churning out 2.2 billion litres annually and there was a concerted effort to sell more milk into the Republic. At the same time, there was further consolidation in the industry with mergers and takeovers. Lakeland and LacPatrick owned processing facilities on both sides of the border. The same was true for Donegal Creameries, later bought by Aurivo. Over time, it all added up to a lot of milk going back and forth across the border for processing.

But there is another reason a large amount of milk goes south. The milk that goes into your cornflakes is known as 'liquid milk'. It is of a higher standard than the milk that is used to make cheese, butter or powder. It has very specific flavour profiles, and is generally available only from freshly calved cows. For a number of complex reasons, Northern farmers produce more 'liquid milk' than farmers in the South.

Put simply, liquid-milk production in the South is highly seasonal. The liquid milk becomes available when cows calve, and the milk is freshest at the beginning of the lactation curve. In the Republic, there are 1,800 farmers who specialize in liquid-milk production, and two thirds of them calve their cows between January and March. So there's a big surge of liquid milk in the spring, and then a second, smaller surge in the autumn, when the other one third of farmers calve their cows. Because the grass-growing season is longer in the South, the rest of the year cows are put out to grass – meaning farmers don't have to buy feed for them. The model of spring calving and a long grass season is regarded, in the South, as providing optimum efficiency.

In the North, by contrast, the grass-growing season tends to be shorter, and calving is spread more evenly across the entire year. This means that Northern farmers can produce liquid milk year-round. In 2016, they provided 120 million litres a year for the Southern market, or 25 per cent of the Republic's liquid-milk pool – although even this statistic can't be taken at face value. Some of those 120 million litres of Northern milk heading south will actually have *originated* in the South: after going north to be processed in a co-op such as Strathroy in Omagh, they will have been sent back down to the South to be sold by retailers.

'Milk flies right, left and centre,' says Catherine Lascurettes, Executive Secretary of the IFA Dairy Committee. 'Brexit will play havoc with all of those flows.'

Specifically, if the UK is forced to revert to WTO rules post-Brexit, Northern suppliers will need EU approval to supply the market, and raw milk will face tariffs of up to 50 per cent.

'If you have to pay a tariff like that,' says T. J. Flanagan of ICOS, 'it would put you out of business.'

Some steps are being taken to allow the Northern milk sector to adapt. Even before Brexit, LacPatrick had invested €45 million in its processing plant at Artigarvan, near Strabane. The plant provides most of the powder LacPatrick exports. The plant had two 40-year-old driers to make the powder. Instead of replacing them, LacPatrick built an entirely new facility alongside the old one, meaning that within a few months capacity could rise from one million litres of milk being processed per day to 2.5 million litres. The two ageing driers could still be used in the meantime. 'This is the biggest single investment ever in the dairy industry there,' says Gabriel D'Arcy. With the new capacity, 'We could, in fact, process the whole Northern Ireland output so that no raw milk crosses the border.'

Of course, the implications of Brexit work in the other direction too. A position paper submitted by the IFA to the European Commission Brexit Task Force in March 2017 revealed that, in 2016, the Republic of Ireland exported 72,222 tonnes of milk and cream to the UK. It also exported 25,674 tonnes of milk powders, 21,772 tonnes of whey and 61,995 tonnes of butterfat, including 40,688 tonnes of actual butter.

But the really eye-popping figures relate to cheese, and in particular to Cheddar. In 2016, Ireland sent 125,669 tonnes of cheese to the UK; of that, 77,651 tonnes were in the form of

Cheddar. That's nearly two thirds of all the Cheddar we produce. 'It's pretty unique,' says Lascurettes. 'There are no other member states where Cheddar cheese constitutes such a significant proportion of consumption. In terms of tradition, taste and market, it's a British Isles thing. And we have traditionally been the biggest supplier of Cheddar cheese into the UK.'

Like beef, Cheddar is a valuable commodity. British consumers pay a decent price for it and consume large volumes. The difference is that they probably don't realize it's Irish. A lot of Ireland's Cheddar is sold through Ornua Foods, whose portfolio includes Kerrygold, Dubliner, Forto, Shannongold and BEO milk powder. Glanbia, now a global food and nutrition company, is another major supplier, both directly and through Ornua. Much of Glanbia's Cheddar ends up as part of Waitrose's or Sainsbury's own-brand cheeses. The second biggest Cheddar brand in the UK is Pilgrims Choice, which is owned by Ornua. The Cheddar is produced in Ireland, packaged into 25-kilo blocks, shipped to Adams Foods in Leek, Staffordshire, repackaged there, and distributed throughout the UK. The packs say the cheese is sourced in Britain and the Republic of Ireland. Ornua says that some of their Irish Cheddar is 'redistributed' by UK retailers back to Ireland and sold there.

Post-Brexit, in the absence of a free-trade agreement, would those packs of Cheddar therefore face tariffs in both directions?

Irish cheese companies have invested millions in processing plants. A number of these facilities were created exclusively for selling to the UK. The clarion call today, with Brexit coming, is that Irish producers must look to markets beyond the UK. Part of that diversification will require processors to adapt their facilities to cater for the non-British palate. The problem is that only the British eat Cheddar in such large quantities, and that the machines that make the Cheddar can *only* make Cheddar.

Catherine Lascurettes explains how Cheddar is made: 'You warm up the milk to a certain temperature (you might pasteurize the milk first, depending on what kind of cheese you're making). You add a reagent, which will curdle the milk, you then separate the curd from the liquid whey which is left behind. The liquid whey is very sexy, nutritional stuff, used to be fed to pigs, now goes into sports nutrition. The curd is then hoovered up into these towers which compact it all together.

'The plants are so specific that they can only produce Cheddar. You will end up in a situation with plants which are very highly specialized, and you can do sod-all else with [them]. So you're left with milk for which you have to find another outlet.'

Those parts of Ireland now having to figure out what to do with all that milk, and all those stainless-steel Cheddar towers, are found in a heartland south of the Dublin–Galway line, heading down west of Bandon, south of Macroom and into the West Cork peninsulas that stretch their toes into the Atlantic. One of the most prominent companies in that belt is Carbery.

The Carbery Group began life in 1965 as a joint venture between four creameries and Express Dairies in the UK. Within two years, it was producing 1,400 tonnes of cheese, and it was the first processor in the world to install ultra-filtration technology to produce whey-protein concentrates.

By 2002, Carbery had acquired a huge flavour-ingredients company in Wauconda, Illinois, and in 2005 the company launched a flavours division under the Synergy brand, which in turn opened facilities in Brazil and Thailand. When EU milk quotas were abolished in 2015, meaning farmers could produce as much as they wished, processors like Glanbia, Dairygold and Lakeland installed new driers with an eye on the growing global powder market. The sky was the limit.

Then Brexit came along.

One of Carbery's best-loved creations was launched in 1996. Dubliner cheese was an attempt at a sophisticated Cheddar for the urban Irish market. It has flourished in Ireland but also enjoys big sales in the US. Dubliner was a result of Carbery's tinkering with its Cheddar towers. The tinkering may have produced a new brand, but Dubliner is still Cheddar. There were attempts by other co-ops to try to develop different kinds of cheese for a mass market. Tipperary Co-Op started to produce Emmental, which, on the Continent, is the go-to cheese for grating and baking. Emmental is now one of the company's export mainstays to the European market (Tipperary has a subsidiary, Tippagral, in France, which develops the product there).

'Our focus changed the week after the referendum,' says Carbery Group Chief Executive Dan MacSweeney, who joined the company in 1992. 'Brexit became the biggest issue we would be dealing with. We're hoping for the best but preparing for the worst. That sounds glib, but that's exactly what we're doing.'

MacSweeney is, like everyone else in the agri-food sector, watching every bleep on the Brexit radar. Any statement from the British or EU negotiators can have an impact on sterling (and, instantly, on margins) or provide a distant smoke signal for how Brexit might play out. 'What's the worst-case scenario for the Cheddar industry? If in two years' time there's no agreement at the end of this divorce discussion, then we fall into a WTO tariff situation immediately. Everyone hopes that won't happen. If it did, you would have a tariff of just over 50 per cent on all cheese products going into the UK. If you're dealing with a tariff of 50 per cent, you're not really in business,' he says. 'The challenge then for the cheese industry is to find a new home for one billion litres of milk.'

It would also be a challenge to keep employment in West Cork. Carbery provides business for 1,300 dairy farmers and employs 230 people directly, not counting all the others along the supply chain.

Carbery is researching other markets and looking at alternative product mixes, especially those that might attract lower tariffs. 'There are other things you can do with milk, but it's not easy,' says MacSweeney. 'Finding a new home for a billion litres of milk won't be done in a year or two.' Sports nutrition has been a big growth area, but the volumes involved are no match for the Cheddar behemoth.

MacSweeney is more sanguine about trying to sell Cheddar on the Continent. 'Germany is starting to eat more Cheddar than it used to,' he says. 'It's becoming a more complex product. There is a whole different range of flavours that weren't there in the past.'

To keep Cheddar and other products ahead of the Brexit curve, producers like MacSweeney place enormous faith in one fundamental resource. 'Dairy farming is about producing *grass* rather than producing *milk*,' he says. 'If you can produce a lot of grass, and produce it efficiently, you have an efficient animal that can convert it to milk. That's the basis of the industry. It means we can produce milk more cost-effectively than other countries. It gives us a certain amount of prominence. You see

Kerrygold products all over the place. You can produce butter and cheese from grass to get a different product. Cows in Germany, Holland, Denmark or France are housed indoors for most of the year. Cows in Ireland are outside up to 24 hours a day for nine months of the year.'

The best-case scenario, says MacSweeney, is a free-trade agreement between Britain and Europe that preserves the status quo for the Irish dairy industry. Failing that, he would hope for a three-to-seven-year transition period to allow producers to prepare for a future beyond the UK but that would keep trade flowing in the meantime. He's realistic: 'You wouldn't find a home for 80,000 tonnes of Cheddar that has come out of the UK. But there's a big world out there. There are developed countries which purchase added-value products based on our natural and grass productions. Developing markets have increased consumption every year: China, South-East Asia, Mexico, North and Sub-Saharan Africa, the Middle East.'

T. J. Flanagan of ICOS sees the problems posed by Brexit as systemic. 'It's the island of Ireland economy,' he says, 'all these supply chains. It's the milk, it's the live cattle, it's the feed-stuffs, the straw, the entire agriculture economy, the ability of a local milk-machine technician to service all his neighbours.

'Once he used to drive out of his gate and turn right or turn left, whether it was to drive into Monaghan or into Fermanagh. Suddenly, if there's a hard Brexit, he can only turn right.'

Nigel Heatrick will also have to figure out which way he turns when he drives out from his 250-acre farm, nestled between the villages of Glaslough and Middletown. From 2019, the external border of the European Union will run *right through* his farm.

'If they put customs on the border it will literally be at the end of our lane,' says Heatrick. 'Potentially every time I leave the house I would be going through customs. On average that would be three times a day.'

Glaslough is in the Irish Republic, in the County Monaghan bulge that pushes its way into UK sovereign territory. Middletown is actually geographically to the south of Glaslough, but it is in County Tyrone. The Heatricks, who bought the farm in 1961, have been living with these complexities for decades, through conflict and peacetime.

Heatrick receives two CAP payments: one for the part of his farm that is in the Republic, the other for the part in Northern Ireland. After 2019, he will no longer receive payment for his Northern endeavours, at least not from Brussels. The farm has 200 acres for beef and dairy cattle in the Republic, and 50 acres solely for beef in Northern Ireland. On the Southern side he has 50 Friesian cows that provide, during the spring, around 1,000 litres of milk per day, and these go to LacPatrick in Monaghan. So the milk is produced in the Republic and processed in the Republic. But the LacPatrick tanker crosses the border twice on the way there, and twice on the way back.

Heatrick is aghast at the inability of the British and Irish governments to provide clarity. 'You'd like to see the English or the Irish government coming out with a clear indication as to what's going to be there. For other people it's not going to have a major effect, but when you're living on the border it's going to affect us, and you have absolutely no say on it.

'We're more or less waiting around to see what happens. You hear people saying it's not going to be a hard border, but we don't really know. We just have to wait and see.'

7. Our Own Private Idaho

If you take a walk along Gerrard Street, in London's China-town, you pass restaurants with racks of cured, wind-dried duck carcasses on display in their semi-steamed windows. You might assume, naturally enough, that the ducks have been spirited in from the distant mists of Asia.

In fact, almost every one of those ducks has come from a farm in Emyvale, County Monaghan, right on the border with County Tyrone.

Once you know that, you might imagine that Silver Hill's dominance on Gerrard Street is owing to its position within the EU. But this isn't entirely true either. The company has also carved out market share much further afield. Every week, it sends a container load of ducks to Singapore, sup-plying forty high-end hotels and restaurant chains. Malaysian duck is one third of the price, but buyers want Silver Hill because they demand the same duck that is sold in China-town in London.

'We're never going to be the cheapest product,' says Barry Cullen, Head of Sales at Silver Hill Farm. 'We've probably turned away more business in the past five years because it didn't meet the criteria. We have margins. We have markets we want to get into. But if it doesn't tick those boxes we stay clear.'

Silver Hill's route to Asia says a lot about the weird world of global food trends. To Brits and tourists, Chinatown is a taste of the Orient. Step inside, order Peking Duck, and your Asian dining 'experience' is complete. But so famous has

Silver Hill's wind-dried duck become that Asia itself wants a taste of the version of Asian food as appropriated by London's Chinatown. And somewhere along the way, the restaurateurs forgot to mention (or didn't realize) that it's actually Irish duck. So in Singapore, restaurants are selling Asian duck from Emyvale, and on the menu it's called either Royal London Duck or London Fat Duck.

How did this come about?

Silver Hill saw an opening in the market to provide a very particular kind of duck for the Chinatown market, and after 15 years it dominates that market. The method relies on a combination of breed, feed, tradition, space and an awful lot of cross-border activity. The Silver Hill breed must be blemish-free because the surface texture is key to a particular Chinese culinary tradition. There is also a high fat content. As such, the ducks live pampered lives in a high-security environment in County Monaghan. They get as much access to water and food as they want, and live in much more spacious surroundings than those usually provided by the average poultry operation. When it comes to laying eggs, ducks are creatures of habit. Every day the same staff, wearing the same clothes, must come in to tend to them. 'If someone different goes in wearing different clothes,' explains Cullen, 'if there is too much noise, that will put the ducks off for an hour or two.'

Post-Brexit, if the movement of animal products across the Irish border is complicated by County Monaghan being in the EU's animal-health regime and County Tyrone being outside it, then Silver Hill would be badly exposed. Silver Hill eggs are laid in the North in Aughnacloy and hatched in Emyvale in the South. They mature either in the North or in the South for seven weeks, and are then processed in Emyvale. 'When we say we have a cross-border business, we absolutely have a cross-border business,' says Cullen. 'I'm from the North, I live in the North, I work in the South. We have 200 staff here. Twenty to thirty would live in the North and travel to the South. Some live in the South and travel to the North. There are farms, offices, production plants, hatcheries: all of it is within 30 miles of Emyvale on both sides of the border.'

One can barely begin to quantify the tariff, customs and EU animal-health implications: the feeding, the breeding, the hatching, the growing, the processing, and the shipping of one million ducks at any given time, all back and forth over the land border, and then over the sea border to the UK.

Overall, Barry Cullen is remarkably sanguine about Brexit. 'We would be philosophical about it,' he says. 'Where we're based, we have been through hard borders before. We're fairly flexible. We took it on the chin and said we'll deal with whatever comes our way. We would have a certain amount of expertise in tariffs and trade around the world.'

Five years ago, 75 per cent of Silver Hill's business went to the UK; now it's 40 per cent. The company says it is ready, post-Brexit, to wean itself off the UK and focus on Asia. In the meantime, though, there are serious implications. Tariffs on duck meat could be as high as 39 per cent. 'We've done the modelling,' he says. 'We've looked at the costing. If there are tariffs to be added on, we'll take that into account.'

The company is considering keeping the ducks raised on the Northern side of the border for the UK market. Cullen says that he would hope that if the birds are raised in the North, then processed and 'packed off' in the South before going to Chinatown in London, there might be some kind of 'dispensation' and that it would be regarded as, 'to all intents and purposes', a UK product.

The EU is, however, allergic to dispensations or carve-outs for particular industries.

Brexit will be disruptive. Silver Hill's advantage is the foothold they have in Asia. As the Irish food sector contemplates the potential trauma of having to diversify away from the reliable, high-value market right on its doorstep, Silver Hill will be better placed than most. But not all companies will have that edge.

The Republic of Ireland exports a remarkable 90 per cent of the food it produces. This is possible because of a revolution, over the past three decades or so, in Irish food production, processing and marketing.

The UK is the destination for 37 per cent of Irish food exports. That is a huge figure; but it also means that 63 per cent of food exports go further afield. 'There is huge growth in Asia and emerging markets,' says a senior civil servant in the Department of Agriculture, Food and the Marine. 'We had already been looking at spreading our risks, spreading our wings in terms of where exports were growing. That has come much more sharply into focus now in terms of the need to reduce the dependence on the UK market.'

The most recent figures would suggest that Ireland is well placed. Since 2010, food and drink exports have grown by 41 per cent, or €3.27 billion. When the financial crash almost crippled the economy, food and drink exports kept doggedly growing. In 2016, exports to the UK actually fell by 8 per cent because of Brexit-related sterling weakness, while food exports to the rest of the EU grew by 3 per cent thanks to stronger sales in beverages, seafood, prepared foods and meat. Growth in all international markets was 13 per cent, driven especially by North America and China.

The risks of Brexit to the food sector were well flagged in advance of the referendum. A dedicated unit was set up in the Department of Agriculture, Food and the Marine to assess the impact, with the minister, Michael Creed, chairing a committee of the key agri-food stakeholders. Bord Bia created an internal Brexit group that meets on a weekly basis, and has been plugged into the department's own subcommittee. The agency will spend €3.6 million in helping companies to withstand the impact, improve efficiency and find new markets. 'We're in the biggest relearning experience of our careers,' says Tara McCarthy, the newly appointed Chief Executive.

But conceiving of the scale of the exposure across the entire food industry has been challenging, and anticipating the political impact daunting to say the least. 'Food is a hugely connected industry in Ireland,' says a senior Bord Bia source. 'Everybody is in some way connected to the land, and to food. It's the 250,000 people who are employed: if you multiply that up by four people per family it's suddenly a million people, or 25 per cent of the population, and even more if you look at the connected services.'

Out of that sphere have emerged some titans. They began at the close-to-the-soil level, but through graft, luck, good marketing and ambition are now global powerhouses. Glanbia, which came about as a result of a merger between Waterford Foods and Avonmore, is a case in point. It is big in Ireland, processing 2.5 billion litres of milk, of which 200 million will go to Irish consumers via brands like Avonmore and Premier. The other 2.3 billion litres are mostly converted into powder and exported as an ingredient for the global food and beverage markets. But that's just the start of its global footprint. Buy a Domino's or Papa John's pizza anywhere in the world and the topping is most likely made with

Glanbia cheese thanks to a joint venture with the American firm Leprino Foods. Glanbia processes over 4 *billion* litres of milk in the US. It is the number-one producer of Cheddar cheese in America, some 300,000 tonnes worth in 2016. It has the largest cheese and whey plant in the world in New Mexico and is in negotiations to open another in Michigan. That plant will produce the equivalent of two thirds of the entire output of cheese from Ireland. Glanbia has four plants in Idaho. In fact, outside the public sector, Glanbia is the largest employer in the state of Idaho.

The Kerry Group has an equally colossal presence. What began on a greenfield site in Listowel in 1972 has flowered into a global behemoth with annual sales of convenience, specialized and nutritional products worth €6.1 billion. In the world of hypersensitivity to all of the things that modern, prosperous humans want to eat, Kerry's website captures the zeitgeist: 'Consumers want great-tasting products created from trusted, authentic and wholesome foods and flavours. We understand the fundamental science of taste: flavour, appearance, texture, aroma, mouthfeel, stability and sensorial experiences.'

But, mouthfeel and sensorial experience aside, there are genuine fears gripping the Irish food sector. Ireland is different because of our reliance on exports. Agra Europe estimates that 45 per cent of Irish agri-foods are exposed to the UK, compared to an EU average of 9 per cent. Irish food producers might enjoy nine months' supply of local produce, but for the other three will need produce from the UK. For security of supply, some companies need two suppliers, one in each jurisdiction. For all these reasons, those firms looking for entry into the UK and European markets, or who are looking to expand, can often struggle to access long-term finance.

When it comes to Brexit, the concerns are threefold: first,

if there is no free-trade deal at the end of the negotiations, high tariffs will make Irish exports to the UK more expensive. Second, Irish food exporters may have to comply with new food standards laid down by the UK, effectively meaning compliance with two sets of rules. If the UK wanted to import cheap food from elsewhere, it could relax its standards – and an influx of cheap food from elsewhere would have its own depressive effect on the market. Equally, if the UK wanted to protect its own sectors, it could change labelling, packaging and certification laws to complicate access for Irish exporters. Third, currency fluctuations: this has had a deleterious effect both before and after the referendum, and many exporters believe it will be a factor for years to come. A drop in sterling to 90p to the euro would, according to Food Drink Ireland (FDI), translate to a loss of €700 million in food exports and about 7,500 Irish jobs.

Bord Bia has tried to make sure exporters know where the risks lie and how to mitigate the impact. One week before Theresa May triggered Article 50 to launch Britain's exit from the EU, the Minister for Agriculture, Michael Creed, launched the Brexit Toolkit, developed by Bord Bia with PwC Ireland. The project poses 100 questions across six specific risk areas to several hundred companies who are most dependent on the UK market. The questions deal with their routes to market, their customs and tax experience, how they fit into supply chains, how well they can hedge in terms of currency, and how well they are prepared in terms of staffing levels. As each exporter goes through the questions, a feedback process informs each one how badly exposed they are.

Irish food and drinks companies went through an intensive period of increased efficiency after the financial crisis. They've had to deepen their capital base and generally become much leaner. Most food processors, therefore, have limited opportunities for further tightening. At the same time, the so-called 'hard discounters', the Aldis and Lidls, have doubled their market share to 20 per cent over the past six years. The result has been good for consumers, but, according to the Small Firms Association, hard on domestic food processors.

The other concern is the geographical spread of SME food producers. Most agri-food production takes place where other kinds of employment are sparse. FDI estimates that over half is located in areas that are in the bottom 60 per cent of those regions designated by the EU, for statistical purposes, as poor and sparsely populated. Half of the employment in agri-food is in parts of the country where GDP per capita is below the EU average. FDI argues that GDP is, in any case, a poor measure of an area's poverty, as it is skewed by the presence of huge multinationals in the economy. If the measuring term Actual Individual Consumption (AIC) is used instead, FDI argues, those poorer parts of Ireland that are so reliant on agri-food would be poorer still.

A senior civil servant in the Department of Agriculture, Food and the Marine adds: 'There's a huge regional spread of employment, and if you have a huge impact on what is the most exposed sector, then that's going to have huge ramifications economically, socially, and environmentally.'

Every day, thousands of litres of milk are collected from dairy farms north and south of the border and brought to a Glanbia processing facility in Virginia, County Cavan. There the cream is taken off the milk and then transported south to Dublin, or north to Mallusk, County Antrim. In Mallusk, the cream is blended with whiskey to produce the world's most famous cream liqueur: Baileys Irish Cream.

Baileys has been manufactured in Dublin since its launch in 1974. The site at Nangor Road still produces the full range of Baileys products – including Baileys Chocolat Luxe, Baileys XC and Baileys Hazelnut – in all bottle sizes.

But the Mallusk plant, which opened in 2003, does the big volumes. It produces Baileys in the key bottle sizes for global sales (70cl, 75cl and one litre) and it does so at very high speed. According to Diageo, which owns the brand, the Mallusk plant 'contains the fastest liqueur bottling line in the world, capable of producing up to half a million bottles per day'.

Mallusk produces around 70 per cent of all the Baileys sold worldwide. Some 97 per cent of the liqueur made there is exported. Having one foot in Dublin and one in County Antrim gives the company a backup should there be any major outages at either site.

The cream that ends up in Baileys comes from farmers who supply only Glanbia, the owners of the Virginia facility. Glanbia in turn has the exclusive contract to supply the cream from the milk to Diageo. It's a supply chain that is both simple and complex. 'It is absolutely seamless as it stands,' says one Glanbia source.

Now Brexit is threatening to disrupt that seamless operation.

One of the reasons Baileys chose Glanbia is because it has a policy of always being able to trace dairy products back to the farm. With Brexit, there is the possibility of dairy tariffs at around 50 per cent. That would immediately hit the milk going from Northern producers to Virginia, and then the cream heading back across the border and travelling up to Mallusk.

Producing Baileys is a major operation. The company requires more than 275 million litres of milk supplied from 40,000 dairy cows grazing on 1,500 accredited farms in the

Republic and in Northern Ireland. This is the equivalent, in recent years, of between 4 and 5 per cent of Ireland's total milk production.

Again, this involves an awful lot of border crossing. Diageo confirms there are about 5,000 crossings a year by trucks in the direct Baileys supply chain, moving raw milk, cream, whiskey, bottles and corrugated paper.

Quite apart from the prospect of tariffs, and of border checks that would slow down the movement of perishable cream, Baileys would have to create a new supply-chain agreement, replacing Glanbia with a Northern supplier.

At the other end of the spectrum is Seamus McMahon. 'We're never going to be Diageo,' he says. 'We're a craft product, landing a higher price.'

Seamus runs Brehon Brewhouse, a craft brewery next to the dairy farm he has worked on since he was 18. Like Silver Hill Farm, a 45-minute drive away, his operation is about as cross-border as you can get. The Brewhouse is 8 kilometres from Crossmaglen, County Armagh, on the periphery of Monaghan and Louth, and 15 kilometres from Dundalk. 'I grew up during the Troubles,' recalls Seamus. 'This past 10 to 15 years have been idyllic. You travel to Belfast, you travel to Dublin in the same time. We're a strong GAA family. We go to most of the Monaghan games. It's just a case of going up the road to Belfast or Dungannon. There are no problems whatsoever. That's the way we want to keep it.'

Seamus started the microbrewery in 2013. The first year was a struggle, but since then it has been growing steadily, with the dairy business as a cushion. Seamus and his team of five can produce 33,000 litres of beer a week. Brehon Brewhouse products are found on the shelves of SuperValu on both sides of the border, as well as in Dunnes Stores and

Marks & Spencer. Beyond that, they're selling into France and Luxembourg. 'There's a big move to get more exports off the island,' says Seamus. 'We're looking very much towards the American market, New York, Washington, into Canada. We're twinned in Monaghan with Prince Edward Island in Newfoundland. There are major links between the two areas. We'll be trying to muscle into that.'

But Brexit has already had an impact.

The slump in sterling forced Seamus to lower his prices and to think hard about where his inputs come from. Brehon would prefer to source ingredients locally. The grains come from Haggardstown outside Dundalk and the bottles come from Cavan. The labels were made in Swords, County Dublin, but they have switched to Portadown, County Armagh, because they are 'half the price' due to the weakness in sterling. The hops, the yeast and the caps are also now sourced in Britain. 'Our malts may follow suit and come out of England as well,' Seamus admits. 'We'll keep a close eye on our ingredients because of sterling. I think that issue is there to stay, I don't think it's a blip.' Of course, the prospect of tariffs and a new UK regulatory regime now threatens this model.

Somewhere in between Brehon Brewhouse and Diageo you might have a company like C&C Group, which will potentially be a serious casualty because of a supply chain that incorporates all parts of the two islands. C&C is tax-resident in Dublin, but also listed in London, with a market capitalization of just over €1 billion. Some €591 million of €633 million in net revenue is generated in the UK and Ireland.

The company buys 80,000 tonnes of apples each year to press into cider: 60,000 from England and Wales, 10,000 from Northern Ireland and 10,000 from the Republic. The apples are fermented in Clonmel. The C&C brewery in Glasgow, meanwhile, sends beer to Clonmel to be distributed throughout Ireland. In a written submission to the House of Lords Select Committee hearings on Brexit and Ireland, the company said: 'We will deliver cider from Ireland and beer from the UK to customers in a single load, on the same delivery lorry. This is possible because both production sites are operating within the same market with no tariffs or barriers.'

Despite its healthy balance sheet, C&C fears for its own operations and those of its apple suppliers. 'Apple growing is a marginal agricultural activity,' the company said. 'It is not the remit of wealthy farmers. We have a long-term relationship often stretching back generations with our apple growers. If Brexit reduces our ability to source apples from the UK in order to press them in Ireland, then hundreds of the farmers will be adversely affected.'

Some agri-food processors are bracing themselves for a rethink by UK producers and retailers who start to review their supply chains. 'If currency movements or trade barriers increase the price of Irish goods, Ireland's attractiveness as a supply base for UK customers will fall,' says the Small Firms Association.

In order to sidestep currency fluctuations, tariffs, regulatory problems and customs delays, some Irish food producers are thinking about moving production altogether to the UK, partly because they are being encouraged to do so by some UK customers. Equally, those companies which have manufacturing investment in Britain could move back to Ireland. Ornua, the huge Irish dairy concern, employs 1,000 people in five separate businesses in the UK. 'You could see a new interdependency and a reorientation,' says one Bord Bia source. 'Whatever has to be done, business will do. But it's just a massive burden.'

Some operators are bullishly optimistic. Country Crest is a north County Dublin-based family business going back four generations to 1910. Today, it is one of the biggest suppliers of pre-packed vegetable and chilled ready-made meals in the country. Managing Director Michael Hoey believes Irish producers can capitalize on the loss of farm subsidies and the EU labour pool that have sustained UK production. 'Brexit will be a massive advantage to Ireland,' he told a Bord Bia panel discussion. 'Primary producers in the UK are on their knees at the moment. Their cost base will get higher. They're facing inflation. They're going to get less labour. We have an advantage in that we can receive people from Eastern Europe. When EU subsidies dry up for people in the UK, how are they going to produce cheaper food? There is capacity here to fill that gap. There is a professionalism in Irish food production that I don't see in the UK.'

Hoey believes Irish producers will step in to supply products that have hitherto been imported from the UK. But one senior figure in the business disputes this. 'We sell Britain food worth nearly €5 billion every year,' says Larry Murrin, Chief Executive of Dawn Farms. 'Britain sells Ireland food worth €3.2 billion. It's not the same food. We buy things from Britain that they have best competency in. Britain buys things from us that we have best competency in . . . There are completely different products, categories, manufacturing processes.'

Murrin is well placed to take the long view on Irish food. He is one of a handful of pioneers who looked around the Irish marketplace in the doldrum years of the mid 1980s. Back then, the Central Statistics Office categorized the food industry as 'beef, dairy and other'. Along with the founders of companies like Rye Valley, Green Isle and Perri Crisps, Murrin realized that they had to export or stagnate. He recalls: 'When we set this business up in the mid eighties, it was an SME. We didn't know what we didn't know. When we realized the Irish market wasn't big enough for what we had ambitions for, we went looking to see where we could sell cooked meats elsewhere. We quickly realized there was not one, but *hundreds* of companies like us in the UK. So that wasn't going to be the solution. But food as we know it was starting to change. People's lifestyles were starting to change, and the sophistication of foods that were starting to appear on supermarket shelves with conveni-ence as their emphasis was also starting to change.

'We could see that the people who were driving that change, the brands, the Finduses of this world – they were going to need qualified outsource companies to feed ready-made, customized ingredients into them. So it's a bit like the guy who makes the engines for BMW – that was our oppor-tunity. That is what we have specialized in for 30 years.'

Dawn Farms now ships to 42 markets around the world, exporting 97 per cent of what they produce: value-added foodstuffs and confectionery, value-added meat products, meat- and dairy-based ingredients, and, says Murrin, 'high-value-added products which take a step closer to the consumer, from jelly beans to cooked meats'. The company employs 1,100 people in three manufacturing plants, two in Ireland and one in the UK.

Dawn Farms is the perfect illustration of how tightly inte-grated the Irish and UK food industries have become. Its products are either assembled in Ireland using Irish, UK and other sourced ingredients, or the company sends highly spe-cific ingredients to the prepared food industry in the UK and beyond. 'We have an inbound supply chain, and an outbound supply chain,' says Murrin. 'After that, we put the ingredients through some pretty sophisticated manufacturing processes that get the product into the shape, form and flavour that our clients want it in. And then we have to feed that back into the markets. It's a sophisticated supply chain. It's a very regulated supply chain, because meat is a very heavily regulated product at production level, from farm all the way through. Food, if not properly cared for, can hurt people.'

Dawn is the largest producer of pizza toppings anywhere in the world, outside the USA. 'If you buy a sandwich in England,' says Murrin, 'there's a one in three chance that you're eating protein that we produced. If you buy a recipe dish or a ready meal in the UK, there's a significant chance you're eating protein that we produced.'

Murrin is uncompromising about the need to defend access to the UK. 'We've got to maintain our market share in Britain while all of that's happening,' he says. 'We just simply have to maintain it. You will not diversify the €5 billion in market share that has taken 50 years to create in Britain. You will not replace that in 10 years . . . We have to maintain market share, while at the same time build market share elsewhere for the overall Irish industry. But those markets should be predominantly in Europe. There will be markets in China, for things like infant formula, and some meat products, but that won't apply in general for the Irish food industry.'

Murrin goes so far as to challenge the state's determined alignment with the European side in the Brexit negotiations. 'The UK market is the most sophisticated in the world bar none. I know of no other geographic market in the world where you'll get the extent and breadth of short-shelf-life innovation on supermarket shelves than you will get in Britain, and Ireland has a pretty important place in that supply chain. It has taken all that time and money and effort and years and years to create. We wouldn't want Britain to be forced into a corner and then say to itself, as it does have this sophistication, that they will just have to re-create that supply chain in some other corner of the world.

'There's no point in having trade talks as part of the EU27 or Ireland looking to be a special case for the next two to five years if by the time we get to the talks Ireland's market share is already cut in half,' he says.

8. Is There Such a Thing as a British Fish?

Sometime after 3 a.m. on Sunday, 15 January 2012, Abdelbaky Mohamed was awoken by a sudden bang.

The 24-year-old Egyptian had only just got to the berth to grab some sleep. For most of the night, he had been either working on the engine or sorting a haul of prawns and whitefish that the crew of the MFV *Tit Bonhomme* had pulled from the Celtic Sea. The trip had been dogged by problems. Even before the trawler was clear of Glandore Harbour in West Cork, it had gone aground just 400 metres north-east of the pier, resuming its course only after the rising tide eased it off the bottom.

On the Saturday evening, the weather had deteriorated. There were strong south-south-westerly winds, and, as the drizzle turned into heavier downpours, visibility declined even further.

In these cold, unpleasant conditions, Abdelbaky Mohamed and his brother Wael, 32, were working in the fish hold. At around 7 p.m., Mohamed noticed the bilge water in the hold was high and would have to be expelled. He suggested to the skipper, Michael Hayes, that he start the bilge pump. After five minutes of pumping, however, the water wasn't receding. Hayes switched to the auxiliary pump, and this seemed to do the trick. They hauled anchor and headed deeper into the Celtic Sea in search of prawn.

At 11.23 p.m. the vessel stopped a second time. Even though the auxiliary pump had taken over, the main bilge pump would have to be repaired. This time the pumping duty was transferred to the auxiliary engine, which was fitted with a bilge pump. While Hayes attempted the repairs, Mohamed went up to the wheelhouse to keep watch. The skipper changed the bilge pump impeller, but was unable to get suction. While he was grappling with the pump, Hayes noticed a second problem. There was an oil leak in the main engine. He alerted Mohamed, and both men went down to the engine room to try to fix it. Mohamed spotted oil leaking from the top of a steel pipe attached to the lubricating oil pump. Hayes looked for a replacement part but none could be found.

At 2.06 a.m., when the *Tit Bonhomme* was 15 nautical miles off the south coast, Hayes decided to call it a day. The fishing had been poor, and the problems, while not terminal, could not be ignored in such weather conditions. For all their efforts, they had only around 42 boxes of prawn. Eight minutes later, Hayes restarted the engine, and they headed back towards the West Cork coast, travelling initially at two knots so that he could keep an eye on the oil leak. After 45 minutes he increased the speed to four knots.

As the *Tit Bonhomme* was making its way back to shore in increasingly difficult conditions, Mohamed turned in to his bunk on the upper berth. Below him was Dubliner Kevin Kershaw, a 21-year-old apprentice on his first fishing trip. On the starboard side were Attiy Ahmed Shaban, another Egyptian, and below him Mohamed's brother Wael. Michael Hayes's cabin was fitted portside aft in the wheelhouse.

The *Tit Bonhomme* was a sturdy, 123-tonne, 21-metre steel-hulled twin-rig trawler. It had been built in 1988 by the French company Chantier Naval Union et Travail in Les Sables-d'Olonne on the western French coast. It was a freezer trawler constructed with a raked stem, a shelter deck and a transom stern. Michael Hayes himself was a seasoned 52-year-old skipper from the Ring in County Waterford, and had been fishing out of Glandore Harbour for 10 years. He had a Special Certificate of Competency and was a qualified three-module long-range fishing certificate holder. On Wednesday, 11 January, two days before the *Tit Bonhomme* set off, Hayes had arranged for routine engine repairs in Union Hall, the small fishing village on the western side of Glandore Harbour. The seawater cooling pump had been replaced with a reconditioned unit, and a leaking gasket on a section of flanged steel pipework attached to the lubricating oil cooler pipe had been repaired. The engine was tested after the repairs were completed.

Of the crew, only Abdelbaky Mohamed was fully qualified. He had been issued with a BIM safety card and had completed a STCW-95 Elementary First Aid training course two years previously. He also had a fire-prevention and fire-fighting certificate from the Arab Academy of Science and Technology and Maritime Transport, which he brought with him from his home in Alexandria.

The *Tit Bonhomme* made it to the mouth of Glandore Harbour around 5 a.m. Standing sentinel at the mouth, close to Sheela Point on the western shore, is Adam's Island, a perilous 27-metre-high rock that bisects the inlet into two channels. Just over a kilometre further into the harbour is Eve Island, a smaller obstacle. The local maxim – 'Avoid Adam and hug Eve' – is generally adhered to. In winds that were now up to Gale-Force 7, the trawler suddenly found itself stranded on the southern side of Adam's Island, veering calamitously towards the rocks.

Abdelbaky Mohamed, having fallen asleep, was jolted awake by a sudden noise. The *Tit Bonhomme* was rolling violently. Immediately Kevin Kershaw and Attiy Ahmed Shaban scrambled out of the berth, up on to the main deck and through to the wheelhouse via the internal portside companionway. The Mohamed brothers also made it to the main deck, but they went through the starboard side emergency escape hatch, hauling themselves on to the deck next to the battery-storage compartment.

In the chaos that followed the lights went out and the emergency lighting also failed (Abdelbaky Mohamed later described seeing the operating batteries strewn all around the deck). Wael Mohamed attempted to cross the deck to the portside entrance to the galley. It was a desperate gambit. Debris from the sea was surging in from the rear of the trawler. Abdelbaky clambered back along the starboard side, hauling himself up a ladder to the access hatch and up to the shelter deck. He reached the wheelhouse through its only entrance and closed it behind him.

According to the Marine Casualty Investigation Board report, all five crew members had made it to the relative safety of the wheelhouse. Michael Hayes was wearing his own personal flotation device, and was handing out others to the crew from the stowage locker on the starboard side. Kevin Kershaw was on his mobile phone, frantically trying to contact the emergency services. Crew members were also grappling unsuccessfully with McMurdo hand-held VHF radios found in a drawer. The recorded details of two phone calls were later played in Courtroom 2 at the Cork Court House.

'Yes . . . we're at . . . helicopter, please.' Kershaw is heard shouting. 'We're after hitting the island off . . . going into Union Hall, boat is aground . . . the vessel . . . ah shit . . . is the *Tit Bonhomme*, please hurry . . .'

In a second, chaotic exchange, Kershaw and Hayes struggle to convey an increasingly desperate situation to the operator and then the Valentia-based Coast Guard. 'What is the nature of your emergency?' asks the Coast Guard. Kershaw shouts back: 'We need a boat, we need a helicopter.' The Coast Guard asks again: 'What is the nature of your emergency?' Kershaw replies: 'What is the nature of our emergency? We're sinking, we're going under water.'

The Coast Guard responds: 'Right, you're sinking – what is your position?' Kershaw is desperate: 'We're three quarters under water . . . please . . .' The Coast Guard again asks for the position. Kershaw makes a final plea: 'Ah . . . we're at . . . we're at Union Hall . . . come on, we're going to capsize . . .'

Hayes managed to give the position. The emergency response was triggered four minutes later. Coastguard helicopters from Waterford and Shannon, as well as lifeboat crews from Baltimore and Courtmacsherry, were all scrambled.

The *Tit Bonhomme* was now rolling heavily and violently. Suddenly the wheelhouse side windows shattered, and a salvo of sea and glass punched its way in. Someone shouted to open the door to let the water out. At 6 a.m., Abdelbaky Mohamed grabbed his lifejacket, forced open the wheelhouse door and was swept out on a swell.

Mohamed was a strong swimmer. He struck away from the vessel in the darkness. The waves by now were up to four metres high. Mohamed saw another light ahead of him, which he took to be that from a life jacket.

Rescuers from the Toe Head Coast Guard found him in a small cove outside Long Point, some eight cables to the north-west of Adam's Island. He had lain with a broken collarbone for over two hours and was found wearing only a t-shirt, boxer shorts, and a life belt that was barely attached. He was winched off by helicopter at 8.08 a.m. and transported to Cork University Hospital. The MCIB report concluded: 'The crew of the Coast Guard boat showed considerable courage in this rescue given the sea state.'

The rest of the crew all drowned.

A colourful entry in the Marine Institute's 2009 *Atlas of the Commercial Fisheries Around Ireland* shows the sea-floor topography of Europe's most westerly islands. Presented from on high, Ireland and Britain recline at an angle on a powder-blue surface that could almost be the sheet of a conjugal bed, but is, in fact, the Continental shelf. To the west and south, the bed tapers off to form the outline of a furrow-browed canine. Then, over the edge of the shelf, intricately ribbed cliffs drop sharply into a darker, colder blue. Along this nexus of Continental shelf and seabed are the most productive fishing waters in Europe.

According to the atlas: 'Over the last number of centuries fisheries have developed and expanded from coastal waters initially, throughout the shelf in the last century, to the deep sea and oceanic waters in the last few decades. In 2007, an estimated 1.9 million tonnes of fish were taken by the fishing fleets of EU member states from the waters around Ireland. Ireland landed 185,000 tonnes of these fish, or 10 per cent of the international landings.'

The largest and most valuable migratory pelagic stocks in the North-East Atlantic, including mackerel, horse mackerel and blue whiting, all spawn in these waters. Large stocks of hake, anglerfish and megrim also spawn along the slope to the west and south. Herring, cod, haddock, whiting, plaice and sole spawn in the Irish Sea and the Celtic Sea. 'The shelf area and coastal waters are important nursery areas for young fish,' the atlas reports. 'Shellfish stocks such as prawn, crab, lobster, shrimp, scallop, whelk and cockles are also abundant regionally or locally.'

Further east, there are also plentiful stocks of prawn: the Irish fishing industry's second most valuable catch. Michael Hayes and his crew on the *Tit Bonhomme* were regular visitors to these waters.

Today Michael's widow, Caitlin Ní Aodha, sends a 25-metre freezer trawler to fish for prawns throughout the season. Caitlin hasn't been on a trawler at sea since her and Michael's three children were born, but for her crew it is a gruelling vocation. It is also a very lucrative one. The prawns are frozen on board Caitlin's trawler to −25°, landed in Rossaveal in Connemara, offloaded in three-kilo cartons, hand-picked, hand-laid and put into 12-kilo master cartons, taken to a buyer in Clogherhead and transported within days to restaurants all over Italy.

Caitlin and Michael Hayes met through fishing. Caitlin's family had fished for generations, and she bought her first boat at the age of 22. 'I did my ticket,' she says, 'and got my own 40-footer.'

After the tragedy in Glandore Harbour, Caitlin had a stark choice: sell the licence and turn away from the trade that had just claimed the life of her husband, or take over the business and start from scratch. 'I was left with Michael's licence,' she recalls. 'Like anyone else, I wasn't prepared. I could have sold it a hundred times over. But I really didn't want to. I kind of felt it was something that my family had done for centuries. My three brothers all sold their licences. I was the last one left. It wasn't financially viable for them. One retired early, the other two gave up because there had been a lull for a few years. I needed to earn a living. I had three kids in college. I thought for a long time. If I was a farmer's wife, would I sell on my farm?'

Caitlin kept the licence. She bought the *Newgrange* in Clogherhead, renaming it the *Dervla*, after her eldest daughter. She picked up where Michael left off, focusing on prawn, which now makes up 90 per cent of what the *Dervla* brings in. Caitlin employs a skipper/manager from Donegal, a relief skipper, also from Donegal, two Filipinos and an Egyptian. The *Dervla* operates in and out of the Irish Sea, and over various banks to the south and west of Ireland: the Porcupine Bank, the Smalls, the Jones and the Labadie. In a good year, there might be 10 fishing trips, but the weather in December and January can be so bad that there is very little fishing. The real harvesting time is from the middle of March until the end of July. By August, the prawns start to disappear and fishing grounds are closed to allow females to breed and the stocks to recover. On a good trip, the *Dervla* can land three to four tonnes of prawn. If they are landed on a Friday, they will be in a warehouse in Rome no later than the following Tuesday, and then distributed throughout Italy.

'The Italians like them because of the colouring,' she explains. 'We preferably get them from the Porcupine and the Labadie.'

The Porcupine Bank is in Irish waters; but the Labadie is British.

If Caitlin is to keep seducing the collective palate of Italian diners with the tender flesh and Mediterranean hue of her prawns, she will need continued access to British waters.

In 2015, the Irish prawn sector was worth an estimated €50 million, and anything up to 40 per cent of those prawns – *Nephrops* is the name given to the genus – are caught in UK waters. According to figures supplied by the Marine Institute, between 2011 and 2015, 64 per cent of the mackerel landed by Irish vessels, both by weight and value, came from UK waters. Across the industry, a drumbeat of fear and militancy is thickening over how Brexit will hit Irish fishing communities. The stakes are high: British waters might be closed, and the European fleet might spill over into Irish waters as a consequence.

But the impact of Brexit goes beyond a calculus of access and quotas. It has stirred up a long-simmering resentment over the European Union's Common Fisheries Policy. There is an industry-wide debate about what Brexit will mean, and the debate has exhumed a strongly held, if contested, notion that Ireland was given a raw deal on fisheries when it joined in 1973. As a percentage of GDP, the contribution of fisheries to the Irish economy is relatively small, but, politically, the industry has always punched above its weight. On 15 February 2017, when the government was convulsed by the latest Garda whistleblower controversy, Enda Kenny still met fishermen for an hour to discuss Brexit. The sector employs 11,000 people, and exports fish worth €150 million. There are 161 companies in the processing business.

'Politicians pay attention to fisheries,' says a senior civil servant in the Department of Agriculture, Food and the Marine. 'It's emotive. Everybody likes fishermen. It's a hard, dangerous job. Politicians will never attack people who appear as characters in children's books. Fishermen and postmen are the good guys.'

Some in the Irish fishing industry have called for Ireland to follow the UK out of the European Union. During a dialogue between stakeholders and the government on how to confront the Brexit threat, Patrick Murphy, the CEO of the Irish South and West Fish Producers Organisation, raised the issue of reopening the quotas that Irish vessels can target and what should happen if Ireland faced resistance from other member states. Murphy declared: 'If this is the case, we believe that Ireland has no future inside of the EU.'

The idea that Brexit provides an opportunity for Ireland to

right supposed historical wrongs and to allow Irish fishermen to catch more fish appears, however, to be a minority view. 'Of course we'd like access to more fish and access to more of a percentage of fish in our waters,' says Lorcán Ó Cinnéide, National Secretary of the Irish Fish Processors and Exporters Association. 'But this is exactly the wrong time and the wrong thing to be doing in the context of Brexit. Simply put, we are in a fight – and a fight it is – with the UK. We have 26 other member states with us. The people who propose to open up the share of our waters are saying, essentially, let's turn around and have a major row with the guys on our own side. This would be completely, totally and utterly mad.'

Although there are differing views within the industry on what to do about Brexit, concern about the future is universal. And the biggest concern is that Britain will be able, with few impediments, to exclude foreign vessels from its waters once outside the Common Fisheries Policy. If there is no agreement between the EU and UK, or if there are no transitional arrangements in place, from 2019 all EU vessels will lose access to the UK zone, as it will no longer be part of what are termed 'Union waters'.

'If we were excluded from British waters completely,' says Caitlin Ní Aodha, 'I don't think our [prawn] fleet would survive. If we were excluded and other countries are too, then where does that displaced fleet go? Are they going to then be sent up off the west coast of Ireland?'

On 30 October 2016, the British Minister for Agriculture, Fisheries and Food, George Eustice, told the *Daily Telegraph* that after Brexit, British fishermen would be able to catch 'hundreds of thousands of tonnes' more fish. It was a bold statement from a prominent Leave campaigner who had once (unsuccessfully) stood as a European Parliament candidate for UKIP. It cheered the British fishing industry no end. Of all the interest groups in the UK economy, the fishing industry has been the most unstinting in favour of Brexit.

The Common Fisheries Policy has been loathed by British fishermen down the years. According to a study by the NAFC Marine Centre at the University of the Highlands and Islands in Scotland, the value of the fish caught by EU boats in UK waters is four times that of the fish caught by UK boats in other EU waters. British fishermen voted in huge numbers to leave the EU. UKIP and a group called Fishing for Leave campaigned relentlessly, and successfully, in coastal constituencies, and the fishing industry largely fell in behind them. While many other sectors of the economy opposed Brexit, or at least want Britain to remain as close to the EU single market as possible, there is no such ambivalence in fisheries. In a submission to the House of Lords Select Committee hearings on Brexit, Fishing for Leave declared: 'It is CRITICAL, for either political convenience or a minority of industry interests, that the CFP is not replicated into British law.'

The Scottish Fishermen's Federation insists that Brexit will mean 'a sea of opportunities'. Outside the CFP, Britain will be able to devise its own sustainability policies, negotiate for access to fishing grounds with North Atlantic neighbours and enjoy a 'cordial' rapport with Europe, but only on its terms. Bertie Armstrong, the Federation's Chief Executive, told the House of Lords Brexit Select Committee: 'We can have access to French waters, of course, and they can have access to our waters, of course, but on our terms. Everybody else needs access to us . . . [the UK has] a fine hand of cards if there is the political backbone to chase this grand prize.'

Irish observers agree that the British have a strong hand

with regard to fisheries. 'Brexit is going to be seen as a historical suicide note,' says Lorcán Ó Cinnéide of the Irish fish-processing industry. 'However, this is one of the few areas where they do have – on paper at least – a relatively strong hand. The industry ambition is that they would regain control over their very large, 34 per cent share of North-East Atlantic waters. They would basically redress the historic injustice to their industry. They would then selectively trade access to other countries in exchange for trade and whatever they need.'

The sentiments expressed by British fishermen have been noted with growing alarm in Ireland. 'The fishing community in the UK,' says Ireland's fisheries minister, Michael Creed, 'has had its expectations heightened more than anybody else. [The Leave campaign] deliberately went after the fishing community. I've had bilateral meetings with [former and current UK ministers] Andrea Leadsom and George Eustice. They want to pull the drawbridge up behind them and take fish in UK territorial waters for UK fishermen. That's a disaster for us.'

Ireland joined the EEC on 1 January 1973. Fisheries was the first speed bump on the road to entry.

The negotiations for the EEC accession of Ireland, Britain and Denmark began in Luxembourg on 30 June 1970 (Norway was part of the same batch but it eventually declined to join). On the very first day of the negotiations, Dublin expressed alarm at a Commission regulation, adopted the day right before talks began, that fleets from the founding six countries would get access to Irish in-shore waters. As Brigid Laffan and Jane O'Mahony claim in their book *Ireland and the European Union*: 'The legislative act would not have been passed if the four candidate countries, which included Norway, were already in the Union.' Ireland resisted the demand,

and accession talks were deadlocked for 18 months. The head of Bord Iascaigh Mhara (BIM), Brendan O'Kelly, recommended a moratorium on the Commission's demands until after Ireland joined. The Commission declined, but eventually agreed a 10-year extension of Ireland's fishing zone to a 12-mile limit (that concession remains in place).

In 1983, the Commission launched an elaborate quota-based system designed to give each country fair access to the fish in European waters, and to help sustain fisheries through the application of scientific advice on stock levels. The Common Fisheries Policy, as we know it today, was born. Under an arrangement called Relative Stability, catch quotas were informed by each member state's historical patterns of access, sometimes going back hundreds of years. This meant that countries such as Spain and France were allocated substantial quotas in Irish waters, but the Irish fleet got relatively little beyond the UK zone. Meanwhile, scientists would determine the Total Allowable Catch (TAC) for hundreds of fish species. Each member state would then be allocated an overall quota for each species. There were also technical restrictions on the kind of gear fishermen could use, new rules on marketing standards for fish products, tariff quotas for imports from outside the EU, and funding for fishermen and their communities.

Every December, fisheries ministers arrive in Brussels for three days and two nights of haggling over TACs and quotas. There is a ritual hue and cry from environmental groups claiming stocks will collapse unless quotas are cut, and from fishermen who say their livelihoods face ruin unless quotas are increased.

There is a widespread view within the Irish fishing industry that the EEC underestimated the scope of the industry when setting up the Relative Stability mechanism, and that

Ireland did not negotiate effectively – with the result that Ireland has never been allocated as much quota as it deserves. A separate but related view is that the very premise of Relative Stability was flawed, and that the quota regime should have been guided not by each country's historical fishing activity but by its territorial claims.

In 1976, the foreign minister, Garret FitzGerald, began negotiating what he hoped would be a better deal for Irish fishermen in their own waters. 'The logic for it,' explains a senior civil servant, 'was this: because our industry wasn't as developed as some of the other industries, we said it's not fair to base it totally on traditional fishing practices because we never had the opportunity to expand our fisheries. So here we are now allowing new access to resources that we could and should be claiming, so we want a payment for that.'

In 1978, that payment was agreed at a meeting in the Netherlands. The so-called Hague Preferences were born – a complex formula whereby, in situations where stocks of a particular species were vulnerable, Ireland would be exempted from cuts in the quota. While the government regards the Hague Preferences as an important concession, fishing organizations feel they are small beer. The other problem is that they are not automatic: each December in Brussels they have to be renegotiated.

Now, with Brexit looming, many in the Irish fishing industry fear the prospect of British waters being closed, worry that Ireland won't be properly represented in the Brexit negotiations, and feel a certain envy of British fishermen who are 'taking back control'.

Caitlin Ní Aodha says: 'Of course [British fishermen] are going to do what we would do if *we* were leaving. That is to get the very best deal for their boats.'

'The whole Brexit thing is the best opportunity we've had since we joined the EEC,' says Niall Duffy, Editor of the trade journal the *Skipper*. 'The problem is the Irish industry is very fractured. Different sectors want different things. They tend not to speak with a unified voice.'

Irish officials take a more sanguine view of the coming negotiations. Michel Barnier, they say, is negotiating on behalf of member states, including Ireland, and as a former fisheries minister he will have the interests of European fishermen at heart. Lorcán Ó Cinnéide insists that Ireland *will* have a final say. 'We have actually got a veto on the eventual settlement,' he says. 'The EU can't ignore that. This will be voted on by national parliaments or governments.'

The *Western Viking* is a 1,150-tonne, 56.5-metre-long trawler, built in Denmark in 2015 at a cost of €18 million. 'That's a big investment,' says Frank Doherty, who started fishing with his six brothers in Donegal in the 1960s and who owns the vessel. 'It has been a worthwhile investment. We've been doing reasonably well now for a long time, but the future is something which is hard to be very sure about.'

From October to April every year, Frank Doherty's son Enda sets off from Killybegs with a crew of 10 or 11 and heads north – to Shetland, or sometimes as far as Norway. The *Viking* is at sea throughout the winter months in conditions that Frank describes as 'fairly horrendous'. Its main target is mackerel.

Irish consumers are not fond of mackerel. But it is the nation's most valuable species – for export. The brightly striped fish spawn off the south-west of Ireland, head up to Scotland and then back south again to Spain. Although they will cruise past the west coast of Ireland, that is not where

Irish boats go. The fish are at their fattest and oiliest at the point in the cycle when they are off the coast of Scotland.

The *Western Viking* catches 3.5 thousand tonnes of mackerel each year. They are processed in Killybegs, frozen and then shipped to Nigeria, Ghana, Greece, France, Japan and China. Frank Doherty employs 80 staff in the processing plant, with a wage bill of €3.5 million.

Now, Brexit is throwing a spanner in the works.

Between 2011 and 2015, some 64 per cent of the mackerel caught by Irish vessels was caught in British waters. 'We could catch it in our own zone,' says a department official, 'because it's a migratory species. But it would affect the market, the supply chain, the dynamics of the market.'

John Nolan, who runs the Castletownbere Co-Op, says: 'If we were disallowed access we'd still catch the quota. But we'd catch it off Castletownbere instead of off the Isle of Skye. It would still be mackerel. But the fat content would be less, so it wouldn't be worth the same amount of money. Twenty-five per cent of it would go to the smoking industry. Down here, 15 per cent would go to the canning industry. The price you'd get would not be the same.'

It looks like a disaster for Irish fishermen, but, like everything else in the world of commercial fishing, it is not that simple.

On Wednesday, 7 September 2016, a group of scientists and British industry representatives appeared before the House of Lords Select Committee on the EU for another set of hearings on the impact of Brexit on fisheries. The Labour peer Lord Rooker asked Professor Richard Barnes from the University of Hull the following question: 'Do I take it from what I have read that there is no such thing as British fish?'

This was not a facetious question. The *identity* of the fish in

British waters goes to the heart of how daring, or cautious, the UK government will be in breaking free from the CFP. Fish do not recognize borders. They spawn in one location and migrate to another. Whether Fishing for Leave likes it or not, ownership of sovereign waters does not equate to ownership of the fish in those waters. There are legal and conventional protocols that require countries to cooperate with their neighbours on managing those stocks that migrate, those that are shared and those that are susceptible to overfishing.

When Britain was in the European Union, all those concerns were governed by the CFP. Under Brexit, a complicated new dispensation will have to be negotiated.

According to a senior Irish official, the swagger with which the British fisheries minister, George Eustice, boasted about hundreds of thousands of tonnes of extra fish has since given way to caution. 'He's pretty careful in what he says,' says the official. 'The UK industry since the referendum has gone nuts. They think that every fish in the UK zone at the moment they're going to get. About 58 per cent of the fish caught in UK waters is caught by non-UK vessels. So if they close their waters they could more than double their industry overnight. There are two simple issues: (a), they don't have the capacity to catch that amount of fish, and (b), they don't have the ability to sell all that fish.'

According to figures supplied to the House of Lords European Union Committee by Britain's Department for Environment, Food and Rural Affairs, in 2014 Britain exported 66 per cent of its catch to the EU. If the UK closes its waters post-Brexit, the EU27 would most likely retaliate by closing market access to British exporters. 'What we and other fishing nations are saying is,' says a senior Irish official, 'if you want to shut us out, fine. But you're not selling any fish into the EU.'

Pro-Leave fishermen have piled pressure on the British government to act tough on fisheries in the 12 months following Brexit. The initial steps open to London are straight forward. The UK could simply invoke the relevant UN rules on fishing waters, assuming full fishing sovereignty within the 12-mile limit for UK vessels only, and more limited sovereignty within the 200-mile limit. The UN rules oblige countries to manage their stocks sustainably and to cooperate on management of stocks that move between territorial waters. For Britain, this would affect species such as plaice, cod, haddock and sole, which move in and out of national waters, and pelagic fish such as herring and mackerel, which migrate over long distances.

Out of the 50 stocks that Irish vessels fish, 47 are shared with the UK. The problem for Ireland is that international law is not as robust as the government would like. At present, the EU works out how to manage the stocks it shares through bilateral negotiations. Would Britain agree to be bound by such arrangements? The government is sceptical. 'There is a cooperation there, but it rarely works,' says one senior source. 'There's the North-East Atlantic Fisheries Commission [NEAFC]. In and of itself, it doesn't do a whole lot.'

The NEAFC provides a structure for negotiations between so-called Coastal States. The European Commission, for instance, negotiates with Norway, the Faroe Islands, Iceland, Greenland and sometimes Russia on member states' behalf. But the process is not entirely successful. 'The Commission will say, "This is what the scientific advice says, but we want a 50 per cent share,"' says the source. 'Then Iceland will say, "We want a 55 per cent share." Then it all adds up to more than 100 per cent. What do you do? There's no enforcement mechanism. They've been trying to come up with some binding allocation system, similar to the EU's, but they've never managed to agree it because everybody wants a bigger share.'

The most dramatic failure of these arrangements has been over mackerel. For years, Iceland had been pressing the EU and other neighbouring states for a bigger quota, especially following the country's banking collapse in 2009. The EU, Norway and the Faroe Islands had reached an agreed management plan, but Iceland decided to remain outside of it. Iceland then unilaterally set its own quota for 2010, at 130,000 tonnes. Not surprisingly, the Faroe Islands was unhappy with that, so it too pulled out and set its own quota of 85,000 tonnes (tripling what it had been granted in the EU–Norway agreement). ICES, the international stock management council, argued that the maximum catch should have been 592,000 tonnes. Instead, 900,000 tonnes were caught that year. Eventually, an EU–Norway–Faroe Islands deal was struck, and, once again, Iceland remained outside of it.

Irish fishing organizations worry the UK will take a similarly bullish attitude.

'In the new scenario,' says Sean O'Donoghue of the Killybegs Fishermen's Organisation (KFO), 'you'll have the UK sitting at the Coastal States table. Given that mackerel is very important to them – especially the Scottish fishing industry – they'll say, "Well, we're no longer prepared to live with the share we had when we were part of the CFP, so we feel there's more of the mackerel in our waters than in others', so we want an increased share. If you're not going to give it to us, we'll fish it anyway." There's nothing we can do in relation to that. They'll say they're fishing in accordance with the scientific advice, except they're taking a bigger share of it.'

The EU's options are limited.

'It's more difficult for the EU to play dirty if that's what the

UK decides to do,' says an Irish official. 'Everything the EU does is bound by the terms of the Common Fisheries Policy.'

Part of that policy is the concept of Maximum Sustainable Yield (MSY), a management system to ensure the sustainable exploitation of fish stocks. The objective of the CFP is that all stocks should be at MSY from 2020. For stocks under EU control, this is a legally binding commitment. 'When it comes to negotiating with third countries, which the UK will be,' says the Irish official, 'it will be a *morally* binding commitment. The EU has put itself on the high moral ground. It would be very difficult to get off that.'

The European Parliament has strong opinions on the sustainability of fish stocks, and it would be alert to any move by the European Commission to get into a tit-for-tat spiral with the UK that would put stocks at risk. The UK would face its own environmental lobby. 'They have a very strong NGO sector,' says the official. 'They would come down on them like a tonne of bricks. But they'll also be under huge pressure from the fishing industry to get higher quotas. They'll have to try to square a very difficult circle.'

Ireland has four main priorities post-Brexit. First, it hopes for continued access to British waters right down to the 12-mile exclusion zone. Ireland landed 775,000 tonnes of fish from UK waters in 2015, worth €87.7 million. That amounted to one third of all landings and one third of the total value of what Irish boats catch. The second priority is to avoid displacement, whereby European vessels would be kicked out of British waters and into Irish waters.

The third priority is to hold on to the Hague Preferences. Britain also availed itself of the Hague Preferences, but, with the UK out of the CFP, Ireland would be the only country left, and fishing organizations fear other member states would seek to scrap the mechanism altogether.

The fourth priority is to maintain access to the quotas that Irish fishermen currently enjoy. Britain could get into a species-by-species scrap with the European Commission, demanding an increase in quota here and there in return for access for European vessels. 'If the UK try to mess around with the shares,' says one senior civil servant, 'any gain for them is a loss for us. Our existing quota shares could go down, or you could have a scenario where the UK says, "Right, at the moment we have, say, 50 per cent of the entire amount of *Nephrops* caught in the UK zone." The Brits then say, "We should have 100 per cent of that quota." But that 50 per cent has to come off us, or off France. So ours goes down. It would be like Iceland did with the mackerel: "It's ours. We're taking it."'

We can see how this would work out in the prawn fisheries, which are so crucial to people like Caitlín Ní Aodha. 'We could argue with them and say, "Well, we don't agree, and we'll sit down like gentlemen and we'll talk it out,"' says the Irish official. 'But at the end of the day if they dig their heels in, what do we do? We could throw trade sanctions, maybe, or we could stamp our feet and get very cross about it, but in reality there's not a lot we can do. The danger is that if we say we're not accepting that and if we keep catching at the level we think we should fish, then it's over 100 per cent [of the quota] so we're all overfishing and we're *all* screwing the stock.'

The potential for Britain to fish more in its own waters is clear and present, even if there is a degree of pre-negotiation posturing.

Once out of the CFP, the UK will not be bound by any restrictions on the size of its fleet. It will then be free to build up its capacity, and that's what its industry expects, even if it won't happen overnight. Of course, if Britain expels European fleets from its waters, British boats can expect to be excluded from European waters in return. But that threat may have little impact, given that, as we have seen, the EU catch from UK waters is currently at four times the value of the UK's catch from non-UK EU waters. The UK has, in this respect, more to gain than to lose.

Although Ireland's fleet will be the most directly affected by whatever happens next, other EU countries stand to lose as well. France's largest fishing port, Boulogne, relies heavily on British waters, with its larger trawlers spending 80 per cent of their time there. 'It's all we've got really,' fisherman Olivier Leprêtre told the *Financial Times* in February 2017. 'There will be bankruptcies if they do take back the waters, no doubt about it. And here, if fishing falls, everything falls.'

These, then, are the arguments that will go to the heart of the fisheries issue. How they will play out in the Brexit negotiations is wrapped up in ancient grievances, local political pressures, the hard realpolitik of trade, and how cleverly – or cynically – the UK plays its hand.

How hard will Britain push, given that its fishermen still need access to European markets, and will need to cooperate with its coastal neighbours? Another consideration is that Britain imports a significant amount of fish for its own processing sector, which had a turnover of £4.2 billion in 2014. As noted by the Irish government, the British authorities have become more nuanced in their expectations on exactly how much control they can take back over their waters. George Eustice told the House of Lords Brexit Select Committee: 'When it is said, "We are going to take back control of our Exclusive Economic Zone out to 200 nautical miles or the median line," it sounds perhaps more dramatic than it might be, in that even having established control of our EEZ we would then still engage in international negotiations around mutual access rights, mutual shares and the like.'

A scrap over quotas with EU member states would most likely spill over into higher tariffs, and Europe will still hold a considerable number of cards in that department. The House of Lords report concluded: 'The vast majority of witnesses . . . agreed that preferential or tariff-free access to the single market for fish products was essential.' Some of Britain's fish exports to the EU are extremely valuable: in 2014 Britain exported 54,564 tonnes of salmon worth £268 million.

The choreography of all these moving parts will be crucial. The British fisheries organizations want the issue to be dealt with separately in the negotiations, and preferably after an overall trade deal has been done. The Irish government wants the opposite: fisheries should be part of the big overall trade agreement, so that London will have to confront losing out in other areas if it plays hardball. Ireland's concern is that in the clamour to get an overall trade deal, the EU may ultimately not want to burn too much energy or capital on a sector that not all member states have a stake in, and that contributes a relatively small amount to Europe's overall economic power. The irony is that British fishermen fear the very same thing from their own government. For that reason, most of the focus from the British side will be on getting an increase in their quota, and that will ultimately hit other European vessels, including the Irish.

The UK's impending departure has also opened up the highly sensitive issue of Relative Stability, the method devised to establish quotas based on historical activity before the Common Fisheries Policy came into being in 1983. It is through the Relative Stability mechanism that other EU vessels can access substantial quotas across a range of species in Irish waters (because they argued successfully they had historical rights to fish there). The Irish government's policy is that it is not seeking a renegotiation of the CFP in general, or Relative Stability in particular. But some in the industry believe they should.

One advocate is John Nolan, head of the Castletownbere Co-Op, a €60 million company selling fish across the globe. The co-op has eight prawn boats at sea, directly supplying the huge Spanish supermarket chain Mercadona as well as the Italian restaurant trade (like Caitlin Ní Aodha) and in the summer months has a fleet fishing tuna off the Azores for the French and Spanish canning industries.

He describes Ireland's terms of entry into the EEC as 'disgraceful'. 'We have to blame ourselves as well as anybody else,' he says. 'We had no vision for what the potential in our waters was.' At the same time, he feels the quota regime is fundamentally unfair. 'I can never accept that, in our waters, whatever about not getting quota in French waters, or Spanish or German waters, or Dutch waters, that we can't have a more equal share of the quotas of fish in our waters. In our waters, in the 200-mile exclusive zone, we have 5 per cent of the monkfish quota. The French have 50 per cent. In French waters we have zero. In Spanish waters we have zero.'

This analysis is disputed by the Department of Agriculture, Food and the Marine. 'The percentage only tells you half the story,' says one official. 'How big is the stock? How valuable? How dependent are we on it? We have 86 per cent of Celtic Sea herring. We have 85 per cent of boarfish. People say we have 5 per cent of this and 5 per cent of that. But these aren't stocks we're dependent on anyway. It's comparing apples with oranges.'

Niall Duffy of the *Skipper* believes there are winners and

losers under the CFP, and that tends to influence the way they view Brexit, and what posture they believe the Irish government should adopt. 'You have Killybegs and Castle-townbere, which are flying,' he says. 'But then you have places like Burtonport and Baltimore – even Dingle – down to three local fishing boats, where there used to be a fleet of fifty or sixty. Burtonport – it's a ghost town. Back in the eighties the place was booming. There were half a dozen bars, great night life, now you go in and there's one pub left in the place, and half a dozen boats left at the end of the pier.'

Duffy argues that the CFP is directly responsible for the bust in some ports and the boom in others. In Burtonport's case, it was the restriction of the dogfishing sector; in Dingle, it was the consolidation of licences. With a capped resource (i.e. the quotas Irish fishermen are allowed to catch) and a reduction in the size of the Irish fleet, licences keep increasing in value, meaning bigger operators buy smaller ones out. This has the effect of concentrating the industry in fewer ports.

Like John Nolan, Duffy believes that, whether the Irish government likes it or not, Relative Stability will have to be opened up. This idea is already on the EU's radar. 'Should the UK complete its withdrawal,' concludes a report prepared for the European Parliament's Committee on Fisheries, 'it would profoundly change the circumstances that justified relative stability and enabled its continued application over time.' In other words, Relative Stability *should* be up for grabs. It was a highly political and contested concept that gave certain EU fleets highly coveted quotas. Advocates will argue that the circumstances that dictated the quota system back in 1983 will have changed significantly by the time Britain leaves the EU, and that Ireland should seek a different quota regime when it comes to putting the pieces of the CFP back together.

The KFO is adamantly opposed to such an approach. 'Ninety per cent of the industry don't want to go down that route,' says CEO Sean O'Donoghue. Instead the KFO has engaged in something unheard of in the highly adversarial world of European fisheries: transnational cooperation. 'We have a lot of problems with the Common Fisheries Policy,' says O'Donoghue. 'But so do *others*.'

On 22 March 2017, the KFO joined fishing organizations from Belgium, Denmark, France, Germany, the Netherlands, Poland, Spain and Sweden to form the European Fisheries Alliance (EFA), claiming to represent over 18,000 fishermen and 3,500 vessels, with an annual turnover of €20.7 billion. Their intention is to lobby against a hard Brexit. For organizations normally on opposite sides of the annual quota scrap, this was quite a development. 'Every one of us agreed to park the CFP to see if we can get a reasonable deal for everybody.'

The creation of the Alliance has mirrored a move by member states with important fisheries sectors to lobby in tandem. The Irish minister Michael Creed has met his Dutch, French and Danish counterparts, and on 21 April, Taoiseach Enda Kenny discussed the issue with the Dutch and Danish leaders in The Hague.

'Alliances are vital,' says a senior Irish civil servant. 'If we're seen by the others as going off on a solo run [on Relative Stability] they'll cut us loose.'

The overriding objective of the Brexit alliances, both at government and industry level, is to ensure that the fisheries aspect of Brexit is not dealt with separately in the divorce negotiations.

'Don't be tempted to do a deal with them on fisheries,' stresses a senior Irish official. 'Fisheries has to be included in the wider negotiation issues. It's one of the few sectors in which the UK do hold a lot of the cards. In pretty much every other sector they're weak. If they play hard ball on fisheries, they'll get hurt on something much bigger.'

Michael Creed agrees: 'In fisheries the UK holds all the aces. We've been very active in that space, trying to forge alliances across member states that would be equally affected, who would fish quite a percentage of their quotas in what would be termed UK territorial waters. Fisheries should be part of a broader trade negotiation because then we can leverage some results.'

Other observers suggest the very weakness of Britain's negotiating hand will prompt an irrational focus on their fishing industry. 'There is an ambition being set for it which bothers me,' says Lorcán Ó Cinnéide. 'In the normal course of events this would be horse-traded. People will see sense, and things will be fine. But this is a situation where Britain is going to get screwed. This is one area where they may choose to make a stand. It might be Pyrrhic or symbolic. But it's a trophy area: "We put up the flag and we gained our waters." There is a focus on it which is out of proportion to its importance, and it's all the more important to them in light of all the major losses they're going to have in other areas. And they know it.'

Ultimately, Brexit threatens long-term disruption to the agonizingly structured and bitterly contested CFP. Whatever fishing organizations say about the CFP, it has helped some major stocks to recover, such as North Sea cod. If British negotiators follow UKIP logic, Britain may well take back control of its waters, but unless the new regime is governed by multilateral negotiations, key stocks are at risk of being overfished.

If Britain does agree to enter into multilateral agreements to avoid overfishing, what will the management landscape look like?

Since 1980, the EU and Norway have negotiated an elaborate set of agreements over shared stocks. These agreements cover 12 species. But reaching bilateral agreements with the UK would be of a different order of magnitude for a simple reason. There are a lot fewer species in colder waters: whereas the EU–Norway agreements cover 12 species, the EU and UK would have to negotiate deals potentially covering 140 species.

Overall, the fate of the Irish fishing industry heading into the Brexit negotiations does not command the unity of purpose of the agri-food sector. Organizations and fishermen are divided. The government is determined to safeguard mackerel and prawn, the most valuable species to the Irish industry, but ones that are largely sourced in UK waters. 'Is the minister focused on saving the mackerel and prawn sector at the expense of all the other sectors?' asks Niall Duffy of the *Skipper*.

Caitlin Ní Aodha, one of those operators dependent on the prawn that live in British waters, will watch the Brexit negotiations with trepidation. Having lost her husband Michael in the *Tit Bonhomme* disaster, she defiantly turned her face back to the sea to keep making a living, and to hold true to the rugged spirit of generations. Now she is facing another daunting challenge.

'If we're out of those waters, where do we get our quota to survive? It could have a very, very serious and detrimental effect on the travelling fleet, and that then would put pressure on the smaller in-shore fleet. What would the rest of the European fleet do? Where would they go? They're not fishing much in Spanish or Portuguese or French waters. They're fishing here. This is the area the rest of European boats are in. They are in Irish, or English, waters.'

9. Room 201

On 4 January 2017, a senior figure in the Brexit drama sat down to write a letter.

Sir Ivan Rogers, the UK Ambassador to the EU, had spent Christmas and the New Year with his family at their holiday home in Dorset. The seasonal cheer had been overshadowed by a story broadcast by the BBC's Political Editor, Laura Kuenssberg, on the night of 14 December, right before a critical summit of EU leaders in Brussels.

Before running the story, Kuenssberg contacted Sir Ivan by text message, and also left a voicemail, saying, in a somewhat apologetic voice, that his life was about to be made miserable. The next day Kuenssberg reported that Sir Ivan Rogers had told Theresa May's government that the Brexit negotiations could take 10 years and *still* fail.

There was an outpouring of venom from the pro-Brexit press. Theresa May and her ministers had been saying with some confidence that the UK could exit the EU, and wrap up a successful trade deal, within two years. Now a British civil servant, with a well-known European pedigree, was talking the idea down.

The *Daily Mail* declared that 'knives were out last night for Britain's Ambassador to the EU'. Dominic Raab, a Conservative eurosceptic MP, dismissed Sir Ivan's 'gloomy pessimism' and accused the Foreign Office of always being 'very pro-EU, and very anti-leaving the EU'. Nigel Farage, the former UKIP leader, declared that 'the old guard all need clearing out, every single one of them. [Rogers] is top of the list.'

Kuenssberg's report was based on a briefing note Sir Ivan had presented to the Cabinet in October. The note distilled what he had been hearing from senior figures, both within EU institutions and other EU delegations, and from Berlin and Paris. Sir Ivan conveyed the widespread belief that Britain would be heading out of the EU single market and customs union, and that the talks on a free-trade agreement would not start before the end of 2017, at the very earliest. Those talks would take at least three or four years, and another two years for governments and national parliaments to ratify the deal.

It would, therefore, be the early-to-mid 2020s before any such trade agreement was in force. Not exactly the 10 years of Kuenssberg's report, but not two years either.

Rogers was unsurprised by the 'gloomy mandarin' accusation: it came with the territory. He saw it as his role to tell what he thought were unvarnished truths about Europe's hardening attitude towards Britain, and how it contrasted with the breezy 'win-win' attitude that May's ministers displayed wherever they went.

It was a particularly gruelling period for Rogers. He travelled to London on 26 occasions between September and Christmas. No one in Theresa May's inner circle, or in her Cabinet, seemed to be sympathetic to his reporting, or to take his analysis seriously. On the contrary, they were becoming hostile to it.

So, when Laura Kuenssberg's story broke on 14 December, Rogers was in no doubt that she had been briefed by someone inside Downing Street who wished to undermine him. This was obvious even to a number of his fellow EU ambassadors with whom he spoke at the European Council meeting on the 15th: surely, they said, this was Number 10 briefing against him? Sir Ivan did not reply, or confirm his suspicions. But he did tell his wife that evening that if he was being deliberately briefed against by the Prime Minister's inner circle during the most vital period for British diplomacy in generations, there was only one possible course of action.

Rogers spoke at length to Theresa May at the summit. According to a source familiar with the conversation, it was 'a good chat'. May was 'quite effusive'. When Sir Ivan spoke of his feelings about the Kuenssberg story, May reassured him with words to the effect of 'I know, it's all fine' and 'Happy Christmas'.

But the encounter failed to douse his suspicions. Rogers had further discussions at the highest level in Downing Street and the Foreign Office. He was not sure if the Prime Minister had authorized the briefing against him, and he did not think it his business to ask. He discussed the issue with his family over Christmas. The only way to quit was to do it without telling anyone in advance, so that it could be done quickly and cleanly, without any leaks. In fact, on 4 January, he didn't even tell his own superiors until the hour before he formally tendered his resignation by email from Dorset.

After resigning, Rogers circulated a note to staff at the UK Permanent Representation in Brussels, informing them of his decision and wishing them well in the negotiations to come. He spoke to his opposite number, Ireland's Declan Kelleher, by now a close friend.

Rogers delivered a parting shot in his note to staff. He urged them to 'challenge ill-founded arguments and muddled thinking' and never to be afraid to 'speak the truth to those in power'. The clear inference was that he did not have a high regard for the thinking of Liam Fox and Boris Johnson, and the former Home Office officials with whom Theresa May surrounded herself. He personally believed there was no small degree of self-delusion at work in Downing Street, as well as a misunderstanding of how European leaders thought about fundamental issues such as the EU's single market and customs union.

It was a view shared by the Irish government. Dublin could draw only one conclusion from Sir Ivan's resignation: Downing Street was drifting further towards a hard Brexit.

Theresa May's government was still sending mixed signals. In an interview with a Czech newspaper on 15 November, Boris Johnson said the idea of the free movement of people as a fundamental EU right was 'just bollocks'. Johnson said Britain was 'probably' going to leave the customs union, only to be corrected by Downing Street, who said a decision had not yet been taken.

Charlie Flanagan, Ireland's Minister for Foreign Affairs, was meeting Johnson once a month at EU foreign ministers' meetings. Flanagan was desperate to find out what the British position was on issues of vital importance to Ireland, and to understand the division of labour within the Brexit government. Who was in charge? Was it Davis? Fox? Johnson? 'I really didn't get a grasp of what their ask was,' says Flanagan. 'We were getting slogans like "Brexit means Brexit." What does that mean, Boris? "No return to the borders of the past"? I wasn't getting an awful lot of detail.'

In fact, Flanagan found himself being buttonholed by both British *and* EU ministers. 'I was struck by the number of EU colleagues who approached me in the margins and asked me to relate to them what was really happening in the UK. "What's the real story here? Does Brexit mean Brexit?

What do you think? We can speak to you in a way that we can't speak to the UK." Correspondingly, there were occasions where UK ministers were saying to me, "What's the story in Europe? Are we going to be punished? When they say we're not going to be punished, is this the real story?"'

Theresa May had told the BBC's Andrew Marr on the morning of her party conference speech that she would trigger Article 50 sometime 'before the end of March'. Under Article 50, a two-year time frame is envisaged for the divorce proceedings. But the process, according to a strict interpretation of the Article, concentrates on the divorce first, and not on Britain's future trading relationship (the Article 50 process would only have to take '*account* of the *framework* for its future relationship with the Union'). Britain wanted the processes to happen in parallel, and the Irish government had its own reasons for wanting those trade talks to get under way quickly. But the view of other member states was that only when they were convinced of Britain's bona fides on the issue of the bill it would face on leaving, and on the issue of the rights of EU citizens living in Britain, could those trade talks be approached – and certainly no earlier than October 2017. In the meantime, the European Union, the UK business sector, and, not least, the Irish government, farmers, dairy producers and convenience-food exporters, were all desperate to know what that future relationship would be, and under what rules those trade flows could continue.

Until Theresa May spelled it out, it was all guesswork. The Prime Minister and Cabinet ministers defended her policy. She had told her party conference in October that it was 'too early to say what agreement we will reach with the EU' and that she wouldn't be giving a running commentary. Critics, however, wanted to know the general direction. Would

Britain leave the customs union? If it was leaving the single market and the customs union, on what basis would it trade with the EU? Would there be a transitional period between the end of the two-year divorce talks and the conclusion of a trade deal, or would exporters face the dreaded 'cliff-edge'? Her message in October had been that she wanted an agreement that involved 'free trade, in goods and services', with British companies having 'the maximum freedom to trade with and operate within the single market'. But to critics in Brussels (and Dublin), these aspirations were either vague or contradictory: the only way to have maximum freedom to trade with and operate within the single market was to be a *member*. Even if Britain had declared that it did not want a Norwegian-style relationship (i.e. to be a full member of the single market but obliged to accept free movement of people and pay into the EU budget), or a Swiss arrangement (sectoral agreements across the single market, again requiring free movement of people), there were recent free-trade models it could copy, such as the EU–Canada or the EU–Ukraine agreements. But London would say only that it wanted a bespoke, and not an off-the-shelf, arrangement.

On the customs union, Britain seemed to be leaving its options open. Between September and January, British ministers from the departments of International Trade and the Foreign Office visited China, the Philippines, Serbia, Kosovo, Turkey, Australia, South Sudan, Ukraine, New Zealand, Colombia, Mexico, Pakistan, Hong Kong, Georgia, India, Argentina and Kenya. Britain was open for business, they all said, and the world was Britain's oyster.

The view in Dublin was more circumspect.

'The UK is testing their relationship with third countries,' said one senior Irish negotiator. 'They're getting mixed messages. It will be hard for them to get promises of good trade agreements. If they believe leaving the customs union is a fertile track, then they'll pursue it – it's still an open question. Now they're seeing life outside the single market and customs union. They didn't realize that that's what Brexit meant.'

Sir Ivan Rogers had intended to quit on Monday, 9 January, but rumours were growing that Theresa May was about to make an important Brexit speech. Rogers expected it to happen on the 6th or 7th. If he quit on the 9th, it might be perceived that he was resigning in protest at the Prime Minister's speech, a perception he was keen to avoid.

So he decided to go early, on the 4th.

In the event, the Prime Minister's speech didn't happen until nearly two weeks later, on 17 January, at Lancaster House, a splendid Grade I listed building next to St James's Palace.

It was an ambitious address, and a radiant example of Britain's core philosophy in the first year after the referendum: having one's cake and eating it.

May declared that Britain would control its own laws, control immigration, end the jurisdiction of the European Court of Justice (ECJ) and no longer pay 'vast sums' into the EU budget. Brexit would be a catalyst, a 'great moment' to fundamentally change the United Kingdom. The referendum hadn't just been about leaving the EU; it was about reordering the national story to make the country 'stronger, fairer, more united and more outward-looking than ever before'.

Those who feared it had unleashed demons of xenophobia and English nationalism needn't worry. Britain was one of the most 'racially diverse' and 'multicultural' countries in Europe. 'I want us to be a secure, prosperous, tolerant country – a magnet for international talent and a home to the pioneers and innovators who will shape the world ahead.' Britain would be truly 'global', and 'the best friend and neighbour to our European partners'. There would be reforms to education, infrastructure would be developed, lives would be improved.

For the EU, she had an emollient message. 'It remains overwhelmingly and compellingly in Britain's national interest that the EU should succeed.' Britain wanted to trade with, study in, and travel to Europe. 'We want to buy your goods and services, sell you ours, trade with you as freely as possible, and work with one another to make sure we are all safer, more secure and more prosperous through continued friendship.'

Britain would, however, be leaving the single market, as staying in 'would to all intents and purposes mean not leaving the EU at all'. Instead, she wanted a bold and ambitious free-trade agreement, with special concessions for the automotive and financial-services industries.

Regarding Ireland, she said the Common Travel Area should remain. 'The family ties and bonds of affection that unite our two countries mean that there will always be a special relationship between us.' On the question of a hard border, May repeated that 'nobody wants to return to the borders of the past, so we will make it a priority to deliver a practical solution as soon as we can.'

Britain would cooperate with the EU in crime-fighting, counter-terrorism and security, and would like to continue to share in research and innovation cooperation. The overall deal – the divorce and the future trading relationship – should be done within two years, with transitional arrangements where necessary. Any attempt to 'punish Britain' would be 'an act of calamitous self-harm' and 'not the act of a friend'. If there was only a poor deal on offer, Britain would walk away. 'No deal for Britain is better than a bad deal for Britain.'

Britain, she said, would leave the customs union, as it would 'prevent us from striking our own comprehensive trade agreements with other countries'. But she did want a customs agreement. As to whether it would be a completely *new* one, or Britain becoming 'an *associate* member' of the existing union 'in some way', or remaining a signatory 'to some elements of it', she held 'no preconceived position'.

The Prime Minister's ambiguity left Dublin in a state of perplexed hope. Being completely out of the customs union would guarantee a hard border; being partly in left some hope that a 'creative' solution might be found to avoid those checks.

The next day, Theresa May travelled to the Swiss alpine resort of Davos. In her speech to the World Economic Forum, she said Britain was coming out of its EU shell to take on the world. She referred to a 'global' British destiny no fewer than 13 times.

There was no reference to Ireland, but she and Enda Kenny, who was also in Davos, did meet by chance the night before in Altes Schäfli, a cosy, log-cabin restaurant on Mattastrasse with a popular line in traditional fondue. The pair spoke for 10 minutes before returning to their separate tables. It was not clear how deeply they got into Brexit, but the next day the Taoiseach welcomed what he called 'some clarity' from the Prime Minister. Kenny also confirmed that Irish officials had been working on 'technical papers' to see how a hard border could be avoided.

There were further talks in Dublin on 30 January, 12 days after the Altes Schäfli encounter. This was the annual bilateral summit, first instituted by Enda Kenny and David

Cameron in 2011. Theresa May was accompanied by James Brokenshire, the Northern Ireland Secretary, while Enda Kenny was joined by Charlie Flanagan. The Irish side was pleased that May had made the trip to Dublin, but the results were disappointing. 'The visit,' recalls Flanagan, 'was very businesslike. It was . . . oh, if I say it was minimalist rather than informative? But, nevertheless, the bare essentials were discussed, and the bare essentials were acknowledged and appreciated. There was certainly no meat on the bones. But the bones were evident. She said quite clearly that she didn't want a return to the borders of the past. On further enquiry as to what that meant, the detail was lacking.'

In fact, Irish Revenue Commissioners had been travelling regularly to Brussels for discreet talks on the borders of the past. They took place on the fifth floor of the Commission's Berlaymont headquarters with members of the Article 50 Task Force, and staff from the Commission's taxation directorate. The fruits of those meetings would not be known for some time, but they involved looking at how, perhaps, number-plate-reading technology could avoid the need for customs controls. Combine Theresa May's 'associative' idea and clever technology – might there be the outline of a solution? Irish officials were sceptical.

On 2 February, May published a White Paper on Brexit. It spelled out exactly how the customs union worked, and how professional Britain's customs and revenue commissioners were. The UK would have to leave the customs union if it wanted to negotiate its own new trade deals around the world.

The reason is that membership of the customs union requires the acceptance of what's called the EU's common external tariff. Any country wanting to trade with the EU must comply with that 'external' tariff. Once it complies, it can trade *inside* that customs perimeter with all 29 members of the customs union (the EU28 and Monaco). That external tariff is negotiated by the European Commission on behalf of all the member states. For that reason, Britain could not be both a member of the customs union *and* negotiate its own trade deals around the globe. And because Britain wanted to negotiate its own trade deals, it would be leaving the customs union. What about the UK's access to the customs union, in that case? Being outside meant Britain itself would have to negotiate access back into the club it was about to leave. The White Paper said Britain wanted a 'new customs agreement' that enabled UK–EU trade to continue to be 'as frictionless as possible'. There were a number of options. There could be a completely new agreement, or the UK could 'remain a signatory to some of the elements of the existing arrangement', the precise form of which would be subject to negotiation.

Again, a hint the UK wasn't shutting the door completely.

'They need to spell out what they mean by an associative relationship,' said one weary Irish negotiator. 'Most of Europe will say, "That's fine but you can't have that very close relationship with the customs union and be off doing unilateral or bilateral trade deals all over the place." You want a very close relationship with the EU, but you're also bringing stuff in tariff-free or low-tariff from other regions. How do you manage moving goods into the EU with those low tariffs as well?

'It's unlikely [Britain] will turn around and *join* the customs union. But I wouldn't categorically rule it out. There's enough of a chink of light in her speech and the White Paper to allow for that. They probably think some kind of tailor-made or bespoke approach is more likely. But then you absolutely are into the tension of how much flexibility there is on that.'

It soon became clear Theresa May's government didn't actually know themselves what they meant by an 'associative' relationship. One Irish official found himself at a meeting in the Department of International Trade, the engine room of Britain's new buccaneering global-trade ambitions. Teething problems were evident. 'The department has gone from a unit of 40 to 220,' says the official. 'There aren't enough seats for people. They're wandering around. It's fairly chaotic. The vast majority are new, so a clear policy is by no means articulated. They state things that are total conundrums, things you can't have, matter and *anti*-matter in the same sentence. We want to stay as close to the single market, but actually we're not going to be really. We want to be part of the customs union, but we realize that what we say we want to do isn't compatible with that either.'

Another Irish official was contacted by her British counterpart, who asked her what she had been 'hearing back' from the EU about the idea of an 'associated membership'. (This was still before Article 50 was triggered, so Britain could not engage directly with the EU.) She replied with some incredulity: 'What am I going to *hear*? What does associated membership even *mean*? Like, what *is* it?'

Her counterpart replied: 'Oh, right. Okay.'

Room 201, on the fifth floor of the European Commission headquarters in Brussels, looks out at eye-level to the glass-and-chrome citadels of the EU institutions: the Charlemagne and Lex buildings, and the newly opened Europa Building, now the headquarters of the European Council, with its pale-wood mullioned façade housing an enormous lantern-shaped centrepiece. Below is Kitty O'Shea's, the legendary Irish pub on the corner of Boulevard Charlemagne and Rue

Stevin, and, next to that, the Old Hack, frequented by UKIP MEPs and Irish Commission officials alike, especially if there is a rugby match on.

Room 201 is on a stretch of corridor commandeered by Michel Barnier as the nerve centre of his Brexit Task Force. Entry to the corridor is strictly controlled by fingerprint biometrics, but that did not stop an enormous amount of Irish traffic.

The Task Force had begun its work on 1 October 2016. Nina Obermaier, a German recruited from the Switzerland and Israel desk of the European External Action Service (EEAS), the EU's diplomatic arm, had been appointed the lead on Irish issues. For the next eight months there would be a regular flow of Irish delegations making their way to Room 201. On most occasions, official teams were led by Émer Deane, a senior diplomat from the special Brexit unit based on the fourth floor of the Irish Permanent Representation in Brussels, headed by Ambassador Declan Kelleher. Deane would provide continuity as officials from various government departments in Dublin came back and forth with their queries and demands. The relevant attachés in the Permanent Representation would also be present.

The Task Force functioned as a clearing-house before the actual Brexit negotiations began. The concerns, ideas, dilemmas of any member state (except the UK) or sectoral lobby group were all aired before it. The raw material would be processed and filtered, so that Barnier, as the EU's Chief Negotiator, could get an understanding of the key issues and a feel for what position should be taken. In the days before the Irish team arrived on 24 January, a Spanish government delegation passed through wanting to know about the rights of Spanish citizens in the UK. A German delegation wondered about financial services. Belgian and Dutch officials worried about customs checks at the ports of Antwerp and Rotterdam.

But no one beat the Irish. 'We are the country with the biggest number of people knocking on the Task Force door by a country mile,' says one senior Irish official.

'The Irish delegation always comes in flocks,' says one European Commission source, who was either bemused or impressed. 'There are always at least a dozen.'

These were official delegations (there were five big meetings involving the civil service) or groups of stakeholders (at least 12 meetings in total). In general, when it came to industry representatives, only pan-European organizations had access. But that wasn't the case for Ireland. 'The Irish had privileged access. We have to make this very clear. For other stakeholders the criteria had to be that it was a pan-European association, because we simply don't have the time to talk to each and every stakeholder in each and every member state. The Irish came well prepared, and with a wish-list. They were *impressively* well prepared. Almost all of them, with very few exceptions. They were very aware of what's at stake and what the issues are. A number of them could have *worked* for the Task Force straight away.'

Fianna Fáil was hosted, as was the Irish Farmers' Association, the co-op lobby ICOS, the employers group IBEC, Bord Bia, the European Movement Ireland (EMI), Ornua, the Irish Feed and Grain Association, Meat Industry Ireland, Lakeland Dairies, Lough Egish and many others. On most occasions, the meetings would be with members of Barnier's team. But on 16 January 2017, Barnier himself met the Killybegs Fishermen's Organisation as part of the European Fisheries Alliance, and on 4 April he met the IFA.

On one occasion, the Sinn Féin MEP Martina Anderson arranged a cross-border delegation under the Brexit Border Communities banner, but she was politely informed that as an MEP from a 'British' constituency, it was 'not appropriate' for her to be included. The UK was still subject to the no-negotiation-before-notification rule.

Every Brexit issue, from data processing to the single electricity market to aviation, could be explored in Room 201. But agri-food dominated: the movement of animals and dairy products, the border, fisheries and customs posts. 'The message,' says one Commission source, 'was that this is unprecedented, this is extraordinary, we need extraordinary support.' But officials had to remind Irish delegations that they could only listen and register. The Commission assumed Britain was leaving the customs union, but until they were sure of that, and knew more about how Britain was going to contribute solutions to the Irish problem, answers were in short supply.

Those arriving in Brussels, though, wanted to be heard, and they brought useful information. 'I remember people from the meat industry,' recalls a Task Force official, 'telling us all about the flow of products from Ireland to the UK, how it was no longer carcasses and was now chilled cuts. This was useful to us. You don't get a picture of this when you just read trade statistics. They also told us about the different steps needed to export a processed product into an EU country compared to one outside the customs union. These were bare, practical concerns. For selling to the EU, they said, all the different steps fitted on one page. Exporting *outside* the customs union took *three* pages. We knew this stuff in principle, but having them present it in such a way was useful.'

Irish officials were mindful of the traffic from the private agri-food lobby. One official says, 'We were asking various farm bodies, "Be consistent with the message." We must be getting through to them. Don't be sending mixed signals. Here are our asks: trade between the UK and Ireland should *continue*.'

All the time, however, doubts in Dublin persisted over whether or not Ireland was getting its message across. In a series of columns in the *Irish Times* throughout January, Noel Whelan captured the public mood. 'Any enduring prospect of a soft Brexit disappeared on Tuesday as Theresa May turned the pages of her speech,' he wrote on 20 January. 'All illusions that the impact of the split on Ireland might be limited are now shattered. We must brace ourselves for Britain and Northern Ireland being outside the European Union, outside the single market and most likely outside the customs union ... Our input in the renegotiation of that relationship will, as things stand, be extremely limited.'

'The Irish government has to provide solutions,' says Micheál Martin, the leader of Fianna Fáil. 'The feeling has come back to us from Brussels that that's the case. The government's [Cabinet sub-]committee is too unwieldy. Sometimes there are fifty people between ministers and officials. I also wonder have they tapped into external sources, people like [former European Commission Secretary General] Catherine Day. They should have set up a steering group of former civil servants, people who would have had long experience of Europe, just as a sounding board.'

In early November – after questions had been raised about the lack of an Irish member of the Commission's Brexit Task Force – Tadhg O'Briain, a civil servant who had joined the European Commission from the Northern Ireland Department of Finance in 2008, and who had been working in the energy directorate, was appointed. Officials were at pains to point out that having an Irish person on the Task Force did not mean that he or she would be negotiating with the British on *Ireland*'s behalf. The Task Force deliberately had a 'flat' structure that was there to provide expert knowledge to the senior negotiating team, led by Barnier. Whether the Task Force official was Irish or Greek made little difference. Their professional responsibility was to the Commission, and not to the member state.

Ireland's situation was, in any case, getting on to the radar. 'It was not on people's minds in June or July,' says a senior Task Force official. 'But the scale of the problem and the challenge filtered through. The prominence of the Irish issue is not least due to the effective information campaign by the Irish government.'

Ireland's strategy had been evolving over very bumpy terrain since the referendum. The essential message was that Ireland didn't want anything to change. Ireland would have to be able to trade freely with the UK, without any tariff or non-tariff barriers, and customs posts were not going to be acceptable. The Northern Ireland peace process and the Republic of Ireland's economy depended on it.

But the message on its own was not enough, even if Theresa May and Enda Kenny had repeatedly insisted, either jointly or individually, that there would be no return to the borders of the past.

The Task Force had a clear mandate. It had to listen to ideas, but also spell out what was acceptable and not acceptable under EU law. Another senior Task Force official says some home truths were pointed out. 'Frozen pizza *without* cheese will cross the border more easily; otherwise there will be rigorous checks. Every consignment that is animal-based will need to be checked.' What was the reaction from the

Irish delegations when they were told this? 'Dismay,' says another Task Force official. 'Absolutely. What do you expect?'

Irish delegations were coming with issues that were highly technical. How could Irish trade, particularly in the agri-food sector, avoid the disruption of a hard border? Were there any ways around the need for animal-health, food-labelling and traceability checks, given the volume of animal and milk traffic heading back and forth? The Task Force was having to call in expertise from deep within the EU's civil service. One query might lead to half a dozen others, and deeper into the bureaucracy the query would go.

In the midst of all the Room 201 meetings, a tension was setting in. A senior European Commission official confided: 'The plan in Dublin is a long way from completion. The objective is to ensure tariff-free trade and border-free trade. We're trying to remind them, this is not *just* a common travel area between Ireland and the UK. This is a common travel area between a third country and the EU. One cannot assume there won't be a problem simply because Britain and Ireland issue a statement saying there won't be a problem.

'We have to protect food standards. Arguments that Ireland is a special case are all very fine. Will they fit into a European context? Irish stakeholders claim they have a special case. How do you think that will travel? There's no doubt that people are sympathetic, but sympathy only gets you so far. You may not find sympathy when you start proposing solutions. Will they be acceptable to the other 26 member states? If there are protections for Irish farmers, it's not much consolation to a beef producer in France who sells into the UK market and who wants to compete on a level playing pitch.

'Barnier is not going to come up with solutions,' the Commission official concluded. 'Ireland needs to come up with solutions. Problems are understood, and the circumstances are understood. What the [Irish] government doesn't want to do is submit a proposal that is then blown out of the water. IBEC and ICOS can submit proposals, there's no credibility problem for them.'

In fact, Ireland had been suggesting solutions. And one *had* been blown out of the water.

Early in the process, according to Ireland's EU Commissioner for Agriculture, Phil Hogan, a suggestion came from Dublin that Ireland and the UK should simply have a bilateral free-trade agreement for agriculture. That would instantly overcome any tariff, sanitary and phyto-sanitary and cross-border animal and dairy movement problems.

'I was deeply concerned,' says Hogan. 'I had to put a stop to such ideas. There will be *no* carve-out for agriculture for any member state, including Ireland. That was one of the suggestions being put forward by the Department of Agriculture, Food and the Marine, which as it happens is illegal. The department mentioned this as a possibility on a number of occasions, that they wanted to have a carve-out for agriculture in Ireland and effectively a bilateral relationship with the UK. It is illegal under WTO rules and illegal under EU law.'

A senior Irish minister concedes that the idea *was* suggested. But it was because the Irish government was deliberately suggesting ideas as close to the status quo as possible. 'It was a scoping thing,' he concedes. 'There have been all sorts of other things scoped.'

There were other problems in getting the Irish message across.

Farm organizations were highlighting the damage customs posts and EU sanitary and phyto-sanitary checks on the land border would cause the industry. One Irish official present was exasperated. 'The people sitting opposite us in DG SANTE [the Commission's division dealing with animal health and food safety] were around in 2001 for the outbreak of foot and mouth. They're old enough to remember that. We'd probably never sealed the Irish border as tightly as we did back then. We were buying equipment to put into British ports to wash trucks. Having to run around now and say, "Ah, Jesus, there's a crisis!" It's a *credibility* issue.'

The point was that European Commission officials knew full well that, when it suited, Ireland had no problem sealing its borders when there was a risk to Irish agriculture, as happened during the foot and mouth outbreak in 2001. Irish organizations lobbying the Task Force, therefore, had to temper their arguments.

Another idea was that there would somehow be a *separate* trading situation on the island of Ireland. The island would become a single customs entity, with no barrier along the land border, so that trade could flow back and forth from the North to the South. It would require Northern Ireland to remain in the EU customs union while the rest of the UK departed from it.

A senior government adviser explains: 'The idea has been mentioned, but I have to say, these things always come up against the problem that you're either in the internal market or not, you're either in the customs union or you're not. If Northern Ireland is in the customs union, then the customs border is in the Irish Sea [as Great Britain would be out of the customs union]. That may be a *possibility*. It may be the sensible thing. But there are political difficulties with that.'

It was clear from the outset that neither the DUP nor the Conservative government would accept any situation that placed Northern Ireland on a different footing from the rest of the UK. Pushing the customs barrier on to the Irish Sea would mean controls at Belfast Port or in Belfast's two main airports.

'The problem,' says the adviser, 'is that you have to have a border somewhere, for customs purposes, for animal and health purposes.'

According to Phil Hogan, the idea remains in the ether, not quite rejected, but showing little promise of political acceptance. 'Moving the customs line off the island is still in the system. You're effectively saying that the four freedoms of the EU would apply on the island of Ireland. And that the border would be down the middle of the Irish Sea. I would say the DUP would have some political difficulties with that.'

A senior European Commission staff member put it another way. Having a single agriculture space on the island would be one thing. But if Northern Ireland were still outside the single market, then animal checks would have to be carried out, again, at those Northern Irish ports. And who would carry out those controls? 'You would have to have *Irish* vets and customs officials doing those checks,' says the official. 'They'd have to be there at Larne.'

Furthermore, if there were no checks on animal movements from Great Britain, which would potentially be doing trade deals with South American countries, what would happen if poorly regulated animals or unregulated beef were brought into Northern Ireland from the rest of the UK? 'The Irish would be out of their minds if they decide to put their national herd at risk,' said the official.

Over time, the Room 201 process developed into an exhausting, detailed game of push-and-pull. Irish officials would highlight a Brexit-related problem. The Task Force would ask the Irish side how *they* planned to get around it.

Ireland wanted the status quo to remain. The European Commission wanted whatever was suggested both to comply with EU law *and* to be acceptable to the 26 other member states. Often there was an inherent contradiction between the two.

At another level, though, Irish officials believed they were making progress with the Task Force. One Commission official brought down from the agriculture directorate to discuss the animal-health/hard-border dilemma, told an Irish diplomat: 'Look, at the end of the day, we can be *astonishingly* creative.'

'That's what we need,' the diplomat replied. 'That's what we want to hear.'

Following one meeting on 4 March 2017, at which 13 Irish officials were present, an Irish agriculture official reflected on the process of trying to avoid animal-health checks on the border: 'I rely on Dublin to have vets go through the wad of EU legislation. But at a macro level we already know what we want, and that's as soft a border as possible. We want to be able to have the controls as easily as we can in terms of electronic options, preferably in the food business. For example, what if we did the animal-health controls in a meat plant? We already have a veterinary officer in every meat plant, since you can't slaughter cattle in Ireland without a vet present. So, yes, please. Can we do the controls there? That means we don't have to have an army of people on the border.

'So, we explained to them technically where we are. We didn't expect them to say, "Yeah, we can do that for you." They said, "You come to us and tell us where in the legislation we can come up with imaginative solutions."

'Then we say, "Don't look at us, you *drafted* the thing!"'

Sometimes, when Irish officials came up with a solution,

an objection would be raised, not from someone from within the Commission, but from within another branch of the *Irish* civil service. The idea of allowing animal checks in Irish abattoirs was a case in point. An Irish customs official pointed out, 'If you stop an animal at the Irish border coming to the South and it has foot and mouth disease, the headline is: "Foot and mouth outbreak prevented at the border". But if you check the animal at an abattoir in Mullingar, the headline is: "Outbreak of foot and mouth disease in Mullingar".'

At a private lunch in March between a European Commission source and a senior Irish official, the Commission official remarked: 'At some point the EU 26 will say, "Fine, so tell us what's the plan?"'

The response from the Irish official was: 'We were working on technical solutions. But word has come from the Taoiseach that it has to stop. It has to be a political solution.'

The Commission official was aghast. 'This isn't *political*. It's technical! You want to know what your technical solutions are for phyto-sanitary issues and animal welfare. Otherwise, the potential for fraud is *huge*.'

At a certain point in the Brexit curve, between the summer of 2016 and the spring of 2017, there was a shift in the Irish posture towards Britain and the Irish question. There had been technical talks in Room 201 in Brussels, and an intense exploration of the issues by British and Irish civil servants in the Locarno Suite in London in October. There had been political meetings between Irish and British ministers, and there had been two high-level meetings between Enda Kenny and Theresa May.

The Irish government was realizing that if Irish and European Commission officials were working away diligently, scoping out technical solutions, looking at ways of getting around customs checks and requirements regarding animal health, food safety and rules of origin as a way to soften the Irish border, then the main beneficiary was the UK.

Having come to this realization, the Irish undertook a subtle distancing from London. It began at the end of 2016 and was increasingly discernible in the first part of 2017. 'If you look at how it all started,' says a senior Irish negotiator, 'it was all about visits to London and phone conversations with Theresa May, Oireachtas committees, House of Lords committees, ministers going to London. Then you just see it changing, somewhere around October, November.

'The main shift is away from a complete focus on the UK for the answers . . . to turning the aircraft carrier around. To realize, actually, they *won't* have the answers. They *can't* have the answers. And we can't even *talk* to them about this because they have no idea what they want themselves.'

It also meant a shift in the chemistry, or the geometry. Ireland would no longer be stuck between London and Brussels trying to look to both for answers. Ireland would have to move completely over to the side of the EU27.

'[Brexit] is a British decision,' says the negotiator. 'So if you look at those elements that are particular to Ireland, Theresa May has made a comment on the Common Travel Area, and on no return to the borders of the past. She's choosing to leave. So what's *her* plan? Great, fine, so Theresa, can you come forward with a plan on that? It would tactically, if nothing else, be a mistake for the Commission and Ireland to be coming up with solutions for something that we didn't think was a good idea in the first place. The Commission had been saying that Ireland needs to find a solution. Well, hang on, really? Why?

'We can have solutions and ideas in our back pocket and in the drawer. But that gets the Brits *totally* off the hook. They don't have to expend any political capital to work this out. We use all our political capital and end up having nothing left. That relationship [with London] has changed since June. We're not in this together. We are both *in* this. But we're not in this *together*. That's a very different thing.'

In other words, by doing the technical work, by constructing an elaborate mechanism to square the circle, Irish and Commission officials would be handing London a negotiating advantage. Britain wouldn't have to shift politically or to take any hard political decisions.

And those hard political decisions would ultimately centre on Northern Ireland. Key to Ireland's strategy would be to ensure that the Commission, Michel Barnier and the Task Force were all on board in the political/technical sequencing, in pushing the problem back across the table to London.

There would be two steps: fully apprising the EU of the complexities of the Northern Ireland peace process, and then turning the Irish position into the European position.

'Both the Commission and ourselves are agreed,' says one Irish diplomat close to the negotiations, 'that the aim is that the EU position and Ireland's position are one and the same on as many areas as possible, so that the idea of an *Irish* position disappears.'

Having the Commission on board would involve optimizing both its technical expertise and its political sense. 'The Commission's forte is the technical and the legal,' says a senior Irish official. 'That's where having a political head of the unit [Nina Obermaier] is really helpful, especially for Ireland, as this is *all* political. We have to get the politics right. The politics is shifting, it's alive, it's dynamic. A lot of our time is spent talking about the politics, just making sure they understand it, making sure that the technical will come. But we just keep reminding them of the politics.'

According to the Irish government's evolving analysis, Brexit's political crucible would be the North. All roads would lead in that direction. The only way to avoid a hard border and to preserve the careful constitutional balance of the Good Friday Agreement would be for Britain to make political choices. Those choices would relate to what kind of Brexit it ultimately opted for, in terms of the ramifications for trade in goods and services, and for the movement of food back and forth across the Irish border. And those political choices would most likely be unpalatable both to unionism and to the Conservative Party.

There was no point in putting technical solutions on the table, according to the Irish analysis, until that political context was there. So the political had to come first, and it was Britain's move. 'There is no context yet,' says the Irish negotiator. 'It's premature. None of the technical solutions can be on the table for the negotiation at this point in time. We're just not there.'

According to another Irish diplomat closely involved in the process: 'We had to make sure we were looking through the right end of the telescope. The technical fixes will ultimately cascade from the politics.'

One powerful advocate for the primacy of the political over the technical was Phil Hogan. Despite his popular vilification in Ireland over the handling of water charges, Hogan's reinvention as the Commissioner for Agriculture and Rural Affairs proved fortuitous for his career, but also, arguably, for the EU itself.

During the Brexit referendum campaign, Jean-Claude Juncker insisted the Commission could not get involved.

The logic was obvious: the first intervention by a Brussels bigwig would have allowed the Leave campaign and the Brexit press to traduce him or her for interfering in a sovereign British decision.

Senior officials, however, wondered if certain Commissioners 'might go down well'. According to a senior British Commission official: 'There were one or two [Commissioners] who had portfolios that were of interest, spoke good English and had a contribution to make. Big Phil was certainly one of them. He had various invitations, which he and his Cabinet turned into a series of visits. He went to Northern Ireland, went to Wales and Scotland as well. He went to agricultural events in England. He spoke very well about the importance of the EU for farmers, both in the CAP and in trading opportunities. But he spoke as an Irishman as well, very eloquently in terms of keeping the UK and Ireland together in the EU. In Northern Ireland he talked about the peace process. He made a real contribution. He might even have swung quite a number of votes.

'Obviously they didn't think of him as a threat. If the UKIP tendency in the Leave campaign and the media barons supporting them thought Hogan was a threat, they'd have gone for him.'

Eight months later, Phil Hogan was trying to limit the damage of the referendum outcome. As well as writing the *Irish Times* op-ed on 9 January 2017, he took a stronger advisory role. He was in close contact with Ireland's EU Ambassador, Declan Kelleher. It's understood contact between Hogan and the Taoiseach had become limited. However, the pair did meet, along with Kenny's sherpa and Brexit Task Force head, John Callinan, in Brussels on 16 February 2017. According to a senior source, Kenny was by then advising any Irish minister passing through Brussels to touch base with Hogan. On 9 February, Hogan arranged for Ireland's Minister for Foreign Affairs, Charlie Flanagan, to meet no fewer than seven EU Commissioners after he had met Michel Barnier and Nina Obermaier.

'You never cease to be amazed,' muses Hogan, 'at the lack of knowledge among some members of the European Parliament and member states who are far removed from this part of the world, who are not familiar with the nuances of what has happened in Northern Ireland, the relationships between North and South and between Ireland and the UK.'

To Hogan, there were a number of political requirements for Ireland's Brexit strategy to succeed. One was to get the other 26 member states to understand Ireland's plight, and to buy into what was ultimately agreed. 'You cannot work up a possible solution unless there is an indication of political support,' he says. Another was to get Britain to spell out its position, and to come up with solutions. The third was to get the EU institutions to be flexible enough in their interpretation of how any ultimate solutions complied with EU law.

'When the Taoiseach said there would be no return to the hard borders of the past, that's a political statement. Whether that stands up in reality will depend on the attitude of the British to the customs union, and on the attitude of the EU negotiators towards whether or not they can accommodate an internal-market set of scenarios of a different configuration on both parts of the island.

'Making a political statement requires you to get some buy-in initially, and then to do the technical work. Does the technology and the technical work support it, and do the other member states agree for this to be a runner?'

*

On 15 February 2017, Enda Kenny delivered an address to the Institute of International and European Affairs (IIEA) in Dublin. The tone was hard and determined. The sentences were short and pugilistic. Kenny conveyed the sense of a nation with its back to the wall. He reached for the totems of Easter 1916, the 'struggle for independence', the quest for economic prosperity. But every patriotic reference point was couched in terms of Ireland's *European* destiny. 'The 1916 Proclamation,' he said, 'recognized that Ireland's place in the world will always be defined by our relationship with Europe, as well as with the United States and with Britain.' The fall of the Berlin Wall meant that the most divisive border left in Europe was that 'between Dundalk and Derry'. Theresa May's name was not invoked once. 'Brexit,' he declared, 'is a British policy, not an Irish policy or an EU policy. I continue to believe it is bad for Britain, for Ireland and for Europe.'

Avoiding a hard border was 'a political matter, not a legal or technical matter'. But, he said: 'let me also make one thing absolutely clear – Ireland will be on the EU side of the table when the negotiations begin. We will be one of the 27.'

That determination was put to the test just three weeks later. On Thursday, 9 March, EU leaders gathered in Brussels for a two-day summit, Theresa May's last before she triggered Article 50 to start the formal process of withdrawal.

Following the customary dinner between the leaders, May and Kenny met on the fifth floor of the European Council building for a bilateral meeting that had been arranged following a phone call the previous Sunday.

The British and Irish delegation rooms are side by side in the new Europa Building. The agreement was that the Irish delegation would leave its room, replete with the Irish Tricolour and the EU flag, and step into the British room, replete with Union Jack, but no EU flag. The meeting lasted 30 minutes. Theresa May was accompanied by three officials; Enda Kenny was accompanied by Dara Murphy, the Minister for European Affairs. The intended focus was the recent Assembly elections in Northern Ireland and the need for the parties to restore the Executive as soon as possible. But Kenny opened by asking May when she would trigger Article 50. Brussels and London had been rife with guessing games, leaks and suppositions. Dates had been pencilled in and rubbed out again. The actual triggering would immediately prompt a choreography of emergency summits and responses from the EU side. There were elections in the Netherlands on 15 March, Kenny was in Washington for most of that week for the St Patrick's Day celebrations, and the EU27 would be gathering in Rome to mark the 60th anniversary of the EU's founding document, the Treaty of Rome, on 24 and 25 March. May had never deviated from her announcement, on Andrew Marr's BBC couch on 4 October, that Article 50 would be triggered 'before the end of March'.

When Kenny directly asked her on 9 March in the British delegation room, May responded with a smile: 'Before the end of March.'

According to a person present, the exchange was relatively good-humoured. They discussed Brexit, the 'borders of the past', and how both sides would work with their European colleagues to ensure that the unique situation of Northern Ireland was understood. 'There was no element of discord,' says the person who was present.

However, as he spoke to reporters the following day, the Taoiseach was asked about his meeting with the Prime Minister. Pressed on whether the Prime Minister had clarified her intentions on Britain's remaining in the customs union, Kenny's impatience was ill-disguised. 'I speak in respect of the Irish government and the Irish people,' he told reporters. 'We didn't cause this,' he said. 'We have to put up with the consequences of it.'

Kenny continued: 'In order to deal with the consequences [of Brexit], we have to know what the relationship that's being sought by Britain is, beyond having the closest possible relationship with the EU.'

The Taoiseach's sarcasm was unmistakable. For nearly nine months, Ireland had been agonizing over how calamitous Brexit might be. None of that would be clear until Britain spelled out what relationship it wanted at the end of the process. Despite multiple meetings on both sides of the Irish Sea and in Brussels, between officials, ministers and the two leaders themselves, all that Ireland had in its hand from the British side was the blandishment that Britain wanted 'the closest possible relationship' with the EU.

May's sunny refusal to tell the Taoiseach when she was going to trigger Article 50 had enraged one Irish official. 'We're their closest ally, their nearest neighbour, the country most affected by Brexit. And yet she couldn't even tell him?'

10. From Bjørnfjell to Svinesund

At a depot near Oslo Airport, in sub-zero temperatures, men from all over Europe load sealed white containers on to a forklift truck, which swivels and hoists the boxes on to a 10-tonne lorry.

Tor Wethal is the owner of the lorry. A stocky Norwegian, his swept-back russet locks and receding hairline give him the look of a *Braveheart* extra. He's sending a consignment of computer parts, pharmaceuticals and clothes to Copenhagen. The single market and its four freedoms are in full effect. The driver will be German, the forklift operator is Polish, the loading crew Polish and Lithuanian, and the supervisor a Dubliner. He's called Pedro.

'My mother jokes,' he says, between barking orders at his crew, 'that I'm a Dubliner, with a Spanish name, married to a Slovak, living in Oslo, eating sushi.'

Pedro is the first cog in the operation to ensure Tor's goods make it to Copenhagen from Oslo, via Sweden, on time and in full compliance with an overlapping set of customs requirements. Had a helicopter filled with politicians, civil servants and customs officials from Ireland, the UK and Brussels suddenly and noisily landed next to the depot, it would have seemed, to anyone interested in Brexit, the most natural apparition. They would have disembarked, clipboards and stopwatches at the ready, waiting for the driver, Matthias Kuster, to adjust his glasses, climb into a vertiginous cockpit and rev up the engines.

Norway is outside the EU customs union, while Sweden, through which Tor's goods will transit, is inside. Post-Brexit, Northern Ireland is likely to be outside the customs union, while the Republic, like Sweden, will be inside. Crossing into the EU customs union requires border controls. There is basically no way around it. But Enda Kenny and Theresa May promised no return to the borders of the past. The answer, some say, is found on the thread of rock, forest and water where Norway and Sweden meet.

Tor Wethal's fleet of trucks range north to Bergen, east to Poland, west to the UK, and south to the great plastic-covered prairies of Spain to collect fruit and vegetables.

Norway is not in the EU, but it is in the single market. It pays into the EU budget, and its people enjoy free movement within the EU. So Tor's trucks have room to roam. But because it's not in the customs union, the goods have to be checked. So, before hitting the E6, Matthias Kuster stops off at Roadfeeders, the shipping agent on Edvard Griegs Veg near Oslo Airport. The late afternoon light is faltering, and the temperature is −3° and falling, but the ice-dusted birches give the facility a festive appeal. Inside, Maritha Gundersen will do the paperwork. Seventy per cent of the shipments she processes are fish, mostly salmon from the fish farms to the north, but also trout, lobster and king crab. The salmon is exported to the United States and Canada. Roadfeeders do plenty of road deliveries, as their name would suggest, but air freight is where the money is.

Gundersen collects the key details: weight, value, content, what the mix is, and the identities of the consignee, the shipper and the agent. Once everything is accounted for, the documents are electronically submitted to customs. If customs are happy, the driver will receive an SMS en route to say that everything is in order.

We head off from Edvard Griegs Veg and are gliding down the E6 when Kuster gets a text message: the paperwork has been approved. When he pulls his juggernaut into the parking bay at Svinesund, just over the border on the Swedish side, he is in and out in a matter of minutes, papers stamped, ready to go. 'It's normal,' he says. 'I go in, five minutes, papers stamped, no problem. Then I drive.'

Our hotel is in Nordby, a tiny stop perched on the Swedish side of the frontier. Nordby is home to the largest shopping centre in Scandinavia, a glass-and-steel wonderdome built expressly for Norwegians who spend one billion krone (about €100 million) there every year in cross-border shopping. Norway has a punitive sugar tax, so the shopping centre has brilliantly lit outlets brimming with candy and chocolate. Almost everything else – food, alcohol, clothes and *snus*, the dried smokeless tobacco product placed under the upper lip – is much cheaper here. The only things less expensive in Norway are, strangely enough, diapers.

The Norway–Sweden border is 1,600 kilometres long. At the very top lies the Swedish town of Kiruna, 67° North, but the first approved crossing is at Bjørnfjell. The border wriggles its way south over mountains where wolves, deer, foxes and brown bears outnumber humans, all the way to the Svinesund customs post, where Carolin Blanco Carlsson, the team leader at the Centre of Excellence for Customs Clearance, is waiting to meet us.

Carlsson demonstrates a small box next to her computer. Throwing a switch, the on-screen display flips from the Swedish customs system to the Norwegian one. So closely have the two countries cooperated on border issues since

1959, that officials are interchangeable. 'We are regarded as Norwegian customs officers,' she explains, 'as they are regarded as Swedish customs officers. So, we're able to enforce all rules and regulations regarding customs and other agencies. We can go 15 kilometres into Norway and they can come 15 kilometres into Sweden.'

As borders go, it does not, perhaps, get more frictionless than this.

Svinesund and Strömstad (on the Norwegian side) represent the busiest crossing point, so there are customs posts on either side. But at many of the 70 other crossings one customs station does the trick. Officials will throw the switch, and become either Swedish or Norwegian customs officers as the situation requires. The seamless cooperation has been enhanced by cultural and linguistic affinity, mutual membership of the Nordic Union and decades of bilateral meetings.

But it is still a border crossing.

Every commercial driver must stop and provide customs documents. There are random spot checks. 'We're looking for discrepancies,' says Carlsson, 'that will result in someone benefiting economically from wrongfully made declarations. We look for things not being declared, or things being declared erroneously, like if salmon is declared when it's cod, if it's swimwear instead of underwear. There's an average wait of five minutes if everything is in order. Businesses with goods to declare need to stop, but a five-minute procedure is not that much of a hindrance.'

Over coffee, one of Carlsson's colleagues points out some of the other restrictions that Norwegians have to put up with. They have to limit their alcohol purchases to 3,000 kroner (€320) in Nordby shopping centre, or twice that if they stay overnight. Carpenters and plumbers who offer their services in Sweden can carry only hand-tools over the border. Norwegians who get their car serviced on the other side have to declare it. 'It's not the same car going back,' says the official. 'The value is different.'

Carlsson gets into her company Volvo to drive us to Strömstad to meet her opposite number, Kristen Høiberget. Before she can start the engine, she is obliged to carry out an in-car breathalyser test, and will have to perform it each time, unless the stopover is less than 30 minutes.

The Norwegian operation is bigger. That is because the flow of suspect material is, naturally, more likely to come from the south, since Sweden is an EU member state and part of the Schengen free travel area. Nonetheless, Carlsson greets Høiberget with a warm hug.

'We're not afraid to recommend it,' says Høiberget. '[Britain and Ireland] should adopt this model. To achieve anything like it, you need a good tone between the countries and the EU, and they have to establish some kind of bilateral agreement that allows this.'

Otherwise, he says, the border would end up like the EU–Turkey frontier.

Turkey is in the customs union, so trucks crossing into the EU do not have to pay tariffs or duties. But Turkish drivers need a permit to pass through every European country they transit. The global body for international road haulage, the IRU, reports average delays of two hours and 45 minutes for trucks at the Kapıkule crossing between Turkey and Bulgaria, with delays lasting as long as eight hours. A report in the *Financial Times* has spoken of 30-hour delays and 17-kilometre queues, while Turkish media reports pointed to bribery investigations by the Bulgarian police and periodic construction as all contributing to long delays.

Høiberget's take on Ireland's Brexit problem is not simply the result of an inquisitive mind. He and Carlsson have already hosted a number of officials from the Revenue Commissioners in Dublin.

One year before the referendum, a nine-strong team of customs officials was assembled at Revenue Commissioners headquarters in Dublin. Their task was to explore the implications of an eventuality that most people thought unlikely. A senior official involved recalls: 'We sat down and said, "Brexit might not be likely. But if it happens, this is going to be big. What's involved?"'

The team started with the basics. Who would need to be checked? What would the increase in volume be? What would the impact on the Revenue's IT systems be? What systems across Europe would the UK be excluded from? Where or how would they manage a land frontier? What were the legal implications?

Following a year of preparation, the team produced a draft that was supposed to remain a historical curiosity.

The team looked at the existing volumes: the value of trade between Ireland and the UK was roughly the same as between Ireland and non-EU countries. 'We thought, "Sure, that's a 100 per cent increase in volumes,"' says the official. 'We realized to our horror,' he says, 'if you bring in an oil tanker from South America, that's *one* transaction. You bring in a lorry from the UK with split consignments and that could be *five hundred* transactions.' In other words, the contents of the oil tanker would attract one tariff, but a split consignment lorry from the UK could have dozens of different products, all of which might attract different import duties. 'We quickly realized that 100 per cent was a complete underestimate. We started looking at figures in the order of 500 per cent to 800 per cent instead.' (The figure has since been revised up to 1,000 per cent.)

The next thing to consider was the land border. Sixteen EU member states already border a non-EU country. 'We couldn't really go over to Brussels and say, "This is new, shocking stuff altogether,"' says the official. 'The answer they gave us was, "Just read the chapters of the legislation that haven't been relevant to you until now. It is all there. The EU customs code."'

The team then began looking at parallels. The EU–Switzerland border was relatively soft, whereas the EU–Ukraine border on Poland's eastern flank was a hard one with notoriously long waiting times (eight hours for both exit from Ukraine and entry to Poland, according to the State Fiscal Service of Ukraine). On paper, the most attractive option was the Norway–Sweden border. 'The Swedish and Norwegians say the customs can be cleared on average between eight and thirteen minutes,' says the official. 'We want to turn it into *one* minute. Technologically it's not difficult. It's basic carpark IT infrastructure.'

But the technical infrastructure is the easy part. The Norway–Sweden border is underpinned by a thicket of bilateral legislation. Although the Irish land border is just a third the length of that between Norway and Sweden, there are more unauthorized crossings, known as 'unapproved roads' on the Irish border. It's also hard to imagine daily hugs between Southern customs officers and their Northern counterparts.

Setting up a customs border would require an EU legal basis that both Irish and British officials would have to sign up to. 'EU law is not something that appears overnight,' says the official. 'There would be a major challenge in getting the IT systems in place, even when you got round data-protection issues. You would have the challenge in training people, not just in their *own* legislation, but also in the *other* country's legislation.'

While politicians and academics were breezily talking up Nordic efficiency and hi-tech wizardry, the Brexit team within the Revenue Commissioners was looking at real-world facts.

A new Irish customs regime could use Automatic Number Plate Recognition (ANPR), or e-flow, technology. The truck driver sends the electronic declaration, which includes the number plate. The driver arrives and the number is read quickly by the ANPR camera. Customs contact the database. 'If the machine comes back to me and says, "He's okay, we can let him go," I can have the answer to the driver in 30 seconds. The question is, do I need him to get out of his truck and come into the office?'

Another possibility would be to send a text message with a barcode once the electronic registering is approved. 'You have that on your phone,' says the official, 'so when you roll up to the toll booth you just stick your bar code under the reader.'

The second option would be more reliable, and cheaper. But the first is more politically attractive because it would be quicker.

'[EU] officials are not necessarily *against* the [hi-tech] options,' says the team member. 'Those are merely more efficient ways of doing the necessary processes. So they would not say, "You can't do that." On the other hand, if we say we'll have nobody at the border and that we'll do everything from Athlone – at that point we would expect them to start looking very strangely at us.'

However, one senior European Commission official says: 'Border Inspection Posts (BIPs) don't have to be in Dundalk. They can be in Balbriggan or Swords. There will be the *illusion* of frictionless travel, but if you are a haulier you are still likely to end up in a 40-acre road station. There will still have to be physical examinations. There may be less pain and paperwork, but the notion that it can be done without physical inspections is fanciful.'

And Brexit, as we have seen, does not just mean customs controls. Any food or livestock being exported from Northern Ireland over the border will have to comply with EU food safety and animal-health regulations, the so-called sanitary and phyto-sanitary rules. 'Phyto-sanitary?' says the Revenue official with an audible gasp. 'They're in a world of pain. That's where the trouble is going to be. It's agriculture, Food Safety Authority of Ireland [FSAI], environmental-health officers, the entire legion of these various authorities.'

There was also the question of whether Britain would start importing cheap food from countries whose standards are not EU-compliant.

'If they flood the UK with cheap food from third countries,' says the Revenue official, 'then obviously we have a problem if that kind of product is floating around north of the border.'

The team was also intensely aware of the political winds swirling around the issue. 'The Taoiseach was saying,' recalls one member, 'there would be no customs at the border, and that he had a deal with Theresa May to this effect. That was an interesting statement. Does he or Theresa May have the authority to make that decision?'

Again, the technical work of officials, in this case the Revenue Commissioners, who have their own independent mandate, was at odds with the political imperatives of the Irish government. Dublin was reluctant to have technical solutions on the border put up in lights: that would take the pressure off the British government to declare its direction of travel, and it would create the impression in the eyes of Ireland's EU partners that it was preparing a fix that was some distance from the status quo. In the first months of 2017, the Revenue team was told in no uncertain terms to scale back their explorations. 'There is a pace to the political discussions,' says a senior Revenue official. 'It is easy for technical groups to get ahead of the politics, because we're not distracted by the political conversation.'

In fact, the government was worried that due diligence by the Revenue Commissioners was actually hampering the Irish diplomatic effort.

'The Revenue Commissioners went off to study models up in Sweden and Norway,' says one Irish minister. 'They did it on the basis of contingency. They did it off their own bat. They are independent. However, it was unhelpful to us because our starting point was the status quo. It's a very difficult balance to talk about contingency, and have it not then framed as if we're planning for something. It was unhelpful for us because we have been saying to our [EU] partners: nothing. We don't want anything. We're not having *any* physical manifestation of a border.'

The draft report, meanwhile, was regularly updated to take account of fresh information from the Irish export sector, and from EU customs officials in Brussels. It was entitled 'Brexit and the Consequences for Irish Customs'. By March 2017, it was running to 56 pages.

The findings were sobering.

The report first identifies the huge volumes of trade between the UK and Ireland, works out the numbing layers of bureaucracy and compliance now required, and then assesses the resources that both the authorities and the private sector will need.

The implications are almost impossible to grasp on one reading. But some findings immediately stand out.

In 2015, goods worth some €17.8 billion were imported to Ireland from the UK. 'As all of these goods will be subject to the Customs Import Procedure in the post-Brexit era,' the draft states, 'the administrative and fiscal burden on the traders involved cannot be underestimated.'

The same year, goods worth €15.5 billion were exported by Ireland to the UK. These will have to be placed under what's called an export procedure. 'The administrative and fiscal burden on the traders involved will be significant.'

Anyone importing goods from the UK will need an Authorized Economic Operator (AEO) certificate under the terms of the EU's Union Customs Code. These were introduced by the World Customs Organization after 9/11 as a way to mitigate security risks in the supply chain. Certificate holders have to have proved they are compliant in safety controls. Irish companies wanting customs simplifications will need to have AEO status, or at least 'meet the criteria'. An increase in AEO applications will 'further burden our scarce operational resources'.

Regarding the Irish land border, the document notes that there are 30 million annual vehicle crossings between Northern Ireland and the Republic. 'While some form of common travel area may exist post-Brexit, a completely open border is not possible.'

Compliance costs and paperwork arise at every turn.

Exports need to be covered by a pre-departure declaration lodged electronically via Automated Entry Processing (AEP), the system that handles customs declarations. It would include data for risk analysis, safety and security purposes. If the UK remains in a number of EU-related systems, such as the 'security zone', British customs officials will still be able to do security checks on third-country goods coming to Ireland. But, if they don't, there will have to be further checks on the Irish side. That will require compliance with systems and software that are, in turn, compatible with the Import Control System. 'The current system would not be in a position to cope with this additional volume without investment,' says the draft.

Goods awaiting customs clearance would need to be presented to a pre-designated customs office, or a Temporary Storage Facility. Post-Brexit, an e-manifest would have to be processed and goods withheld 'until all customs formalities have been completed'. The moment goods arrive they will be deemed to be in 'Temporary Storage' and will be permitted to remain in this state for only 90 days, at which point they incur a 'customs debt'.

Because of the UK's physical proximity, there would be an explosion of Temporary Importation Procedures, whereby goods brought into Ireland and out again in a short period of time would have to be cleared for customs through the use of what's called an ATA Carnet.

A typical casualty will be the National Ploughing Championships. The vast outdoor agricultural expo, says the draft, involves 'a significant volume of equipment moved into Ireland from Northern Ireland and the UK for the duration of the event ... All of these products would need to be declared under the Temporary Importation Procedure with guarantees of ATA Carnets required for the period of Importation.'

Transit will be another major headache. Ireland exports huge volumes of goods to the Continent via the UK. The UK is currently part of the Common Transit Convention, agreed between the EU and European Free Trade Association members in May 1987. If the UK remains in the regime, an Irish company importing goods from China could avoid customs formalities when the goods enter and then exit the UK, en route to Ireland, under a so-called transit procedure. But the importer would still need to be approved as an authorized consignee, and a Temporary Storage Operator would be required until the goods are cleared by customs. This would be the 'best outcome' for Ireland.

If the UK pulled out of the Common Transit Convention, we could be in the realm of TIR Convention, the international system for transiting goods through countries. The TIR Convention essentially means containers are sealed during transit so as to avoid smuggling. Only authorized carriers can use the TIR procedure, and they must be formally approved and then reapproved every two years. To cover the taxes and duties at risk during transit, there is a guarantee chain managed by the International Road Transport Union, which prints and distributes the TIR Carnet. The Carnet is a customs declaration and proof of guarantee that the goods will stay on the truck. Under this scenario, a truck leaving Dundalk for Letterkenny, via Northern Ireland, would now have to undergo a TIR procedure.

Dublin and Rosslare ports would need to make major adjustments. In 2013, Irish ports handled 12,000 vessels carrying 46.7 million tonnes of goods.

'Existing physical infrastructure and traffic streaming are

likely to be stretched, if not *overwhelmed*, by the increased demand for customs controls,' the report states.

Passengers at airports and ferry ports will also require checks. In 2014, there were 8.6 million passenger trips to Ireland, some 3.5 million, or 41 per cent, of them from the UK. Of 7 million outward trips, 3.5 million were to the UK, excluding Northern Ireland. 'This would mean that the number of passengers (both air and sea) arriving from the UK and potentially in possession of prohibited goods or with goods in excess of duty-free allowances may *exceed* our existing customs control capacity.'

While the main airports of Dublin, Shannon and Cork would have customs facilities, a number of smaller airfields approved for the arrival and departure of traffic to and from the UK would have to be reapproved for the arrival passengers. This would mean an 'additional, if not permanent, customs presence at such airports, e.g. Weston, Knock and Kerry'.

The problems don't stop there. Currently, only 20 customs officers assess non-EU post at Irish mail centres. Since half of the international post comes from the UK, staffing levels will need to increase.

But the real crunch point is the Irish land border. As a source of political agony, it is unparalleled.

The Revenue draft says that the Norway–Sweden model 'would require extensive retraining of customs officers from both jurisdictions in order to comply with both EU and UK legislation and is probably not a priority in the initial stages of Brexit as any related efficiencies are more to the benefit of customs than trade'.

The e-flow system might work, but 'it would require an interface between both countries' electronic systems, and it is unclear whether any such system could be commissioned and installed in the time available.' Even then, 'The inevitability of certain consignments being routed, other than green goods, or documents having to be examined would still require investment in suitable facilities at *all* designated crossing points.'

The report then confronts the nightmare scenario: locating customs controls on the busy M1 motorway. 'A particular issue in this regard,' the draft states, 'may be the logistical challenge of placing permanent controls on the M1 route from Dublin to Belfast.' The draft report records that in May 2016, at the Ravensdale crossing in County Louth, some 372,726 vehicles crossed into the North, and 359,800 travelled to the South.

Dungiven is a small town nestling in the Sperrin Mountains on the A6 from Derry to Belfast. It is a strongly republican area. Kevin Lynch, one of the 10 hunger strikers who died in 1981, was from Dungiven, and the local hurling club is named after him.

On Tuesday, 1 December 2015, the *Derry Journal* reported that the Police Service of Northern Ireland (PSNI) had just replaced an ANPR security camera in Dungiven for the *third* time. It had been cut down in mid January, and again in November 2014. Following the January incident, a dissident outfit called the North Derry Republican Group claimed responsibility in a call to the *County Derry News*.

Eleven months after the camera was cut down for the third time, and three months after the referendum, Seamus Leheny, the Policy and Membership Manager of the Northern Ireland branch of the Freight Transport Association (FTA), met officials from the Northern Ireland Office

(NIO). Two months later, he was invited to give a presentation to MPs in Westminster. 'They were keen to learn more on the Northern Ireland scenario,' says Leheny, 'because in the whole Brexit debate there was no emphasis on the North. After the referendum it suddenly dawned on officials in London that the Northern Ireland problem could be the loose thread that unravels everything.'

On 23 January 2017, so concerned were Whitehall officials that they booked a hotel room in Belfast to meet Leheny, a number of NIO civil servants and eight haulage companies. The meeting got straight down to business: how could a new customs frontier on the Irish land border operate? Would ANPR technology work?

An official from the NIO did not mince his words: 'Listen,' he said, 'we're not even *contemplating* hardware like that along the border. Because the day it goes up, it will be down that night. There will be guys out with an angle grinder. The PSNI have already said they will not be policing any customs infrastructure along the border because it will make them sitting ducks.'

This is supported by a senior PSNI intelligence source. 'That is the risk with installing a customs border,' the source says. 'When that happens, what are you likely to respond with? You're likely to respond with surveillance, cameras, ANPR. You're likely to respond by making buildings more safe and protected, maybe armoured glass, fences, fortifications. You're also likely to respond by the use of police officers. And when you put police officers down into a border situation, inevitably they will be carrying guns. They will be using armoured vehicles and they will themselves present a target opportunity for murder, or attempted murder, by dissidents.'

At the end of the meeting the Whitehall officials were

sympathetic, if unsettled. 'They completely understood the mood of the hauliers,' says Leheny, 'and the risks involved of a hard border and vehicles having to be stopped and customs clearance. They totally get it.'

One FTA member who runs 100 vehicle movements a day into the Republic told them that a lot of those movements had 'short lead times'. A driver might get a call at 10.30 in the morning to get a load into Dublin in the afternoon. 'How would you raise that many customs declarations per day,' says Leheny, '*and* do it at short notice?'

ANPR cameras are used for traffic management and crime detection. In some republican areas – not just in Dungiven – they are vandalized or cut down. 'To think that something like that would be mounted on a border crossing and wouldn't be vandalized or destroyed?' says Leheny. 'You know yourself.'

A member of the Revenue Brexit team believes the British government would be highly averse to facilitating customs operations on the border, for obvious historical reasons. 'I'm not sure,' he says, 'how eager the UK are to occupy physical infrastructure at or near that frontier. If I was on their side, I would be very cautious about putting a building with a flag outside it in certain parts of the frontier. The British focus on infrastructure is almost exclusively on the [English] Channel ports [Dover, etc.]. If they could find a way to not have any British official within 50 kilometres of the land frontier, they would feel it was a good result. These are for reasons to do with life expectancy.'

So, everyone is proclaiming no return to a hard border. But everything about the reality, from the EU's non-negotiable Union Customs Code, to Britain's determination to do trade deals around the globe, to the sanitary and phyto-sanitary requirements, all scream 'hard border'. There may be room for tweaks here and there through technology, but the Revenue Commissioners' own professional research suggests controls *will* happen on or near the border. They will require manpower, infrastructure, money and a large degree of patience on the part of hauliers and regular commuters.

And yet the Revenue Brexit team has been under the political direction not to make plans until the negotiations between the EU and the UK yield clarity. The modus oper-andi is *festina lente* – hasten slowly. Even if the British government knew what kind of political relationship they were prepared to accept on the island, it will take years before a conclusion is reached.

But officials can't afford to wait until a deal is done.

'We're going to be looking at customs declarations on day *one*,' says a member of the Revenue team. 'We have to plan on that basis. But we may find that when we have to start, we can't move fast enough.'

The team is discreetly talking to the Office of Public Works (OPW) about the government's land banks. While there is a healthy stock on the eastern part of the border, there is less land on the western side. Revenue is also tendering for a new IT system that will be compatible with the Union Customs Code. This can be funded by the EU, since Ireland collects VAT and tariff receipts on the EU's behalf (Ireland earns €50 million each year in the process). The new system will have to have volumetric capacity *10 times* what officials currently pro-cess. 'The tendering documents don't make any reference as to why we need that volumetric level,' concedes the official. 'It's just that we *need* it. In essence, we're trying to bury the Brexit procurement in the UCC procurement.'

*

One observer with a keen knowledge of border country is P. J. Hallinan, a retired Garda sergeant who worked for 32 years around the Donegal–Derry frontier. He was there before the Troubles started, and retired around the time of the Good Friday Agreement.

'People had to put up with the hardship, the long delays, the queues,' recalls Hallinan. 'The minor roads were closed, bollards were placed on them. They were a bone of contention. People resented them – the people who were living there, or who had land on both sides. They had to make the long journeys around either way.'

He was also around for the BSE and foot and mouth crises, which saw checks on the border again. After that he was a juvenile liaison worker and, when he retired from the force, a youth worker with the Inishowen Partnership Company. Over the years he has brought people together through GAA, boxing, basketball and, later, through the Wider Horizons Programme in projects commemorating the First World War.

'We had those people out there,' he recalls, 'they were away for four or five days, doing the battlefields in Flanders. It was about the futility of war and the futility of conflict.'

By the time of the Good Friday Agreement, the sense of conflict was fading. 'People today wouldn't know where the border was,' says Hallinan. 'The old boys would know, but the young people wouldn't know what you were talking about.'

What might happen if those borders return? 'The worst-case scenario is that they open up the border posts and they carry on as before. That will mean mayhem. The amount of traffic they have at the moment is serious compared to what it was 20 years ago. Any attempt to put a checkpoint in place at the moment, you would have a tailback for a mile within 15 minutes. That's unacceptable.'

P.J. has hosted a group of 200 visitors from Cyprus, another divided island, as part of his peace work. 'They said, "Where is the conflict in Ireland?" They were at the border and they couldn't see it.

'All I see is goodness coming out of the peace process,' he says. 'It takes resources to do that. To build peace.'

The potential for a customs post to set in motion a dangerous sequence of events that would undermine that peace is not entirely fanciful, and not one the authorities on both sides of the border take lightly.

'Brexit is still a couple of years away,' says a senior PSNI intelligence source. 'So much has to be negotiated between Ireland, the EU and the United Kingdom, that it would be presumptive to start doing any planning and threat assessment until we understand the landscape in more detail. But our working assumption is that *any* manifestation – electronic, physical or even legal – of a border will create increased risk. It will require some republicans to take some action because of the very nature of it. They cannot *not* be seen to be doing something around this.'

Another senior PSNI officer agrees. 'Even though people say they don't want a hard border,' says Assistant Chief Constable Stephen Martin, 'and that they want a soft border, depending on the response from people who oppose it, you can very quickly find yourself in a sequence of events that leads to a *de facto* hard border. If it suits their strategic objective, you could imagine the opportunities dissidents would have to politically attack Sinn Féin in the event of the remilitarization, the resecuritization of the border. Even if they, by their actions, were semi-responsible for that, it would give them a wonderful opportunity to attack Sinn Féin, that Sinn Féin were involved in a partitionist settlement, a failed political project.'

11. The Great Disruption

Natural gas rises from beneath the Yamal Peninsula in the Russian Arctic and is piped westwards through the Continental expanse. It also comes up from North Africa, hissing its way to compressor stations in the Netherlands and Belgium, from where it hurtles through subsea pipelines to Bacton in Norfolk. And it comes south from Norway, through a 1,166-kilometre pipeline to the Yorkshire coast.

But much of this gas has a further destination. The offtake from the British national grid happens in the Scottish town of Moffat, at a pressure of 50 bar. The gas is separated into two 36-inch-diameter pipelines and pushed for 30 kilometres (at the much higher pressure of 85 bar), until the pipelines converge and head south-east to Brighouse Bay on the Scottish coast. The gas is compressed one more time, to 140 bar, for its final 200-kilometre journey under the seabed to make landfall in Loughshinny, north County Dublin, and Gormanston in County Meath.

There are other ties of energy that bind Ireland to the UK. The 500-megawatt East–West Interconnector runs under the sea between Shotton in North Wales to Rush North Beach in County Dublin. A 400 kV overhead cable from Charlemont, County Armagh, to Kells, County Meath, has been in the pipeline (so to speak) since 2011.

The EU has been pushing for a more integrated energy market, where, in theory, cross-border energy flows open up competition, reduce prices and attract investment. There is closer cooperation between energy regulators, a common certification for transmission-system operators, and systems to approve interconnectors, manage congestion and transmission charges, and so on. The EU also encourages the pooling of energy as a way to withstand external shocks, such as Russia turning off the gas.

Since 2007, Northern Ireland and the Republic have operated the Single Electricity Market (SEM), a wholesale electricity-trading pool across the island. But Brexit could reverse decades of Irish–UK energy cooperation, and carve a border through the SEM.

Gas piped over from the UK is used to generate 46 per cent of the electricity supply on the island of Ireland. Northern Ireland is heavily dependent on that electricity coming north from Loughshinny and Gormanston. The Republic's indigenous gas supplies are not sufficient on their own. The Kinsale gas fields are nearly exhausted. Corrib Gas began flowing, from a deposit off the north-west coast of Ireland, on 31 December 2015, meeting 55 per cent of Ireland's natural gas needs in 2016. But during the summer of that year, there were only three days when gas from the UK wasn't needed. Corrib will probably provide 103 gigawatt hours per day at its peak (the Moffat-Ireland interconnector can deliver 265), but that will decline to 60 in two to three years.

Within five years there will be no gas storage in Ireland. According to Gas Networks Ireland, the Moffat interconnectors represent a robust guarantee of supply. However, under the EU Security of Gas Supply Regulation, member states are required to share resources at times of energy disruption. Since cooperation predates the regulation, Gas Networks Ireland believes the UK will continue to guarantee security of supply. But post-Brexit, the UK will no longer be legally bound by EU solidarity rules. 'As Ireland is poorly interconnected to other EU Member States,' write Paula Higgins and Roisin Costello in a paper for the Institute for International and European Affairs, 'this could leave the country more vulnerable to energy crises if the UK is no longer required to compensate for supply disruptions.'

Even though the SEM is a bilateral arrangement that does not rely on an EU framework, there are potential problems. A system whereby service providers, distributors and customers communicate freely across the Irish border relies on a wealth of data. But after Brexit, the UK will be outside the EU's data-protection rules. If the UK is non-compliant, write Higgins and Costello, 'the Republic of Ireland would be legally obliged to refuse to transfer the personal data of customers, employees or market participants in the Republic to any data processor (in this case an energy provider, distributor or regulator) located in Northern Ireland.'

The SEM had actually been undergoing reform to comply with the EU's Energy Union rules, including measures to ensure greater awareness about supply, excess capacity and carbon emissions. Implementing the reforms would rectify these deficiencies, but, with Northern Ireland no longer participating in the reform process, there will be less incentive for investment in the SEM.

Indeed, investment is a general concern. Even if future World Trade Organization tariffs will be low, and in any event unlikely, investors immediately took fright after the referendum. Ireland's dependence on the UK may frustrate the country's participation in the EU's strategic energy plans. Under one of these plans, a regional electricity market was to be created involving France, Ireland and the UK. With the UK now heading for the door, Ireland's interconnection will run through a third country, meaning significant regulatory complications. Furthermore, the European Commission has prioritized interconnection endeavours between Ireland and the UK that can benefit from accelerated planning and permit processes, lower administrative costs and access to EU funding. The Greenlink interconnection between Wexford and Pembroke in Wales, and the ISLES interconnection between Coolkeeragh and Islay, Scotland, are two such projects. 'In the new milieu of uncertainty,' write Higgins and Costello, 'it is likely that UK–Ireland projects will face substantial delays and reduced political support at a European level as well as operational delays once under way.'

One enormous imponderable is what path the UK will decide to follow. If it adopts the Norway model, the UK could enjoy continued participation in the EU's internal energy market. That, again, presupposes a role for the European Court of Justice.

Meanwhile, the European Investment Bank (EIB) is rethinking its commitment to UK infrastructure projects such as a North Sea windfarm. But the EIB says it may help Ireland as a result of Brexit-enforced isolation. One project is the €1 billion Celtic Interconnector, a 700-megawatt subsea cable running 600 kilometres from Brittany to the south coast of Ireland. Following President Hollande's visit to Dublin in July 2016, both countries moved the project to a two-year design and preconsultation phase, with a potential launch in 2025.

'Because all of our electricity and gas interconnections are with Britain,' Environment Minister Denis Naughten told Reuters, 'it would be irresponsible of us not to explore all other options.'

In the same Reuters report, EIB Vice-President Andrew McDowell, Enda Kenny's former Chief Economic Adviser, confirmed EIB interest in both the interconnector, and the development of a Liquefied Natural Gas (LNG) terminal at Shannon that would pump up to 28.3 million cubic metres of gas per day into the Irish grid, further reducing Ireland's dependency on the UK. 'The EIB is very conscious that Ireland is uniquely exposed to the economic consequences of Brexit,' he said. 'The need to show tangible European support for Ireland is becoming more pressing and the EIB is part of that.'

The Cheltenham Festival in March 2017 set new standards in Irish participation (and glory) in a British sporting event. Some 60,000 Irish punters travelled to Cheltenham, wagering €125 million. In the event, 19 out of 28 winners at Cheltenham were trained in Ireland.

The Cheltenham Festival is the quintessential British–Irish sporting occasion, one entirely free of malice or begrudgery. It is also testament to how closely aligned the racing and bloodstock industries in the two countries have become.

'In the sporting and social world,' says Brian Kavanagh, CEO of Horse Racing Ireland (HRI), 'horses and horse-racing are the best example you will ever come across of Britain and Ireland being integrated. Throughout the Troubles, you could go to a meeting like Cheltenham or Ascot and there was never a problem. There's a great common passion for horse-racing between the Brits and ourselves.

'That's why Brexit is such an earthquake.'

Within political circles, the horse-racing industry was the dog that barked a little late. The European and Mediterranean Horseracing Federation held a brief meeting with the European Commission in July 2016, but the industry in Ireland has been slower to respond.

On Wednesday, 24 May 2017, a full 11 months after the referendum, the first major meeting of stakeholders took place at HRI headquarters in The Curragh. Everyone was present: English sales companies, trainers, representative bodies, breeders, stud-book operators. The industry was shaken by a series of questions. Might there be a problem with thousands of horses crossing the land border, or crossing to the UK, or even transiting the UK to France, be they race horses or foals being sold as part of Ireland's €225 million bloodstock industry?

'We're none the wiser,' said Michael Grassick, the CEO of the Irish Racehorse Trainers Association, after the meeting. 'That's being honest with you.'

There are 9,200 thoroughbred foals born on the island of Ireland every year, the highest level of production in Europe. Two thirds of them are exported. Of these, 80 per cent go to Britain by boat or by air. The British horse-racing industry relies on Ireland to provide horses for owners to race. If the UK reverts to trading on WTO terms, the tariff on a racehorse would be around 11.5 per cent. There may, however, be exemptions on the export of thoroughbreds for breeding purposes.

The two countries operate as one from a racing-and-breeding standpoint. Horses born in Ireland and Britain are entered into the same stud book. Irish horses, trainers and jockeys compete in Britain and vice versa on a daily basis.

The movement of such a large number of animals would normally be subject to strict EU veterinary controls. However, the Tripartite Agreement (TPA) reached between Britain, Ireland and France in the early 1970s gives all three countries a derogation from EU law. The TPA is essentially an agreement between the Chief Veterinary Officers of all three countries that any racehorses crossing their borders are of a 'demonstrably higher health status' than the normal equine population, so are allowed to travel without the normal veterinary-health inspection.

Under a May 2014 revision to the TPA, however, all horses must now travel with an additional document known as a DOCOM, which permits traceability via the EU's animal-movements database. The new document runs for 10 days, but it is currently not needed for horses travelling back and forth between the UK and Ireland, since the two countries are considered as a single epidemiological unit for equine-health purposes. According to Brian Kavanagh, 'In the absence of that, a horse would require a veterinary examination before it moves, or the checking of identification papers or of the animal's disease status. The fear is that post-Brexit, when Britain becomes a third country, will we still be able to do that?'

Of the 9,200 foals born in Ireland every year, 800 come from Northern Ireland. Those foals carry an IRE suffix, meaning they are considered as Irish, not British. 'That has become an important marketing tool,' says Kavanagh, 'a brand identification. When we're selling horses internationally, the IRE label is an attraction. If a foal is born in Tyrone or Cork, they all carry the IRE suffix.'

The horse-racing industry north of the border is funded and controlled by HRI. There are 24 race meetings a year at two tracks, Down Royal and Downpatrick. They're part of the Irish, and not the British, fixture list. With Britain out of the EU, there may be a question mark over that situation continuing. Some 90 per cent of the runners who take part are from the Republic. What will happen if those horse boxes are stopped at the border to undergo customs clearance and, potentially, veterinary inspections?

'There's a lot of anxiety,' says Michael Grassick. 'Once you stop the truck, the horses want to get off. Being pulled in for an hour or half an hour can discommode the horses. That can upset everything.'

Transporting horses to France either for racing or as breeding stock would be an even more difficult scenario. The horses pass through the UK, spend the night in England and then continue to France. Post-Brexit, they may be stopped at ports going in and out of the UK. 'Some have suggested we transport the horses directly from Ireland to France by ferry,' says Grassick. 'But with the ferry the journey is too long. It's not ideal for the horses' welfare to be a long time on ferries.'

Despite the depth of mutual regard on both sides, the Irish horse-racing fraternity suspects Britain will seek a competitive advantage post-Brexit. In a written submission to the Joint Oireachtas Committee on Agriculture, Food and the Marine, HRI stressed that the two countries compete globally for investment, the sale of media rights, and the location of bloodstock and training facilities. 'The concern is,' the submission stated, 'that once Britain leaves the EU, it could offer a raft of taxation and other incentives which Ireland would be unable to match.'

Brian Kavanagh believes that Ireland can hold its own. 'We have the land, we have the people, we have the climate, we have the natural advantages.'

Britain may adopt wholesale EU rules on animal and veterinary health in the Great Repeal Bill, meaning they could maintain the status quo under equivalency rules. But the UK authorities would have to update their rules as EU rules develop, and abide by the ECJ.

The odds on that appear long, to say the least.

*

In Gallinagh, County Monaghan, one company encapsulates all of the challenges, and even some of the opportunities, of Brexit.

Combilift makes specialist forklift and straddle-carrier machines that allow customers to move heavy loads around narrow-aisle warehouses. A quarter of its exports go to the UK, and the company is part of an elaborate supply chain involving dozens of small firms on both sides of the border.

What happens in Gallinagh is fabrication, design and assembly. Some 450 people are employed directly, and 100 other subcontractors supply fabricated machine parts. The company sources both fabricated parts and operational components from the North. And it buys axles and transmission gear from JCB in Staffordshire (where David Cameron made a key speech on reducing EU immigration ahead of his ill-fated project to win the referendum).

'If we're taking a transmission axle in from JCB, are we going to pay an import duty on that product coming into the Republic? And then the finished products we export out to the UK: are our customers going to pay more because of an export duty or an import duty into the UK market?' asks founder Martin McVicar.

Combilift also supplies the UK with spare parts on a very tight delivery schedule. 'We can ship parts at three o'clock in the afternoon,' says McVicar, 'and they're delivered anywhere in the UK the next morning. If that's being held up by customs, it will become an issue for our customers if they need it urgently.'

The WTO tariff rating on forklift trucks is 4.5 per cent. 'It's not so major,' says McVicar, 'but it's still a significant increase on the supply cost of our product. It's going to mean that our forklift truck will be 4.5 per cent more expensive in

18 months' time. Then you add in the sterling fluctuation as well.'

Another concern is VAT. Under EU rules, when Combilift buys a component from another EU member state, in this case the UK, it is sourced at cost price, and no VAT is payable on import (the VAT is applied when the product is sold on). After Brexit, however, the company will have to pay Irish VAT at the point of entry. 'As a business we can claim that back,' says McVicar. 'But that will increase the cash-flow requirements for our business, and will tie that cash flow up.' It will also increase compliance costs.

Then there's the transit issue. Combilift makes bulky, heavy things that are shipped to mainland Europe through the UK. 'Whatever kind of customs border controls there are, whether they're electronic or whatever, it's going to slow down the transit time. That's a cost to someone, probably the customer at the other end who's paying for it. So it's going to make Irish companies like ours less competitive.'

Combilift already exports forklifts to India, Russia and China, so it's familiar with customs forms and export duties. But smaller, indigenous SMEs, which export only to the UK, and which provide employment in economically vulnerable regions, face a stiffer challenge. Since the referendum, they have dealt with upheaval on all fronts. Irish goods are instantly more expensive in the UK. Even if British imports are cheaper, that might have a worrying knock-on effect. For every biggish SME, there is a smaller plant nearby, employing perhaps 10 to 15 relatively low-skilled workers making parts for that bigger company. Cheaper British imports mean that smaller companies may be priced out, with no other potential clients for their products.

The Small Firms Association (SFA) has been monitoring

business sentiment post-Brexit. 'There was a bit of denial at first,' says Acting Director Linda Barry. 'That idea that we don't export so we're grand. And then gradually the realization has been kicking in in terms of all of those less direct impacts, such as their own supply chain, or a supply chain they're part of, anyone who is involved in holding or transferring data, anyone who relies on customers crossing the border. We saw towards the end of 2016 a real drop in confidence once people became aware of the primary and secondary impacts.'

The SFA has been urging exporters to develop in-house customs and trade expertise, or to hire authorized customs-clearance agencies. Headaches may not just occur when the goods are being shipped out: if controls are slowing everything up, there may be implications for after-care support, reverse logistics costs and delivery lead times, especially for time-sensitive products. Companies are being asked to review their entire operations, to identify variously the flow of goods in and out of the UK, the possible challenge points in supply chains where new costs may arise and the overall administrative burden. How will trade barriers hit profit margins, price-setting policies, the ability to absorb costs and the implications of passing those costs on to customers? Are there alternative routes to transiting the UK? How is currency volatility impacting on your suppliers and customers? Have your IT systems been reconfigured for border controls? If not, how long will this take? How much will it cost?

The deeper into the supply chain you go, the more complex these questions become.

'The EU has made it abundantly clear,' says Simon McKeever, CEO of the Irish Exporters Association, 'that the UK cannot benefit from being outside the single market . . . So what happens to supply chains where bits are made in

Ireland and then get put into finished products in the UK, or where bits are made in the UK and then get put into finished products in Ireland? If there's a tariff of between 5 and 10 per cent every time they cross the border, you're looking at the competitiveness of that supply chain decreasing quite a lot. If it's crossing the border back and forth a couple of times, then we're really looking at something that's very, very uncompetitive.'

An Irish Exporters Association survey of its members found that, by March 2017, only 30 per cent of exporters had done an impact assessment on tariffs, only 26 per cent had costed customs procedures and only 23 per cent had looked at the effect of border controls. Around 14 per cent had looked at the implications of complying with EU *and* UK regulations. Only 12 per cent had looked at the potential for increased competition in the UK due to the higher cost of Irish goods. One third of companies hadn't done an impact assessment at all, but were planning to do so, while 31 per cent were not planning to carry out *any* impact assessment.

The overall picture is one of companies quick to take advantage of the weaker sterling, but slower to carry out longer-term adjustments. Companies are aware of the exposure, and aware of the need to take steps, but some appear almost paralysed by the sheer complexity of it all.

'People haven't even started getting their heads around it,' says McKeever.

One man trying to get his head around the complexity is Andy Leyland, the Supply Chain and Business Development Director of Lifes2Good, a Galway-based health and cosmetics company. The company makes hair and beauty products, cardiovascular food supplements, novelty travel/gym toothbrushes, liquid supplements for canine health and pedicure gadgets.

The lower costs of importing raw materials from Britain are offset by fears that, as the UK economy contracts, sales of optional luxury products such as food supplements will fall. 'From a supply-chain point of view,' says Leyland, 'it's going to be more complicated for UK companies to export, and for us to import. We would envisage delays in stuff coming in while things get sorted out. The worst-case scenario is that the UK applies WTO tariffs on goods, and what the additional cost might be with those tariffs in place.'

Lifes2Good imports raw cosmetics, shampoos and conditioners from the UK, then exports them back under their own brand name or generically to Boots or Holland & Barrett. For the food-supplements business, they use ingredients sourced from other Irish companies, but those companies in turn source the ingredients from the UK. That means if their Irish suppliers are hit with tariffs, they may pass the cost on to Lifes2Good.

Things get really complicated in the physical shipment of goods out and raw materials in. 'We hear there are going to be different grades of classifications, like traffic-light systems,' says Leyland, 'green, orange and red, depending on the classification of goods. That will have implications because a lot of our products come through mixed consignments with different carriers. So, you might have goods on a truck and you have green status, but someone else is red. So the whole truck gets held up.' That may mean couriers are less attractive.

Lifes2Good has a significant presence online. Individual packages are sent direct to the homes of British consumers. 'It's going to be messy where we ship stuff direct to people's homes – individual parcels, where people log on to a website or ring through a call centre. We fulfil those orders from Ireland. We have a warehouse on site. We'll ship them overnight to homes in the UK. The cost of that will go up because each shipment will be subject to import duty in the UK. It's no longer going to another EU member state, which is very clear and very clean. It's going to a non-EU state. You're running up the costs of that. Would it make more sense to bulk ship those into the UK and have a local hub ship the parcels through UK parcel post, rather than shipping them out from Ireland to British consumers' homes? We're trying to look at the numbers to see if that makes more sense.'

The Irish Exporters Association survey found that for companies exporting more than 25 per cent of their products to the UK, there was a temptation to bring the entire production across the Irish Sea to avoid currency fluctuations and the customs hit. 'That's a natural progression,' says Simon McKeever. 'Companies in the services sector are saying, "I'm going to have to base more people in the UK to have access to that market."'

Currently, under EU freedom of establishment rules, there are no tax consequences for restructuring a company and moving it across an EU border. Businesses can establish, relocate and set up branches and offices in any other EU member state. 'It's all tax neutral,' says Brian Keegan, Director of Public Policy and Taxation at Chartered Accountants Ireland. 'But those shelters will disappear the moment the Article 50 process terminates. If a parent company moves the manufacturing branch to the UK, there's an automatic trigger of a capital gains tax because you have a big asset moving to another territory.'

This will not just hit companies moving from the Republic of Ireland to Great Britain. It will also hit companies shifting a couple of miles north or south across the land border.

So far, smaller companies are not rushing to move production. An SFA survey in May 2017 found that just over 5 per cent of companies were planning to move operations. 'It may seem like an attractive option,' says Linda Barry, 'but it's a big lifestyle decision to move your business to the UK, because you *are* your business. It's up to 50 employees, so it's not just you. But it's a big commercial decision to do that. It involves being on a plane, commuting back and forth, or moving yourself and your life and family to a new location.'

Companies that stay will face new costs and obligations. 'They have forgotten about this since 1992 [when the single market fully took effect],' says Brian Keegan, 'because they just haven't needed the expertise.'

That expertise will have to be paid for, but even then the sheer messiness of exporting will cost. 'If you're filling a pallet every two or three months and sending it across,' explains Keegan, 'these are relatively small consignments, and a customs agent is going to charge nearly as much for doing that as for your weekly three or four full containers' worth.

'If it's a mixed load, the guys who do small exports in the back of a white van – nothing wrong with that – but they might be exporting stuff under multiple categories. If you have a consignment of finished industrial goods, there'll be a customs charge of 2½ per cent that will apply to the entire consignment. But if you have a consignment of processed food, some sandwiches, some cold cuts – they actually *all* attract different customs rates. It's not about volume. It's about frequency and the mix of the export – that's what's going to drive customs costs.'

In a report published in April 2017, Chartered Accountants Ireland explored the exposure of different kinds of firms, setting out case-study scenarios based on real-life companies.

A large subsidiary of a US software company based in Northern Ireland just over the border would invoice in US dollars, so the weakness of sterling has been a boost. However, the company employs staff who routinely commute north across the border. They lose out because they're paid in sterling, and because they face delays in getting to work across the frontier. The company already has a staff-retention issue, with some seeking employment within the EU since Brexit. In fact, the company is concerned about a mass exodus, so it is thinking of moving parts of production into the South.

Then there is the data-protection issue. Before Brexit, the UK complied with EU data-protection regulations. These put restrictions on the movement of data between EU member states, and tougher controls on data flowing *outside* the EU. Businesses operating across an EU border depend heavily on the free flow of data between subsidiaries. It might relate to their customer base or simply to human-resources issues. Post-Brexit, the UK will no longer be compliant with data-protection rules, so that data flow may simply have to stop. The UK may copy EU rules into British law through the Great Repeal Bill. But, as will apply in so many cases, the UK may have to accept the jurisdiction of the European Court of Justice where disputes arise. This is something Theresa May's government has vowed to resist.

Even without clarity on that political point, companies that straddle the British and Irish business environments will have to update IT systems to meet changes brought about by the rupture: extra administrative overheads, finance systems that will have to adapt to changes in regulation, customs controls, taxation, employment and contract law.

What will happen to the rights and obligations enshrined in legal contracts between Irish companies and UK counter-parties that run beyond the exit date of March 2019? The SFA has been encouraging businesses to consider their contractual rights and obligations, and how these might be affected by issues such as the free movement of goods and services, dispute resolution, the use of EU funds and so on. Do contracts assume the UK is a member of the EU? Do contract obligations assume the free movement of goods, people and services? Do they allow for price increases in the event of tariffs? With the UK leaving the ECJ, there is the potential for long-term legal uncertainty, especially where there is a supply-chain dispute involving companies in Ireland, the UK and any other EU member state.

Another complex area is intellectual property. The EU has created a Unitary Patent designed to recognize an applicant's rights in 25 member states. Inventors who feel their innovations have been improperly copied will have recourse to a soon-to-be-established Unified Patent Court. The Court is not an EU institution, but in its intended form only EU member states are permitted to join. In November 2016, however, the British government announced that it would seek to join the Court. The ECJ would not be the final arbiter in any disputes, but it would hand down guidance to the new Unified Patent Court as to whether EU law was in question. Brexit will mean further delays in the Court being established, as all sides try to figure out how it will work legally, while the Tory right will want to limit any role for the ECJ.

The freedom for the UK to develop its own laws will be watched closely. Theresa May has promised to maintain, and even expand, EU-derived workers' rights. But both she and the Chancellor, Philip Hammond, have also warned that the UK could walk away from the negotiations and adapt its economic model accordingly. This is presumed to envisage a low-tax, low-regulatory environment, the so-called Singapore model. Irish businesses operating in the UK are advised to monitor changes in employment law so that they not only understand the impact on their business, but also are mindful of their competitiveness against UK rivals.

Already the Irish Congress of Trade Unions has warned that EU employment rights and rules governing equality, health and safety, part-time workers, agency workers, working time and product standards will all be at risk. Its October 2016 Brexit report warns that 'changes to employment rights in the UK could place downward pressure on employment protections across the island [of Ireland]. This in turn could endanger job security, threaten key industries and effectively lead to a "race to the bottom" across the island.'

One big focus will be on the extent to which the UK maintains its standards across a range of areas currently governed by EU regulatory systems. There are over 50 EU agencies that cover a multitude of realms where directives and regulations have an impact, from the Community Plant Variety Office, which governs intellectual property rights for those who breed plants that are sold across the single market, to the European Maritime Safety Agency, which covers things like pollution alerts, hazardous shipments and accident investigations at sea, to the European Chemical Agency (ECHA).

Britain has said it will convert the body of EU law (the *acquis communautaire*) into British law, then keep or dismiss elements of it over time as it sees fit. But in many cases the UK will have to replicate those agencies in terms of staffing, administration, expertise and costs, if it still wants to interact with the single market – even if it's no longer a member.

The Helsinki-based ECHA is a case in point, and is relevant to Andy Leyland and Lifes2Good. It was set up to apply the so-called REACH directive, which assesses the hazards, risks and safe use of chemical substances that companies manufacture in the EU or import into it. On 23 June 2016, British voters voted themselves out of the ECHA. That means the UK will have to create its own agency from scratch to replicate what the ECHA currently does on Britain's behalf. It will have to do it without the cohort of experts to call upon, or the benefit of data-sharing (which allows costs to be shared and to avoid unnecessary testing on animals). It also means British companies will have no automatic licence to market their goods in the EU.

Andy Leyland believes that it is 'not in the UK's interests' to change the classification of the ingredients in the goods he exports, but he accepts the situation is 'unclear'. He is also aware of the risk that the UK could create an agency, or a system of classification, which gives them an inbuilt edge. 'They're going to have to come up with some things that are a competitive advantage,' he says, 'because at the moment everything is going to go against them as it's going to be very expensive to trade there. We don't think we fall into those categories. But we just don't know.'

In another Chartered Accountants Ireland scenario, an e-commerce company trades from Northern Ireland across the whole of the UK with a proportion of its sales in the Republic and in mainland Europe. The business says that even if future arrangements between the EU and the UK are tariff-free, the paperwork needed for shipments will be 'a major block to trade'. Furthermore, the company says, no consumer will want to pay import VAT when collecting their incoming parcel, even if there is no duty. The company worries that 'most legislators and commentators are too far removed from the daily practical realities of trade' to be fully aware of the significance of non-tariff barriers, such as customs controls.

The business does have direct experience of the EU single market from which Britain and Northern Ireland will be departing. It has tried hard to develop business outside the EU as well. But the costs incurred by geographical distance mean the company is far from reassured by the British government's claims that trade with the rest of the globe will easily make up for the loss of access to the single market. As a result, the e-commerce firm believes that 'the social and political isolation and confusion' of the post-Brexit era will be 'more corrosive' than any restrictions on trade.

Enterprise Ireland wants to get more Irish companies into the European market, with a plan to increase exports by 50 per cent by 2020, to the tune of €26 billion per year. 'Companies cannot afford to wait until the Brexit negotiations conclude – they must act now,' CEO Julie Sinnamon said at the launch of the initiative in May 2017. 'While diversifying from the UK might have been a desirable objective for Irish companies in the past, Brexit means that it is now an urgent imperative.'

The agency will support 600 companies, half of which are very reliant on the UK, and the other half of which already export significantly to the eurozone. The plan is to increase R&D spending to €1.25 billion per year to give sufficient added value to Irish goods in Europe. The priorities will be construction, engineering, life sciences and food, but there will also be opportunities in artificial intelligence, management, infrastructure and data centres. The target countries will be the wealthy ones: Germany, France, Italy, Belgium, the Netherlands, Spain and Finland.

Back in Gallinagh, Combilift says it wants to remain a player in the UK. 'We're not going to cut back on our UK marketing,' says Martin McVicar. 'We want to keep growing there because it's on our doorstep.' But he's having to look at things in an entirely different way. Sourcing British components makes sense now because they are cheaper, but it may not make sense if tariffs apply. So Combilift is looking to European markets for more of their components. 'It's not something you can change overnight,' says McVicar. 'It might take six months.'

But the company does see some opportunities. Combilift is a dominant player in the forklift-truck business worldwide, but what it does is *assemble*, and not *manufacture*. It will not necessarily be competing with German competitors that are part of a recognized engineering hub. 'But if I'm a mainland European forklift producer, and I'm selling product into the UK today, am I going to be bothered with the hassle of selling there in one or two years' time? UK customers are still going to need forklift trucks. If we can find a way to do business there, it would mean less competition from European producers.'

Another strategy is to beef up research and development and then charge a higher price. 'We currently put 7 per cent of our revenue into new product,' says McVicar. 'We're intending to ramp that up. We're recruiting electronic- and mechanical-design engineers. If we can develop more innovative products, then we can charge a higher premium, and by doing that counteract the export tariff.'

Overall, the corporate sector's exposure to Brexit is offset by one behemoth on the landscape. The biopharmaceuticals sector accounts for a breathtaking 60 per cent of the value of total Irish exports and 20 per cent of GDP. In 2014, those exports rose by €12.6 billion to €65 billion. The sector contributes €1 billion in corporation tax annually, and employment has grown from 5,200 in 1988 to 25,300 in 2016 (a further 24,500 people provide services to the industry). 'Brexit is not necessarily a burning concern for the sector,' says Matt Moran, director of BioPharmaChem, the IBEC group that lobbies for the sector. 'It's a global industry.'

But the very scale of the industry, and the state's dependency on it, given what it provides in tax receipts, means complacency is not an option. 'Where we're moving product through the UK there's a supply-chain issue,' Moran says. 'It's an issue, but I wouldn't say it's insurmountable. It's quite convenient to export goods through the UK at the moment, so they'll probably have to look at flying them over or going some other way. I reckon it's something they're going to have to manage. They'll try and avoid that route if they can.'

This will be possible because pharmaceuticals are light and thus easy to export by air. Furthermore, raw materials coming in from the UK, while heavy and transported in tankers, are not likely to attract a high tariff. It's only once the value has been added in Ireland that the tariffs start to rise. But will those raw materials comply with the EU's REACH directive? It will depend on what Britain invents to replace REACH and the resources of the ECHA, and on whether the British replacement is recognized by the EU. There's every chance recognition will be slow, or that over time the UK system will diverge from the EU one, or that disputes will hold things up because Britain refuses to accept the authority of the European Court of Justice.

The medical-technologies sector has different Brexit-related challenges. The industry in Ireland employs 30,000 people across 450 companies, and it hosts 18 of the top 25 global companies, including US corporates Medtronic, Boston Scientific, Abbott, Stryker, and Johnson & Johnson. The sector also produces 75 per cent of the world's orthopaedic knees, 80 per cent of stents and 33 per cent of the world's contact lenses.

Those processes are highly regulated. Each production line has to be validated, meaning that if you change a UK component (to avoid a tariff) you will have to wait a year before the replacement is validated. Another problem is that for a med-tech firm to get a product on the market it must seek approval from a notified body (the infected breast-implant scandal in France prompted EU legislation). The legislation is getting tougher, and, in order to tighten controls, the European Commission recently reduced the number of notified bodies in Europe from 80 to 65. That means fewer bodies are doing more work. But with Brexit, the six notified bodies in the UK – which are used by around a quarter of Ireland's med-tech firms – will no longer be acceptable.

Meanwhile, for Lifes2Good, the option of diversifying out of the UK market and into the European mainland has been considered – and rejected. 'We took a business decision three years ago,' says Andy Leyland, 'to focus on the English-speaking markets, such as the UK, North America, Canada and Australia.'

Part of the problem is the nature of what Leyland sells. The food supplements, for example, make strong claims based on clinical trials. Some European markets do not permit the use of these claims. 'You'd have to redesign all the packaging,' he explains, 'come up with different claims. Going into those markets, you need people on the ground. We sell mainly through pharmacies, but there are rules in Germany where you can't own more than one pharmacy. You'd also have to find a good distributor. That's a lot of work, and once you find one you need a lot of volume if you're making a German-specific product. It would take three to four years before you got your money back, and you'd have to get it right.'

This is one of the cruel ironies of Brexit. The impediments Leyland identifies are the very ones that member states like Ireland are forever criticizing at EU level. Whenever any Irish minister or Taoiseach refers to the importance of 'completing the single market', this is what they are talking about. There are still many obstacles that, according to critics, are simply forms of protectionism under the guise of health or cultural sensitivities.

Ireland is not alone in wanting those impediments removed. Denmark, Finland, the Netherlands, Poland and the Baltic states all pursue a more liberal, free-market course. Germany and France tend to be protectionist. Because Ireland needs so much support from those big countries to keep our Brexit exposure centre-stage, it cannot, according to one Irish diplomat, push too many other agendas in the meantime.

There was one member state Ireland could always rely upon to champion greater access for companies to sell their goods and services across the EU.

That member state?

The United Kingdom of Great Britain and Northern Ireland.

12. An Unpleasant Sheet of Water

A month before the official foundation of the Irish Free State, two British Home Office officials travelled to Dublin for delicate talks. Their mission was to persuade their opposite numbers that neither country should impose passport controls on the other.

Ever since the Act of Union in 1801, foreigners entering Ireland had been subject to the same immigration rules as everywhere else in the United Kingdom. In order for the status quo to continue, the new Free State would have to keep participating in the British immigration system.

The Irish officials responded with enthusiasm, 'believing that cooperation was the most effective way for the Free State to control aliens in general and "Bolshevists" in particular', according to a 2001 paper by Bernard Ryan, Professor of Immigration Law at the University of Leicester.

But it was a very sensitive issue. Questions of nationality, citizenship and identity go to the heart of how a new-born state establishes itself. During the Anglo-Irish Treaty negotiations in 1921, the Irish side had suggested the 'reciprocity of civic rights' when referring to British people living in the Free State and Irish people living in the UK; the British side suggested 'common citizenship'. The issue was not resolved.

But after the foundation of the Free State, the two sets of officials persisted. There was another meeting in December 1922, and two months later an exchange of letters. A new understanding had been reached. Both islands would become a single entity as far as immigration from outside was concerned. The Channel Islands and the Isle of Man would be included. The Free State and the United Kingdom would apply the other's rules to anyone entering from outside the British Isles. London would provide Dublin with a list of questionable individuals to be refused entry to the Free State.

British law was amended to make it clear that people who were neither Irish nor British were free to enter the UK from the Free State. The amendment also deemed the Irish Free State to be 'part of the United Kingdom' for the purposes of British aliens law. Because Irish and British people were excluded from the definition of 'aliens' on both sides of the Irish Sea, it did not just mean they could travel freely back and forth. It also meant they *automatically* had the right to reside, work and claim benefits in each other's countries.

Following the British amendment, the Irish Free State adopted its own rules. Any aliens travelling from the fledgling Northern state or from Great Britain would not be subject to restrictions, unless they had outstayed their welcome in Britain or had been excluded or deported. Essentially, if it was okay for them to be in the UK, then it was okay for them to be in Ireland.

Such free movement continued until the Second World War, when Ireland's neutrality changed the dynamic. Controls were needed because Britain wanted to prevent spies entering from Ireland, and Ireland wanted to prevent an influx of refugees.

The wartime restrictions had a side effect. From September 1939, much to the annoyance of unionists, controls were placed on anyone arriving from the *island* of Ireland (not just the Free State), and from June the following year a British travel permit was required for travel in both directions.

Those permitted to travel to Great Britain were generally allowed to do so only for employment purposes. Anyone wishing to travel from the South to the North needed an identity document and, in some cases, a residence permit. In turn, the Irish Free State placed restrictions on the arrival of non-British people at ports and airports. Irish hotels, guest houses and B&Bs were required to hand over lists of non-British and non-Irish guests to the police.

After the war, restrictions were gradually lifted. From December 1946, the Free State allowed aliens to enter from the United Kingdom. However, restrictions still applied between Northern Ireland and Great Britain – to the fury of unionists.

On 28 January 1948, in the House of Commons, the Ulster Unionist MP for South Belfast, Conolly Hugh Gage, expressed outrage to the Under-Secretary of State for the Home Department, Kenneth Younger. 'As everyone knows,' Gage fulminated, 'Ulster is as much a part of the United Kingdom as Devon or Cornwall; yet any person wanting to visit a sick child, or wanting to go on urgent business from Belfast to Liverpool, has to obtain a travel permit . . . Nor does this end the difficulty for travellers, because when they are making the journey they have all the annoyance and worry of queuing in draughty sheds on quaysides in order that immigration officials may stamp their passports before they can get to their destination . . . It would be unthinkable if someone travelling from London to Glasgow had to show a permit, and in my submission it is just as wrong that people travelling from London to Belfast should have to show it. There is no difference in the journey, except that the travellers to Belfast have the dismal task of crossing an unpleasant sheet of water.'

The reason for the restriction was that undesirables could still enter the United Kingdom across the Irish land border because the pre-war arrangements had not been reinstated. Kenneth Younger's successor, Geoffrey de Freitas, told the Commons in July 1950 that the controls that so irritated unionists could only be abolished if 'the Irish Republic would once again join with us in working a common system for the control of aliens'.

In due course that common system came about. There was another exchange of letters in early 1952. As before, both countries would refuse entry to anyone the other side regarded as undesirable, and watch lists would be shared.

The arrangement was further embedded in law when Britain introduced the Aliens Order in 1953. The Order was specifically intended to allow for the influx of Commonwealth visitors flocking to Britain for the Coronation of Queen Elizabeth. By then the Irish Free State had become a republic. Irish and British officials had neatly taken cognizance of that fact through another exchange of letters. The 1953 Aliens Order therefore deftly incorporated those letters into law. The Order also ended identity checks in draughty sheds at Belfast Port, much to the relief of unionists.

The term used to describe the new arrangements spanning the Irish Sea came into being. The Aliens Order of 1953 referred, for the first time in legislative history, to an entity called 'the common travel area'.

In the decades since the Aliens Order, the Common Travel Area (CTA) has grown in stature. The need to safeguard it is the fifth of seven principles set out in Theresa May's letter triggering Article 50, and the fourth of twelve objectives and ambitions set out in her Lancaster House speech. It appears in Paragraph 11 of the European Council's Negotiating Guidelines, and in Paragraph 14 of the European Commission's more detailed negotiating directives. Before that, protocols 19 and 20 of the Lisbon Treaty stated that EU law should not hinder the special travel arrangements between Britain and Ireland. Going back further, it is in lights in the Treaty of Amsterdam (1997), which acknowledges that, because of the CTA, Ireland and Britain could stay outside the newly agreed Schengen Area.

And yet the CTA is as flimsy a legal instrument as you're likely to find.

When the Irish government first brought it to the attention of European Commission lawyers following the Brexit vote, the Europeans were startled. 'Most Commission lawyers,' says a senior Irish official present at the meetings, 'come from a civil law background. They were expecting this thing to be set out neatly in an intergovernmental agreement.'

There is no intergovernmental agreement. The CTA is not the subject of any bilateral treaty. There is no specific law either in Ireland or in the UK exclusively devoted to its functioning. Its evolution has been surreptitious, contradictory and confusing.

In 1952, when Irish and British officials reinstated the pre-war immigration arrangements, the very *notion* of a common travel area was kept secret. In a Department of Justice memo dated February 1952, Irish officials fretted that if the public knew Dublin was handing over passenger lists, then 'objection might be raised . . . on the ground that it would not be in keeping with our position as an independent state . . . Since the proposed arrangements would be entirely informal, it would be undesirable that any publicity be given.'

No reference was made to it in the House of Commons.

In the Dáil, the Minister for Justice, Frank Aiken, suggested that, while Irish officials had been informed of the new arrangements, they were a 'matter for the British themselves'.

Throughout its existence, officials on both sides have struggled to adapt the CTA to the incongruities of history, the partition of the island, conflicting aspirations on the relationship between the two states, Ireland's wartime neutrality, the collapse of Britain's empire and the exigencies of handling colonial immigration.

From the start, both sides got off on the wrong foot. From 6 December 1922, Britain regarded the Free State as having the same legal status as Australia, New Zealand or Canada. Ireland was a dominion whose citizens were natural-born British subjects. The Free State, however, had other ideas. It created a separate citizenship principle in the 1925 Constitution, and consolidated it in the 1935 Irish Nationality and Citizenship Act (the first time Irish citizenship was ever legally underpinned). The Act distinguished Irish citizenship from British subjecthood.

Britain ignored this development. It still regarded Ireland as a dominion, as it was still part of the Commonwealth.

Critically, however, a statutory instrument in the Irish Act provided for reciprocity between Ireland and Britain. The instrument effectively would mean that, in practice, when British nationals travelled to Ireland they would be excluded from the definition of being an alien. That would mean they were not subject to the same immigration controls when they arrived in Ireland that aliens would be subject to. However, the instrument did not spell out actual *rights*.

This delightful ambiguity continued until the British Nationality Act of 1948. That Act acknowledged that those born in Ireland were no longer British subjects, since Ireland was about to become a republic and relinquish its ties with the Commonwealth. Not everyone was happy. Addressing the House of Commons on 7 July 1948, the Attorney-General, H. W. Shawcross, lamented the notion that Irish people should have their *own* citizenship. He preferred the status quo, whereby Dublin believed in such a thing as Irish citizens and London saw only British subjects. 'There is no hostile feeling between the peoples of the two countries today,' he told MPs. 'It has worked perfectly well. We impose our interpretation of the law; they impose theirs. And we have never clashed on it.'

Any change, he argued, would 'inflict a severe and unnecessary affront on the deepest feelings of a section of the population of Éire who have always stood by us in fair weather and foul, and who are proud to regard themselves as loyal subjects of the King . . . What the status of Éire nationals under this Bill is to be, heaven only knows. [They] are not aliens; they are not British subjects . . . That is why we say, "Why not let alone what has worked perfectly well for 13 years [since the 1935 Irish Nationality and Citizenship Act], and let it go on?"'

In the event, Shawcross's sentiments were taken to heart. The 1948 Nationality Act still treated Irish nationals who were in the United Kingdom as if they were British subjects. British law applied to them in the same way as it did to the local population. Irish people were not regarded as aliens, and Ireland was not regarded as a 'foreign' country.

When Ireland then became a republic, it made sense for Britain not to treat it as a foreign country. The preferential immigration rules operated by both sides would not have worked if Irish nationals were treated the same as 'aliens' and subject to the same immigration controls. Britain was also, of course, coming to depend on post-war Irish labour to rebuild shattered cities and infrastructure.

In 1949, Britain introduced the Ireland Act to bind the ambiguity into law. The Act states: 'The Republic of Ireland is *not a foreign country* for the purposes of any law in force in any part of the United Kingdom.'

In the early 1960s, a sudden influx of non-white immigrants from Britain's former colonies was starting to become a political problem. In 1962, the Conservative government of Harold Macmillan introduced the Commonwealth Immigrants Act to limit the numbers coming in. The Labour Party immediately denounced it as racist, calling the Act 'cruel and brutal anti-colour legislation'.

Wincing at the charge, the Conservative government sought, and found, a happy solution. Why not include the Irish in the legislation, and instantly dilute the charge of anti-'coloured' racism? This they duly did. And yet the ambiguity remained. While Irish nationals were technically subject to the 1962 Commonwealth Immigrants Act, they were not *actually* subject to immigration controls when arriving from Ireland, even when the Act was amended in 1971. 'It remains the position under the Immigration Act 1971,' writes Professor Ryan, 'that Irish nationals are subject to British immigration law, although entry from Ireland typically is not.'

The position of British people living in Ireland was somewhat different. In 1956, Dublin revised the 1935 Irish Nationality and Citizenship Act. It now defined a 'non-national' simply as a person who was not an Irish citizen, so a British national was regarded as just like any other person who was not Irish. However, during the transition from

Free State to Republic, a series of legal orders issued between 1949 and 1951 stated that British nationals, and those from a number of Commonwealth states (New Zealand, Australia, Southern Rhodesia, South Africa and Canada), should enjoy the same rights and privileges as Irish citizens, since Irish citizens enjoyed certain rights and privileges both in Britain and in those Commonwealth countries. Those orders were carried over by the 1956 Nationality and Citizenship Act.

Those privileges did not extend to voting in Dáil elections until 1985, however. By contrast, Irish people in Britain were always able to enjoy full political participation.

Whatever about citizenship rights, British visitors had been exempt from Irish immigration rules under the Irish Aliens Act of 1935 (separate from the Nationality and Citizenship Act). 'With minor exceptions,' notes Professor Ryan, 'British nationals have never been subject to Irish immigration law, and it has in particular never been possible to exclude or deport them from Ireland.'

Whereas the Aliens Act of 1935 exempted British nationals, and those from a number of Commonwealth states, from Irish immigration rules, Britain's own clampdown on 'coloured' visitors in their 1962 Commonwealth Immigrants Act prompted the government in Dublin, in the same year, to exclude Commonwealth nationals from the 1935 exemption altogether. The change in Irish rules came about when London raised concerns that Commonwealth visitors could get into Britain using the Republic of Ireland as a backdoor. Dublin promptly responded with two orders that meant that *only* those born in Great Britain and Northern Ireland would be exempt from Irish immigration controls.

In the Dáil, Frank Aiken acknowledged the perception

that Ireland was 'going even further than the British authorities in adopting a policy of racial discrimination'.

In 1973, when Ireland and the UK joined the EEC, the residency, travel and work rights covered by the concept of the Common Travel Area were properly articulated and set out in EU legislation. According to the Irish government's reading of it, EU rules started to *overlay* the rights enshrined in the CTA, rather than supersede them.

Things were working fine until 14 June 1985. On that date, in a small town in Luxembourg called Schengen, five members of the 10 EEC countries signed an agreement gradually to do away with border controls, fixed vehicle checks and visa requirements. The agreement became a convention in 1990, and was formally incorporated into EU law with the Treaty of Amsterdam in 1997.

Britain was determined not to join Schengen, and, because of the Common Travel Area, Ireland decided to stay out as well. (The Schengen Area today has 26 EU members and a handful of non-EU countries.) When the Lisbon Treaty was drawn up in 2009, protocols 19 and 20 allowed Britain and Ireland to stay out of Schengen and to organize their own border controls. Ireland and Britain would, in effect, have their own mini-Schengen.

Cooperation on border controls between Dublin and London deepened. Officials from the two governments would meet on a regular basis to discuss the practicalities of applying common rules. The British–Irish Visa Scheme, for example, allows for visitors from India and China to apply for one visa to enter both countries.

Data-sharing deepened. If someone from Kazakhstan was refused a visa to Britain, the chances are they would also be refused entry to Ireland. Equally, if an applicant had a positive visa history in the UK, they would probably be treated favourably by the Irish immigration authorities. 'This is a win-win from our perspective,' says a senior official from the Irish Naturalisation and Immigration Service. 'It works because we trust each other's systems and we share significant amounts of data.'

Cooperation deepened at ground level. Gardaí would set up temporary checks on the border with Northern Ireland in concert with the PSNI. If the UK Border Force set up checks on ferries leaving Britain, Irish immigration officials would do the same on ferries coming in from Holyhead. These joint operations were ad hoc, lasting for one or two days. The purpose, according to one official, was not to deny access to those entitled to free movement, but to identify those *not* entitled to free movement, 'by and large non-nationals on either side, anyone outside the European Economic Area'.

Since 2005, under Operation Gull, Gardaí, PSNI officers and UK Border Force officials have been carrying out checks on domestic flights from England to Belfast City and Belfast International airports, and on ferries from Stranraer to Larne, with a view to intercepting people trying to enter the Republic, or the UK, illegally. In 2016, some 775 people were arrested, allegedly attempting to abuse Northern Ireland ports to access the UK, an increase of 66 per cent on the previous year. That number included 73 people with criminal convictions who had previously been deported from the UK, and 30 foreign nationals with serious criminal convictions in the UK or abroad.

The Northern Ireland Law Centre has, however, been highly critical of Operation Gull, complaining that it operates with undue speed and without independent oversight.

The Immigration Law Practitioners' Association (ILPA), who gave evidence to the House of Lords European Union Select Committee hearings on Brexit, highlighted the case of a Zimbabwean engineer, legally resident in the UK, who was arrested after flying into Northern Ireland from Great Britain, and who was questioned, photographed, detained and strip-searched under Operation Gull.

How badly could Brexit disrupt the Common Travel Area?

When David Cameron announced the referendum in February 2016, a team in the Irish Department of Justice began a risk analysis. The immediate concern related to protocols 19 and 20 of the Lisbon Treaty. Would those protocols collapse if the UK left? 'Technically speaking,' says a senior official, 'if those protocols were no longer in existence, Ireland could be obliged to join Schengen.'

The other worry was what the UK government was thinking. The hot-button issue in the referendum was 'taking back control' of immigration. Brexiteers wanted out of the EU so that Poles, Romanians and Bulgarians would no longer have an automatic right to travel to, and work in, the UK. But there would be nothing stopping them coming to Ireland and crossing the border into the North. 'Would the UK feel politically obliged to restrict the CTA for their own political reasons?' wonders the official. 'Depending on the outcome, that's what could have happened.'

Contacts were made with the European Commission's legal services. They signalled that, on first glance, the Lisbon protocols *should* be able to survive Britain's departure. The political backdrop was highly relevant: the migration crisis that had gripped the EU from 2014 to 2016 had placed unbearable strain on the border-free Schengen zone, especially its Greek frontier, through which at least a million refugees and asylum seekers had travelled. The notion that, in such a climate, Ireland might somehow be obliged to join Schengen was remote. 'We felt politically,' says an Irish official, 'that no one was going to be looking to expand Schengen when they were looking at kicking Greece *out* of it.'

But there was still the question of the UK's intentions. Perhaps the very first meeting between Irish and British officials following the 23 June referendum was one between the Department of Justice and the Home Office. It took place within days of the referendum. 'Despite what was said during the campaign [about taking back control],' says an Irish source present at the meeting, 'the British immediately assured us they wanted to maintain the CTA.'

Squaring the pitch with London was one thing. Dublin would also have to ensure that the CTA did not fall foul of the other 26 member states. It was doubly sensitive. The CTA didn't just involve border controls and the movement of people. It also provided for reciprocal work, welfare and pension rights for citizens of both countries. Would those arrangements discriminate against other EU citizens post-Brexit?

The Brexit unit in the Department of Justice went through all the EU legislation that might be relevant, with a similar trawl being carried out by other government departments. 'There didn't *seem* to be a conflict between the CTA and EU law,' says one official. 'We would be applying it to what would become third-country [i.e. British] nationals. It wouldn't therefore prejudice the rights of EU citizens.'

It would remain to be seen what the Polish, Bulgarian and Romanian governments thought about it. Post-Brexit, Irish citizens would, in theory, be automatically entitled to work, live and receive benefits in the UK – but their citizens, also from the EU, might not.

In any event, the Irish government began preparing a case that there was no conflict. The objective was, at all costs, to avoid the CTA being drawn into the Article 50 negotiations. The issue was first raised with Michel Barnier during his meeting in Dublin on 12 October 2016. A team of Irish officials then travelled to Brussels to meet the Commission's Task Force in Room 201 on 23 November, and again on 16 December. It was a delicate issue, but an important one. 'Keeping it out of the negotiations would be a major plus for us,' says one official. 'Because it would just have been Ireland and Britain, keeping the Commission informed, rather than having another 26 member states trying to decide what the relationship between Ireland and Britain should be.'

By March 2017, the government was ready to make a formal pitch.

A confidential Irish paper was submitted to the European Commission. It was essentially a history lesson, itemizing all of the acts, orders and understandings that Britain and Ireland had laboriously engineered since 1922 in order to facilitate a system allowing for passport-free travel, as well as for reciprocal work, residency and welfare benefits.

The Europe Commission *appeared* reassured that the CTA was not in conflict with EU law. But some hard questions were asked. The Commission wanted to be sure Ireland would not restrict the rights of EU citizens to travel to Ireland simply to keep them out of Britain. A number of member states also wanted to make sure that service providers from Britain would not use the CTA as a backdoor into the single market.

On the first point, Irish officials insisted there would be

no restriction on EU citizens. 'We said no,' says an official who was present. 'They have a right to come here. We won't stop them. But we will cooperate with the UK.'

On the second issue, the Irish team acknowledged that any British service providers *could* come and work in Ireland, but if they did – be they a doctor, a lawyer, a dentist – they would still be complying with Irish law, which in turn complies with the rules of the single market.

Irish officials admit, though, that the impact of Brexit on who is, or is not, allowed into Ireland will be devilishly complicated.

Ireland will effectively have to operate two parallel freedom-of-movement regimes – the European Union system and the Common Travel Area. One scenario posed by an Irish diplomat in the weeks immediately following the referendum was as follows: post-Brexit, Britain has ended free movement of people from the EU. A Bulgarian travels to Britain on a tourist visa, but then starts working on a fruit farm. The Bulgarian is caught by British immigration officials and then deported. What if that Bulgarian then flies to Dublin, asserting his EU free-movement rights? Will Ireland be entitled to deport him because he is on a British watch list? Or, if not, will he be able to cross the land border and re-enter Britain that way?

The same conundrum was posed to a senior Irish immigration official. If a Bulgarian was kicked out of the UK after working on a strawberry farm, would that be sufficient grounds to put him on a watch list? 'I doubt it,' was the reply.

However, Irish officials are working on the assumption that Britain will not control immigration from the EU at its *borders*, at Dover or Heathrow. 'Our belief,' says the official, 'is that they will do it through in-country measures. In other words, Eastern Europeans will not be able to access services. They won't have the right to work. If that assumption applies, the Common Travel Area should operate pretty much as it currently does.'

In other words, life will be so restrictive for EU citizens who try to travel to the UK to reside and work there that it will not be worth their while using Ireland as a backdoor.

The Common Travel Area survived the conflict in Northern Ireland. It survived the British Prevention of Terrorism Acts of 1974 and 1989, and the Terrorism Act of 2000, all of which provided for border and port controls on entry to Great Britain and Northern Ireland. It was safeguarded in the 2009 UK Borders, Citizenship and Immigration Act. Taking the long view, the Common Travel Area looks like it will survive yet another jolt of history.

Both the British and Irish governments want it to continue, not least for tourism reasons. Great Britain accounts for 47 per cent of all overseas visitors to Ireland and 30 per cent of tourism spend. In 2015, there were 4.5 million British visitors, up 10 per cent on 2014, while the Dublin–London air route is the second busiest in the world. Furthermore, Irish people in the UK have a vote in parliamentary elections, so they represent a political force that cannot be ignored, and one with a strong opinion on the CTA. The arrangement seems to be accepted as a cultural norm by the British public. As an Irish official elegantly puts it: 'The average English person doesn't regard the average Irish person as foreign, in the way that they regard the average French person as foreign.'

The European Commission appears to have accepted that the CTA does not discriminate against other EU citizens.

Other member states appear to accept it will not allow British service providers to undermine the single market, although this may be subject to a stronger stress-test during the negotiations. Irish and British immigration officials believe that the high degree of cooperation at ground level will allow the twin freedom of movement regimes to continue.

Is it a settled issue?

'It's ... *almost* a settled issue,' says a senior Irish Department of Justice official. 'There is a grey area.'

The grey area is that the British government is hedging. The status of EU nationals living in the UK, and UK nationals living in the rest of Europe, will be one of the first, and most sensitive, of the issues in the divorce negotiations. The EU wants European residents of the UK to have their 'acquired rights' fully, and legally, protected by the European Court of Justice. They want those rights (the right to work, reside, access health and welfare benefits) to extend to family members, and to extend for life. On 26 June 2017 the British Home Office issued its opening position with a paper entitled 'Safeguarding the Position of EU Citizens Living in the UK and UK Nationals Living in the EU'. It envisaged EU citizens being allowed to apply for 'settled status' once they had lived in the UK for five years. The paper ruled out any role for the European Court of Justice in protecting those rights. The paper made it clear that the offer was 'without prejudice to Common Travel Area arrangements between the UK and Ireland' and to the rights enshrined in the Ireland Act 1949, which essentially provided for reciprocal rights of residency, employment, healthcare and social-welfare access. 'Irish citizens residing in the UK will not need to apply for settled status to protect their entitlements.'

The view of the Irish government is that the British are holding out on fully declaring their intentions on the Common Travel Area until London sees where the other negotiations are heading. 'What they've been reluctant to do is to clarify exactly what they regard as the rights Irish people would have under the CTA,' says an Irish official. 'What's likely to happen is that they'll kick to touch until the negotiations on what rights EU citizens in the UK will have after Brexit. They're holding that in reserve.'

But the rhetoric is still friendly.

The CTA is an arrangement that long predates EU membership and reflects a cultural affinity that has outlived bitter and violent enmity. It is, the argument goes, a private arrangement between old friends with which the EU need not concern itself.

The reality, however, is somewhat more nuanced.

'The peculiarities of the Irish border,' wrote Professor Bernard Ryan in 2001, 'have been the primary reason for the absence of immigration control. This is partly because of the physical difficulty of immigration control on the Irish border, given that it is 280 miles long, does not follow natural boundaries and cuts across some 180 roads.'

Simply put, Britain maintaining immigration controls on the land border has been unthinkable.

During a debate on the Commonwealth Immigrants Act on 16 November 1961, the British Home Secretary, Rab Butler, told the House of Commons that 'all experience and information indicates how very difficult it is to police the Republic–Ulster border and prevent people getting across it either by day, or, especially, by night. We are, therefore, forced to the conclusion . . . that if we are to operate a control against the citizens of the Irish Republic we should have to institute a control within the United Kingdom itself [i.e. at Northern Ireland ports and airports]. The government takes the view that that would be an intolerable imposition upon British citizens.'

Even during the worst year of the Troubles, 1971, the Under-Secretary of State at the Foreign and Commonwealth Office, Anthony Kershaw, told the House of Commons: 'If we were to try to enforce the inviolability of the land frontier as a military operation it simply would not be on.'

The impossibility of maintaining controls on such a land border still holds true. But this time it is not just British ministers who are invited to look at the prospect and shake their heads.

Now it falls to the European Union, its institutions and 26 other member states to look at the Irish border and figure out what to do with it.

13. Old Habits of Wariness

'Pain wouldn't describe it,' says Donie Cronin. 'This was something I never had experienced before. It was absolutely *excruciating* in the chest. I wasn't able to use my two arms because of the extreme pain.'

It was Saturday, 8 October 2016. Donie Cronin, a 70-year-old security guard living in Newtowncunningham, County Donegal, a few miles from the border, was having a heart attack. Letterkenny Hospital was 10 minutes away. His wife and son drove him there immediately, but staff realized he needed special treatment, so Donie was taken by ambulance to Altnagelvin Hospital in Derry. A consultant discovered a 95 per cent blockage in one of Donie's arteries. He was given an angiogram and stents were inserted. 'In all of the conscious moments,' recalls Donie, 'I felt very well looked after, because I knew you had two very good teams cooperating and deciding what to do.'

The nearest acute service south of the border was Galway or Dublin. 'The cardiologist said I would not have survived road transport to either place,' says Donie.

Three months later, the European Union announced €47.5 million in funding for cross-border health projects. It was part of the EU's overall cohesion policy, which promotes cooperation that is transnational and interregional. The idea behind Interreg funds, as they have become known, is that the single market cannot function properly if there are disadvantaged regions throughout its area of operation. Between

1991 and 2020, some €822 million in funding has been disbursed (or pledged) over five separate programmes for the border area in Ireland.

The announcement covered a range of initiatives. There was funding for counselling services for people affected by sight loss, a trial on healthcare intervention for people living outside major population centres, a project to support greater independence for ageing populations through e-health technologies, and new services for children with Attention Deficit Hyperactivity Disorder (ADHD).

The scale of the activity suggested a highly developed sphere of cross-border healthcare activity in Ireland. But this was a relatively new phenomenon. And it has been broadly enabled by European money.

Those future funding streams are now at risk.

'Border populations suffer from a double peripherality,' says Tom Daly, of the Irish Health Service Executive, and Director General of Cooperation and Working Together (CAWT). 'They're back to back against each other, and very often quite a bit away from the big cities.'

That double peripherality is particularly acute in health. Occasionally in the 1980s, orthopaedic patients in the north-west would have been referred to Belfast for treatment, then sent back to Lifford Hospital to recuperate. But there was no formal cooperation or even contact.

However, in 1992, the chairpersons of four health boards and seven trusts covering Derry, Donegal, Armagh and Cavan got together in Ballyconnell, County Cavan, to deepen health cooperation along the entire border. CAWT was born.

Research was carried out. There were exchanges between

management teams. But it was not until the mid 1990s that the initiative was given oxygen. In 1995, the first EU funding under the so-called PEACE programme was made available. CAWT secured money to conduct three health-research projects. As the prospect for further funding became more widely appreciated, both Dublin and Belfast began to factor in European money when drawing up national development plans.

In one early project, a team from the University of Ulster found that along the border corridor, 70,000 people could get quicker access to a GP out of hours by crossing the border (from either side) than they could in their own jurisdiction. A pilot project was carried out in the Castleblayney/South Armagh and Derry/East Buncrana areas. CAWT was able to prove that the concept worked. 'Absolutely none of that would have happened without European funding, either PEACE or Interreg,' says Daly.

European money became more accessible. In the 2000s, some €30 million was made available for a suite of projects from mental health to intellectual disability, to children's and acute services. Up to 50,000 people benefited.

The concept was changing the way governments looked at health. In January 2009, an interdepartmental group drew up an all-island health strategy. Some observers in the Republic were suspicious that unionist ministers were dragging their feet. But eventually a study was published with 37 recommendations for cross-border cooperation.

Some of those recommendations have borne fruit. CAWT had prioritized radiotherapy services in the north-west and, in November 2016, a £50 million service finally opened in Altnagelvin (the Irish government contributed €20 million in capital funding). The impact on Donegal cannot be overstated: 10 years previously, young mothers with cancer often decided against radiotherapy because they did not want to leave their children behind for six weeks while they went to Dublin for treatment.

Our Lady's Hospital in Crumlin now takes up to 800 paediatric congenital heart patients each year from across the island. In Altnagelvin, the cardiology service used by Donie Cronin actually saved the lives of 26 others from the South in the first nine months of operation. Ambulances in north Leitrim and north Sligo, as well as in Donegal, have been re-equipped so that electrocardiograms (ECGs) can be transferred by paramedics and immediately read by staff in Altnagelvin.

Renal dialysis services in South Down are linked up to the north Monaghan area, as are ophthalmology, ENT, vascular treatment, and oral and maxillofacial services. Prior to that, patients in Cavan and Monaghan had to go to Dublin for an ENT service, with children sometimes having to wait four years for their first appointment. Thanks to an EU funding round of €9 million, two extra staff were appointed to the highly regarded ENT service in the Northern Ireland Southern Trust. That meant a team of six rotating into Monaghan General Hospital, where they did out-patient and day cases. Patients could still cross the border for more complex services, to Craigavon and Daisy Hill in Newry.

Not all cross-border health cooperation is funded by PEACE or Interreg money, but it was instrumental in getting it going. And shared EU membership made cooperation far more straight forward than it would otherwise have been. Today, Belfast surgeons work two days a week in Our Lady's Hospital in Crumlin. The new paediatric hospital in Dublin has been categorized as all-Ireland, with outreach centres in Cork, Galway and Derry.

The Brexit vote was naturally greeted with shock by many in the sector.

'My first thought,' says Daly, 'was what is this actually going to do to the psychology in the public sector in terms of the collaborative work we have been doing over the years? How can we continue to have strong partnerships? They are never more needed than they are now, whether it's inter-agency or interdepartmental. What does it mean for the radiotherapy service in Derry? It is clearly likely to add some more barriers to what existed.'

Ruth Taillon, Director with the Centre for Cross Border Studies, has warned that Brexit could reinstate the border as a cognitive barrier. 'There is a huge danger from all the things that make the border a barrier in the first place,' she told the Joint Oireachtas Committee on Arts, Heritage, Regional, Rural and Gaeltacht Affairs, 'and the problems that has created over time with regard to people turning away from the border. Centralization in Belfast and Dublin is going to be exacerbated.'

Susan McKay, a Northern Ireland native who now runs the Glens Centre, a small community arts centre in Manor-hamilton, County Leitrim, described to the same committee the mental and physical toll that Brexit might now inflict. 'Old habits of wariness still exist in both communities in the North and both communities in the Republic,' she said. 'Manorhamilton, for example, is a town with a significant Protestant minority. We are facing a situation where there may be polarization and a reversion to separatist outlooks, neither of which are helpful to the peace process. We may be facing into a period which will lay waste carefully nurtured relationships as well as risking a massive waste of the many

EU, American, Irish and British funds that have gone into trying to nurture cross-border relationships in a constructive way. Manorhamilton is a very poor town. There are a lot of ruins, a lot of failed businesses, a lot of subsistence and a lot of emigration. One sees schoolchildren in the town but one does not see young people in the 20-to-30 age-group because they have simply gone and not come back.'

Between 2014 and 2020, some €550 million has been earmarked for cross-border programmes under Interreg and PEACE. Beyond that, their future is uncertain. Shane Campbell, CEO of the Irish Central Border Area Network (ICBAN), told the House of Lords Select Committee on Brexit that ICBAN was involved in 14 cross-border projects, to the value of €114 million. 'A lot have been approved,' he said, 'but they are not starting yet because the letters of offer have not been released on the cross-border programmes. Mostly it is because of Irish concerns in terms of what will happen in the middle of these programmes if the UK leaves.'

It is estimated that between 20,000 and 30,000 people commute across the border every day. In its statement to the Oireachtas Committee, the Centre for Cross Border Studies concluded that they will 'inevitably experience significant change in the environment for cooperation and mobility' due to customs controls, and the potential for an increase in both smuggling and other forms of organized crime.

Another concern is mobile-phone roaming charges. In 2015, the European Parliament and the Council of Ministers agreed to end roaming surcharges by June 2017. According to a source in the Irish communications regulator ComReg: 'It may be that the UK after Brexit decides not to continue with those roaming arrangements. That would have heavy implications for people who are travelling to the UK and for people calling the UK. Those are going to end up increasing costs.'

Cross-border social-welfare and pension entitlements are also a source of anxiety. As we have seen, the Common Travel Area provides for reciprocal rights between both countries. If you have contributed during your working life either to the British or the Irish pension systems, and you retire in either Ireland or the UK, each side will recognize the contributions made in the other system. This is not an insignificant issue: the Department of Social Protection reports that 135,070 people in Ireland are in receipt of a UK pension, and 34,238 people resident in the UK are in receipt of an Irish pension.

Social-welfare arrangements cover both contributory and means-tested assistance payments. This is a complex area. Irish payments cover child benefit, domiciliary-care allowance, family-income supplements, back-to-work family dividends, the one-parent-family payment and the non-contributory guardian's payment. The two governments will have to reach agreement on whether these payments can be exported both ways after Brexit. The authorities are also having to work out the aggregation of periods of social insurance completed in Ireland or the UK that will allow applicants to qualify for Irish unemployment or UK jobseeker's benefit.

Beyond that, there is a thicket of complexities facing officials in the Department of Social Protection in Dublin and the Department of Work and Pensions in London. These departments handle old-age and survivors' benefits, such as the contributory state pension, the contributory widow's and widower's pensions, the surviving civil partner's pension and the contributory guardian's payment. They also handle benefits relating to invalidity, partial capacity, illness, maternity, and health and safety, as well as the adoptive and carer's benefits and the health-treatment benefit.

Can the use of UK social-security contributions satisfy PRSI contribution conditions in Ireland? What happens with employees of Irish companies who have a designated home base in the UK? Will the payment of an Irish carer's benefit to people living in the UK continue?

Some of the existing rules relate to the Common Travel Area, and others are governed by EU legislation. Disentangling these things is daunting. Border People, an EU-funded one-stop project that collates citizens'-advice expertise from both sides of the border, has been struggling to cope with enquiries since the referendum. While some come from cross-border workers who fear they will no longer be entitled to work, many more are from people concerned about benefits.

'At the moment most of the benefits would be exportable home,' says Annmarie O'Kane, who manages the project. 'But they're wondering down the line, what if years of contributions go up in smoke? Or if they'll end up with no old-age pension or illness benefit.'

The Border People project is trying to work out the complexity, and is urging applicants to prepare for an unhappy outcome as the negotiations unfold.

'What we're trying to look at on a higher policy level,' says O'Kane, 'is: where do the CTA rights and entitlements begin and end? They're blended in over the years with EU rights and entitlements. We know we have these entitlements, but where do they actually come from? A lot of them originate with the CTA, but the majority of them are grounded in EU law. We can go to a directive or a regulation and that will stipulate which country is responsible for meeting people's social-security needs. But there's nothing really laid down in legislation that we can find in the CTA that secures x, y and z. There's no CTA Act. People assume that the rights under the CTA will continue. We would say, "Assume nothing until everything is signed."'

For those who are neither Irish nor British citizens, and who live and work on different sides of the Irish border, the prospects are particularly uncertain. Unlike citizens of Ireland and the UK, they are not protected by the provisions of the Common Travel Area. Under EU rules, such people are regarded as 'frontier workers'. That means they enjoy certain rights, such as access to medical services – including the right to a medical card – on the side of the border where they work. There are similar rights regarding social-welfare and pension payments.

When Britain leaves the EU, those rights will fall. That would mean that, for example, Lithuanian lorry drivers or mushroom harvesters who live in the North and work in the South (or vice versa) will no longer be regarded as frontier workers protected by EU rights. It is understood, however, that their particular situation will be looked at during the two-year withdrawal negotiations. Any fix, according to one EU legal source, will need to ensure that other EU citizens who might be considered cross-border workers, e.g. a French banker who takes the Eurostar every Monday and Friday to work in the City, is not discriminated against if the same deal isn't available for everyone who is regarded as a cross-border worker.

On 14 July 2009, the Police Service of Northern Ireland was called to the scene of an accident on the Sligo Road, in Enniskillen. The front-seat passenger had suffered 75 per cent burns to his upper body and would remain in a coma for a month. A man was arrested at the scene. He was charged with being over the drink-driving limit, having no insurance and causing grievous bodily injury. The following day he was remanded at Enniskillen Magistrates' Court and two days later granted High Court bail. When his court appearance came around on 8 February 2010, the man failed to show up. It turned out he had fled to Lucan, County Dublin. A European Arrest Warrant (EAW) was issued, and he was arrested on 30 July 2013 by Gardaí and extradited to the North. On 3 January 2014, he was convicted on all charges.

The above case was one of five brought to the attention of the House of Lords Select Committee by the PSNI in order to register the force's grave concerns about Brexit. Once Britain leaves the EU, there is a strong possibility it will also leave the EAW network, which is currently the only legal extradition instrument between the two countries. The PSNI's biggest worry is that terrorism, organized crime and regular offences will flourish within the Common Travel Area if there is nothing to replace the EAW. Since 2004, some 12,000 people have been arrested in the UK under EAWs. 'That's 12,000 dangerous and violent and highly criminal individuals living in our society,' says the PSNI's Assistant Chief Constable Stephen Martin. 'An inability to extradite those individuals creates risks for the UK.'

Between 2010 and 2015, 168 people were arrested under EAWs in the Republic for extradition back to the UK. 'These are dangerous individuals,' says Detective Chief Superintendent Hugh Hume. 'They are wanted for serious crimes, and they may live literally metres away from their victims, just across a line from where they committed this crime.'

The PSNI is worried at the prospect of dozens of new agreements having to be negotiated. 'We can remember the bilateral European arrest warrants,' says one senior PSNI source. 'They were plagued with politics. Plagued with emotion. With extradition between Northern Ireland and the Republic, the EAW has been fantastic in terms of taking it to a European level, and away from a British–Irish context. In doing so, it has made the extradition of the most dangerous people a very seamless process.'

Both the PSNI and the Garda Síochána make use of the Prüm Convention, an instant-access exchange of DNA, fingerprint and vehicle registration records. They also make significant, though not comprehensive, use of the Schengen Information System (SIS II), a centralized database used for law enforcement, immigration and border controls. SIS II contains over 63 million alerts on people and objects wanted by police, and gives live-time access to all wanted or missing persons, stolen vehicles, bail-jumpers, foreign fighters and travelling sex offenders.

The PSNI privately believes that the British government wants to remain in the EAW and Europol, the agency that handles cooperation between police forces. But it is questionable how far the EU will be willing to go to facilitate this. The deal-breaker may come when a dispute arises. If someone believes they have been wrongfully extradited, or their homes wrongfully searched, or if a member state believes their request for assistance has not been met, they can appeal to the European Court of Justice – but the UK has vowed not to be bound by the Luxembourg court.

'It's in our interests to be able to work as closely and efficiently with the UK as possible,' says one Irish source in the criminal-justice field, 'and to be able to exchange as much information about terrorism and security matters. There should be a certain amount of constructive negotiations in this area. But the ECJ issue has to be addressed, because there has to be some form of dispute resolution.'

The EAW is a particularly relevant instrument in combatting child trafficking. 'If you know the UK is out of the EAW,' warns Tanya Ward, Chief Executive of the Children's Rights Alliance, 'I'd be going to the UK [as a trafficker]. If the UK is out of the EAW, it will have to negotiate bilateral agreements with all the other EU countries, either individually or with the EU as a whole.'

The ramifications are equally problematic in civil law. EU rules simplify the acceptance of public documents in the civil sphere for those crossing an EU border to work, live, get married, set up a company and so on. Under current EU rules, a mother can go to court in Ireland to secure a child-maintenance order against a person living in the UK. The maintenance order is automatically recognized by the UK courts. As long as the receiving court is satisfied it's an authentic order, they can take action, and will not question the reasons behind the Irish judgement.

After Brexit, this will no longer be the case. An Irish applicant will have to go through the UK courts from scratch.

One night in Derry in the late 1980s, a young woman lay in wait on the side of the road. She was part of an IRA team poised to ambush eight British soldiers and two RUC police officers with a roadside bomb. She was 21 years old.

Anne Walker's journey was both highly unorthodox and entirely in keeping with a conflict shaped by brutal circumstance. She was born in Wales in 1969, where her Derry-born father had been posted with the RAF. When Anne was three, her father received another posting, this time to Hong Kong. However, a life of wandering around Britain's former colonies was thwarted by violence. On 30 January 1972, Anne's uncle, Michael McDaid, was shot in the face at a barricade on Bloody Sunday, his body tossed into the back of a Saracen. He was 20 years old.

'When we found out, we immediately moved back from Wales,' Anne recalls. 'The whole course of my life changed at three.'

Anne was the elder of two sisters, quickly coming of age in the charged atmosphere of the Bogside. She was quiet, but what she lacked in confidence she made up for in righteous zeal. Life was a balancing act between the public routine of school and a private sense of injustice at the killing of her uncle. Long before the Saville Enquiry exonerated Michael, Anne's family was marked as republican, subject to harassment, raids and arrests. Anne lived through the hunger strikes and attended as many of the funerals as she could.

When she turned 18 she was approached by the IRA. 'I jumped at the chance,' says Anne. 'I had the notion they were our heroes, our protectors, our saviours. They were the only ones doing anything.'

Anne was sworn in, rising to the rank of Quartermaster. Several months later she found herself on active service, on the night of the ambush. What happened that night would transform a life that had already experienced no small amount of upheaval. It was also as surreal as any episode in an increasingly macabre conflict.

As she lay in wait by the roadside, Anne was hit by a sudden, blinding pain. 'It felt like a hammer blow to the back of the head,' she recalls.

An informer had tipped off the security services. But the sudden blow had nothing to do with gunfire.

Anne was, in fact, having a brain haemorrhage.

On 24 October 1990, another IRA operation took place in Derry. This time the modus operandi was more sophisticated. Patsy Gillespie was a Catholic, a 42-year-old cook who had worked in the Fort George British Army base. He had been warned several times by the IRA against serving there. On the night in question, his family was held at gunpoint and Gillespie was driven to a rural location where he was forced into a van packed with 1,000 pounds of explosives. Under orders, he drove the short distance to the British Army checkpoint at Coshquin. As he tried to jump out, the bomb exploded. He and five British soldiers were killed. So fierce was the blast that there was virtually nothing left of any of them.

At Gillespie's funeral mass, the Bishop of Derry, Edward Daly, described the attack as 'satanic'.

Patsy Gillespie's wife, Kathleen, spent years grieving for her husband. When the Deputy First Minister, Martin McGuinness, died in March 2017, Kathleen Gillespie, who, like many others, had held McGuinness ultimately responsible for the killing as he was the presumed commander of the IRA in Derry, told BBC Northern Ireland: 'There's no forgiveness in my heart . . . I don't feel any better because Martin McGuinness is dead. I feel sad for his wife. If she loved him as much as I loved Patsy, then I give her my condolences because I know what's missing.'

Anne Walker also spent years coming to terms with her own experience of violence.

She remained conscious after the haemorrhage struck on

the night of the ambush. 'The fellow I was with realized that something was wrong and he told me to go home, but I wouldn't,' she recalls. 'I said, "I'm not leaving." I stayed until I started spewing my guts up.'

Anne eventually went home, but her parents called the doctor, who suspected meningitis. The next morning she was taken to hospital. Doctors discovered a brain haemorrhage and a blood clot. A week later, Anne suffered a bigger haemorrhage and was rushed back to hospital for surgery. When she was finally arrested and interrogated a few weeks later, she was still shaven-headed, with a prominent scar across the back of her skull. Her lawyer argued she was in a vulnerable state and should be released without charge.

Suffering memory loss and finding herself estranged from the republican movement, Anne left Derry for Limerick in 1993, returning in 2001 with a one-year-old son. 'I was carrying all this pain but trying to act as normal as possible,' she says. 'I was starting to question what I was doing. Was it the right thing? I had this romantic idea of a United Ireland and what the fight would be, but the reality was something different.'

In 2008, an avant-garde playwright from Philadelphia called Teya Sepinuck travelled to Derry at the invitation of the Playhouse Theatre.

Sepinuck had forged a career in the United States by taking real-life testimonies from individuals mired in suffering, and creating cathartic stage performances involving the survivors themselves. Through her Theatre of Witness project, Sepinuck had worked with perpetrators and victims of child abuse, child killers and mothers of children who had been murdered, prisoners and victims of crime.

Sepinuck's first production in Northern Ireland, *We Carried Your Secrets*, was written around fathers who were caught up in the conflict through membership of the RUC, the UDA or the IRA. Participants were introduced to each other and would articulate their memories and feelings. The testimonies would then be synthesized into a stage performance. The production was a revelation. 'We had full houses everywhere we went,' she recalls. 'People were crying in their seats, saying things like, this is heart surgery on the city of Derry.'

One former RUC forensics officer who took part had, it turned out, attended at the scene of the Coshquin bombing. After one performance, Kathleen Gillespie approached him to ask what was left of Patsy's remains. So intense was the blast that there was little left of those killed, but she hoped the officer might be able to tell her at least how much of her husband's remains he could salvage to place in the coffin. She also asked Sepinuck if she could participate in a follow-up production.

Anne Walker, meanwhile, was undergoing counselling when she heard about Sepinuck's project. The second Derry production, *I Once Knew a Girl*, opened on 21 October 2010 in the Playhouse. It focused almost exclusively on women: a serving police officer, a Paisley supporter from Enniskillen, a loyalist from the Shankill Road whose family had burned out the home of a Catholic woman, and the woman whose home had been burned out. But Anne and Kathleen were at the centre of the piece. 'You can imagine what it was like, for them, for me, being in the same room,' recalls Anne. 'We had to make sure we could work together, to get to know each other. If Kathleen felt she couldn't work with me, then I wouldn't have been able to be in the production. But she was the first to accept me. After she heard my story, she put her arm around me and gave me a big hug. She says: "Don't worry, we're going to be okay."'

What made it all possible, however, was a grant from the European Union.

The European role in Northern Ireland has been a rare example of win-win, rather than zero-sum.

In 1995, one year after the IRA ceasefire, three leading Northern politicians – Ian Paisley, the DUP leader, John Hume, of the SDLP, and Jim Nicholson, of the UUP – lobbied jointly, as MEPs in Brussels and Strasbourg, for Europe to play a greater role in underpinning the peace process. The idea was taken up enthusiastically by Monika Wulf-Mathies, the Regional Affairs Commissioner. She insisted that all funding would have to go to cross-community projects.

The result was the Peace Programme for Northern Ireland and the Border Counties, known simply as PEACE. The first programme, PEACE I, ran from 1995 to 1999. It was worth €500 million, with an extra €167 million coming from the two governments. The most recent programme, PEACE IV, will run from 2014 to 2020, and it will have €229 million from the EU and €41 million from national contributions.

After a gruelling application process, Teya Sepinuck was granted €1 million to carry out her Theatre of Witness projects. 'If we didn't know about that grant, there was no way we would have thought about doing this project,' she says. 'Where would they have gotten the money? Nobody had that kind of money.'

The funds are disbursed by the Special EU Programmes Body (SEUPB), set up under the Good Friday Agreement to channel EU funds of a cross-border, regional or peace-process nature. Because it was not American money – which tended to be seen as favouring the nationalist community – there was greater buy-in from the unionist side. 'One of the things that worked was the fact the money was EU, viewed as neutral money,' says an SEUPB source. 'The man in the street didn't have a clue that there was Northern Ireland or UK or Irish government money within the programme. They just saw it as EU money, so people on both sides were much more open to it.'

By 2013, the PEACE programme had supported 1,800 events relating to victims and survivors, and 2,000 work-shops on conflict resolution. In all, some 5,000 people received trauma counselling. As well as Theatre of Witness, the SEUPB supported Skainos Project, a new square in an interface part of East Belfast with an emphasis on a 'shared space' in which loyalists, republicans and immigrants could feel comfortable. There was a similar project in the People's Park in Portadown. The most iconic project was the £14.7 million Peace Bridge, a swerving foot-and-cycle bridge that links the Ebrington Barracks site in the Protestant Waterside area of Derry with the historic and commercial heart of the city, which had always been regarded as a more nationalist space.

When the bridge was officially opened in June 2011 by Johannes Hahn, the EU's Regional Affairs Commissioner, he asked the Theatre of Witness team to be present at the dedication. One of the participants, a former UDA member, spoke, describing himself as a grandfather, a father and a peacemaker, but also as a former terrorist who had tormented his community. Hahn was so moved, according to Sepinuck, that he invited Theatre of Witness to perform in Brussels.

The Irish PEACE programmes are now being presented in conflict zones across the world as best practice. Commission officials who have worked closely on the Northern Ireland peace money have given presentations in Colombia and elsewhere on how PEACE and Interreg funding have helped the process in Northern Ireland. 'These ideas worked. Other countries look at them as an example of what might be possible,' says one official. 'It may well be these programmes become more popular outside the EU than inside.'

Europe's commitment went a stage further in 2007, when Commission President José Manuel Barroso created the Northern Ireland Task Force as a way to support the Executive, which had just been re-established following the St Andrews Agreement. The Task Force brought together 18 departments within the Commission to help the North's economy shift away from a heavy dependence on the public sector. Competitiveness would be boosted through research, education and innovation across a range of sectors. The Executive set up an interdepartmental working group to implement the Commission's recommendations. An official from the regional affairs directorate-general was seconded to the Executive, while desk officers from Stormont were seconded to the Commission, and to the UK and Irish Permanent Representations in Brussels.

For Anne Walker, her involvement in Theatre of Witness was transformative. Encountering Kathleen Gillespie and other victims/perpetrators was gruelling. 'Then all of a sudden we're on stage, and the reaction from the audiences was absolutely incredible,' she recalls.

Anne and Kathleen continued their collaboration. They performed at schools and for women's groups. They collaborated with survivors of the 7 July terror attacks in London, victims of the conflict in Yemen, and those caught up in the Bataclan terror attack in Paris. There was also the Tim Parry–Johnathan Ball Foundation for Peace, set up by the parents of the two boys murdered in the IRA bomb attack in Warrington in 1995.

'I was in Derry watching the TV the night of the referendum,' says Anne. 'I thought, "Oh God, no!" The next day I phoned the Warrington Peace Centre and I said, "How is this going to affect what you do?" Not just for my sake. They work with people in England affected by the Troubles. If it affects them, it affects me. Because I am now part of that.'

Another perspective comes from Ken Funston. A former RUC officer originally from Pettigo, which straddles counties Donegal and Fermanagh, his brother Ronnie was shot dead by the IRA on 13 March 1984. After the murder, Ronnie's killers fled across the border. Funston reflects that the debate over whether the border should be hard or soft misses the point. There never was, nor could there ever be, a properly sealed border, he says. 'A lot of people in border areas have still very bitter thoughts over what went on over the years,' he says, 'and how the Irish government never gave any help to the British to quell the campaign of violence and to prevent a free run for terrorists. The border was never a safety line. There are a lot of unionists who will look at that again and ask, "Would I rather be part of the UK as an independent state, or part of a United Ireland?" And I think the status quo must be maintained for them.'

Brexit has forced these issues back on to the matrix of sectarian politics. For Denis Bradley, the former Vice-Chairman of the Northern Ireland Policing Board and a Co-Chairman of the Consultative Group on the Past, Brexit provides an opportunity. 'It forces us,' he says, 'into a wider debate and a wider consensus about the archipelago which is England, Northern Ireland, Scotland, Wales and Ireland. We have been left to our own devices in the North. It's a really small, petty, inward-looking kind of conflict. But it is best resolved when you widen it out. We are going to be forced, and ultimately politics will be forced, into some kind of consensual understanding of these islands. How that works itself out is far from clear, and I don't think it's going to be clear for a number of years.'

On 23 June 2016, some 55.7 per cent of people in Northern Ireland voted to remain in the EU, against 44.3 per cent who voted to leave. It was, of course, not enough to overcome the Leave vote in the rest of the UK.

The result has upset a fragile constitutional balance. Nationalists worry that their rights under the Good Friday Agreement have been taken away against their will; unionists are hostile to any attempt to weaken the union with Britain through Brexit rearrangements. Identity politics have been reawakened. A survey by Professors John Coakley and John Garry at Queen's University Belfast found that 85 per cent of Catholics supported Remain, compared with only 41 per cent of Protestants. Similarly, 88 per cent of those describing themselves as Irish supported Remain, while only 38 per cent of those describing themselves as British did.

There is a potential powder keg in the return of border controls. 'If we start to see infrastructure at the border,' says Detective Chief Superintendent Hugh Hume, 'if we start to see cameras, buildings, resources – whether it's to do with tariff issues, duties to be paid, or with immigration or security – presentationally that would be viewed very dimly by nationalists. It would be highly foreseeable that there would be a reaction, from protest and civil disobedience, through to potentially active targeting by anti-peace, dissident republican groups. That would manifest itself in physical force.'

In the months after the referendum, the North's vulnerability was exposed, economically, administratively and politically. The public had, arguably, not recognized the danger. Despite the vast sums of PEACE, Interreg and CAP money at risk, and the prospect of business disruption and a stiffened border, turnout in the referendum was 9 per cent lower than in the rest of the UK. In January 2017, the UK Supreme Court ruled that the British government did not require the consent of the Northern Ireland Assembly on how it proceeds. A Joint Ministerial Committee on EU Negotiations involving the devolved administrations appeared to give the North a presence in the process, but the British government said the Secretary of State for Northern Ireland would attend the Brexit Cabinet Committee only 'as required'. When he visited Belfast after the referendum, the Brexit Secretary, David Davis, had to meet the DUP and Sinn Féin separately. While the devolved administrations of Scotland and Wales have both produced detailed studies of the impact of Brexit, no study has been published by the Northern Ireland Executive. The Executive conceded that its civil service had produced a working paper, but it was not forwarded to ministers because it contained 'well-rehearsed arguments which were openly being aired during the referendum campaign and would have added nothing to the wider debate'.

'I've become more and more appalled at their inertia,' says Dr John Bradley, Honorary Professor at Queen's University

Business School. 'Their backward thinking, the lack of urgency. You are dealing with a political administration and a civil service who are not in control of the situation, aren't even sufficiently in control of the analysis of the situation to appreciate the difference. If you know where the flood is going to hit, or where the economic costs are going to be most serious, there is a certain amount of preparatory work you can do, if only to alert people that a hard rain's gonna fall. But they're not even doing that.'

The Executive maintains a lobbying office in Brussels, known as Brussels NI. Despite limited resources, in early 2017 Brussels NI extended a nine-year lease on an office block it shares with Google and other high-profile companies. But all Brexit lobbying by the British government is done through the UK Permanent Representation, with little or no role for the Northern Ireland Executive. According to a source familiar with the operation of Brussels NI, even simple social events undergo excruciating political tinkering from Stormont: when events across Brussels celebrate St Patrick's Day, the Northern Ireland Executive Office can only invite guests to 'An Ulster Fry', with no reference to St Patrick.

One sore issue during the referendum was that the Secretary of State for Northern Ireland, Theresa Villiers, was an enthusiastic Brexiteer. 'It was unfortunate,' says a senior Irish diplomat. 'It meant that the British government minister responsible for Northern Ireland was the one who was wheeled out all the time to say, "Everything will be fine. Trust me."'

After the referendum, the polarized climate rendered a swift response all but impossible. 'The system tends to be such,' Katy Hayward, a Senior Lecturer at Queen's

University Belfast, told the House of Lords Select Committee on Brexit, 'that unionist and nationalist views on any particular issue come to the fore, rather than the collective interests of Northern Ireland.'

This has led to deep frustration in the non-political sphere. The Northern Ireland Confederation of British Industry (CBI), InterTradeIreland (established under the Good Friday Agreement) and the Northern Ireland Food and Drink Association (NIFDA) poured out their concerns to the same committee, painting a stark picture of an economy more dependent on access to the single market and EU funds than any other part of the UK, yet facing abject abandonment by Stormont, Whitehall, Dublin and Brussels. 'The moment we exit Europe,' said Declan Billington of NIFDA, 'we will have a 30 per cent exposure if we do not get the trade deals in place. That is £1.3 billion of our turnover at risk.'

Northern Irish farmers look to be worst affected of all. Under the Common Agriculture Policy, the North secured direct payments of €2.3 billion, and a rural development allocation of €227 million between 2014 and 2020 (9 per cent of the UK's total CAP allocation, despite the fact that Northern Ireland has only 2.9 per cent of the UK's population). Some 87 per cent of Northern Irish farm incomes comes through direct payments from the EU. The Ulster Farmers' Union stayed neutral in the campaign, but a significant number of unionist-voting farmers supported Brexit. Theresa Villiers reassured Northern farmers that they would get even more generous subsidies from Britain post-Brexit, but it remains to be seen whether London will fund what the EU takes away.

In the Conservative Party manifesto for the June 2017

general election, Theresa May pointedly promised to protect the interests of Scottish and Welsh farmers. However, she made no reference to protecting the interests of Northern Irish farmers.

It was not until 10 August 2016 that the First and Deputy First Ministers managed to present a united front. In a joint letter to Theresa May, Arlene Foster and Martin McGuinness highlighted the fact that Northern Ireland would be the only part of the UK with an EU land border, and expressed concern about the free movement of people, goods and services, especially in the agri-food sector. The letter warned against any undermining of the peace process in the event of the border hardening. Notably, it raised concerns about the impact on EU migrant labour and the potential loss of billions of euro in EU funding. While many in the North welcomed the joint approach, it put Foster on the back foot. 'The tone and content of this letter,' said Jim Allister, Leader of the Traditional Unionist Voice, 'is so strongly pro-EU that it is hard to imagine it is co-authored by a party that campaigned for Brexit.'

Throughout the autumn of 2016, positions in the North hardened. There was a stormy debate in the Assembly over a Sinn Féin motion – ultimately defeated – to support a 'special status' for Northern Ireland in the Brexit negotiations. It was all making life difficult for the government in Dublin. Irish officials, who had been struggling for months to figure out the British position, hoped the triangular arrangement would produce a common understanding that could be presented to Brussels. 'We had hoped,' says a senior Irish diplomat, 'that London would talk to Belfast, London would talk to Dublin, and Dublin would talk to Belfast.'

A North South Ministerial Council meeting on 4 July had agreed work programmes at official level, but the politics were becoming ever more treacherous. 'We had to deal with the reality that the DUP and Sinn Féin were on diametrically opposing positions,' says a senior Irish negotiator. 'We could work up the issues, but the politics were always going to be tricky.'

A second Council meeting in Armagh loomed on 18 November. Again, Dublin was struggling to get the Northern parties to engage. 'We needed them to rally around,' says one Irish official. 'To find out, what is the common ground, what can we *define* as common ground, even if it's not going to be a fully-blown common position on every issue.'

The launch on 2 November of the first All-Island Civic Dialogue, the forum that had been trenchantly rejected by Arlene Foster in July, had deepened the frostiness between Dublin and the DUP. Enda Kenny's diary was cluttered with trips and engagements, and pinning down the DUP to a meeting was proving difficult. The only date that Kenny and Foster could meet was the day after the Civic Dialogue, but the mood in the DUP camp was still 'pretty raw'. 'There was a lot of nonsense about Arlene being away,' recalls an Irish official, 'so the upshot was that we met four of the parties – but not the DUP.'

It took another 10 days before the DUP agreed to meet in Dublin. By then the mood had improved. 'It went particularly well,' says the Irish negotiator. 'I think there was a realization that no one was trying to hoodwink anyone. We were just trying to see what were the things we could *say* we agree on.'

The thaw meant the Armagh meeting on 18 November could produce a set of agreed principles that Dublin regarded as a starting point. Both sides said contacts between ministers and officials would intensify. But the mood swings in Belfast were having a knock-on effect in London and, by extension, in Dublin. 'It became clear in further contact we had with the British after October,' says a senior Irish diplomat, 'that they were very anxious for it not to appear that they were talking to *us* about things which they *weren't* talking about to the Executive and the Northern political parties. Given the slowish pace with the parties, it meant a slower pace with the British than we would have liked.'

There was another issue that complicated these relationships: the collapse of the Northern Executive.

A scandal over a botched green energy scheme, set up by Arlene Foster in 2012 when she was Enterprise Minister, had erupted after it emerged that the taxpayer could be on the hook for half a billion pounds. Meanwhile, Sinn Féin nursed grievances over the status of the Irish language and the issue of killings by the security forces during the Troubles. With no sign of Foster stepping down, Martin McGuinness dramatically resigned on 10 January 2017, thereby precipitating the collapse of the Executive and Assembly.

On 22 November 2016, Sinn Féin launched a document called 'The Case for the North to Achieve Designated Special Status within the EU'. The party argued that its plan would protect the peace process and the Common Travel Area, ensure continued access to the single market, maintain EU funding, and protect cross-border employment, social-security and healthcare rights.

The idea of special status for Northern Ireland in the Brexit shakeout was not new. Five days after the referendum, the Secretary of State for Northern Ireland, Theresa Villiers, had ruled it out. An SDLP motion favouring special status was defeated by 47 votes to 46 in the Assembly in October 2016. But the idea lived on, and not solely within Sinn Féin. On 10 March 2017, the 42-page report of the Joint Oireachtas Committee on Jobs, Enterprise and Innovation concluded it was 'essential to argue the case for designated special status for Northern Ireland'. A Dáil motion on behalf of Sinn Féin on 15 February 2017, calling on the Irish government to 'negotiate for Northern Ireland to be designated with a special status', was carried, without binding effect.

In April 2017, Sinn Féin produced a follow-up paper, 'Securing Designated Special Status for the North within the EU'. This time the party spelled out two options: either create a special legal, designated status for the North or achieve a united Ireland through a referendum. Special status would mean Executive ministers attending European Council meetings, the North continuing to have MEPs as well as seats at the EU's Committee of the Regions and the European Economic and Social Committee. Any Irish members of the European Central Bank and the European Court of Justice should have an 'all-Ireland' remit.

Sinn Féin highlighted the Lisbon Treaty as supporting their case. Since citizens of the North can choose to be EU citizens through the Good Friday Agreement, articles 9 and 10 of Lisbon should apply. Article 9 states that the EU shall 'observe the principle of the equality of its citizens', who are entitled to equal attention from its institutions, while article 10 provides for citizens to be 'directly represented at Union level in the European Parliament'. Article 10.3 states that 'Every citizen shall have the right to participate in the democratic life of the Union.'

Special status, says one Irish negotiator, is 'a sort of

meaningless phrase. The task was to make sure there was a full understanding of the complexity of the Northern Ireland issues. And then to establish that they were going to require political solutions, or "flexible and imaginative solutions". Those don't magically appear out of a hat. We need to take this quite slowly and carefully. Because of the politics of the North, whatever sounds like a good solution to one side de facto sounds like a bad solution to the other.'

Nonetheless, there will be potentially 1.8 million people with a right to claim Irish – and therefore EU – citizenship on a piece of territory that will be removed from the European Union. Do articles 9 and 10 necessitate some kind of special status?

A senior EU official specializing in treaty law suggests those citizenship rights will be limited by one stubborn fact. Article 9, which Sinn Féin quotes, makes an unambiguous link between EU citizenship and the *member state*. The article reads: 'Every national of a Member State shall be a citizen of the Union.'

'By producing an Irish passport,' explains the official, 'if they went to another member state and said they wanted to benefit from the right of free movement and get a job, they would get that right. The supposition is that you are *living* in a member state, and you are a citizen of that member state. From there you get your EU citizenship. Yes, they're entitled to exercise their rights as EU citizens, but they'd need to go to an EU member state to exercise them.'

But this would not be the same as Northern Irish citizens having the right to vote for MEPs or to be represented at Council meetings. 'That's like saying if you have double citizenship and you're living in Canada,' says the official, 'that you can force Canada to set up a mechanism for you to vote for an MEP. It's ridiculous. You're living in a third country. So you *can't* exercise that right.'

Both the DUP and the Ulster Unionist Party have strongly resisted any talk of special status. In February 2017, the DUP's Deputy Leader Nigel Dodds said it was a way for nationalists to 'separate Northern Ireland from the rest of the United Kingdom with a border in the Irish Sea'. The Ulster Unionist MEP Jim Nicholson accused Sinn Féin of 'attempting to use Europe to create a false sense of ambiguity about the constitutional position of Northern Ireland'. During Northern Ireland questions in the House of Commons on 1 February, the Secretary of State for Northern Ireland, James Brokenshire, told the DUP's Sammy Wilson that there would be 'some specific factors in Northern Ireland', but that 'concepts of special status' were the 'wrong approach'.

A day after meeting Michel Barnier in Luxembourg on 20 June, Ireland's new foreign minister, Simon Coveney, raised eyebrows when he said: 'What we are insisting on achieving is a special status for Northern Ireland that allows the interaction on this island, as is currently the case, to be maintained. It is not so much about a soft or hard border, it is about an invisible border effectively, that you don't notice as you cross it. To achieve that, we need to draw up a political solution here as well as a technical and practical one, which doesn't really have any precedent in the European Union.'

The remarks drew an immediate and hostile reaction from unionists. An Irish government source said that Mr Coveney had misspoken; a senior Irish negotiator insisted there was 'no change' in government policy. At his first summit of EU leaders two days later, Leo Varadkar, who was elected Leader of Fine Gael on 2 June and then became Taoiseach on

14 June, was repeatedly pressed by reporters on whether or not there was a change in policy, or if Coveney had misspoken. 'I spoke to Simon Coveney last night,' he said. 'We are absolutely, totally on the same page on this. I understand Sinn Féin talk about something a bit different, which is special status within the EU; that is not something we are talking about as a government. We understand that if the United Kingdom leaves the EU, all parts leave. We are talking about recognition for the fact that we have a unique issue and unique difficulty with the border and that we will need special arrangements that recognize that to achieve our objective of normal trade and movement of people.'

Varadkar added: 'What's important is not what it says on the tin – it's what's inside the tin.'

14. The Unity Play

At 9.45 a.m., on 29 March 2017, Sir Tim Barrow, who had replaced Sir Ivan Rogers as Britain's EU Ambassador, stepped out of the UK Rep building on Avenue d'Auderghem and was driven the short distance to the European Council. Inside his briefcase was a six-page letter from Theresa May, formally notifying the European Council of Britain's intention to leave the EU.

Barrow had to attend a routine COREPER (Committee of Permanent Representatives) meeting before handing over the letter to Donald Tusk, the Council President. But the only show in town was the May letter. It would trigger a well-prepared choreography. Within 48 hours, Donald Tusk would issue the EU's response in the form of Draft Negotiating Guidelines. These guidelines would determine the course, content and priorities of the two-year divorce negotiations, and the future relationship beyond the divorce.

The Draft Negotiating Guidelines were many months in the making. The task facing the Irish government was to highlight the damage Brexit would inflict on the island, and to seek the maximum protection. To achieve that, Dublin would have to make sure its concerns were reflected prominently in the Draft Negotiating Guidelines.

The diplomatic effort ran on two tracks. The first was engagement with the European Commission's Task Force, the endless meetings in Room 201 of the Berlaymont Building. The second track was with the European Council, the body that represents the leaders of the member states. While the Commission would be the frontline negotiator, the Council would own the process. If Ireland wanted political clearance on technical solutions, it would have to get the green light from the Council.

In December 2016, senior Council officials asked Dublin for a first list of concerns and issues. At that stage, Irish officials and diplomats were working without detailed political direction from the Cabinet. 'We had to fill the space,' says one senior diplomat.

Engagement had already been happening. 'It was very clear from the outset,' says a senior European Council figure, 'that this for Ireland was of potentially *cataclysmic* proportions. The Irish were the best prepared of all member states, including the UK, which was not prepared. The Irish were among the very first to come to us, to underline their situation and their needs.'

But the Council was also cautioning Dublin that it had to convince other governments. The Council official says, 'It is not our task to guarantee to the others, "Don't worry, this is not undermining the single market, this is not a Trojan Horse for something else." The Irish have to do that.'

In December, Irish officials provided eight bullet points on a single page to their interlocutors in the European Council. 'The points were slightly overegged,' says a senior Irish diplomat.

There was silence from Brussels for a couple of months. Word came back that the list was too long. Like any self-respecting student, Dublin sent back something the same length, but in a slightly different style. The list came back again. It was 'way too long'. As the process thickened into a negotiation, Dublin agreed to shorten the document, but to keep as many of the elements as possible.

The Council had been drawing up internal drafts for the guidelines since the autumn, texts that were not shared with any member state. Dublin had to be reminded that, while their concerns were important, the entire process did not revolve around Ireland. 'We had to say to the Irish,' says a Council source, '"Look, we have four lines on the budget, which is of obvious importance to all member states, we have six, seven or eight lines on citizens' rights, which is important to at least 10 member states." So there are limits to how long a paragraph on Ireland can be.'

The Council was also concerned that the Irish were including potential traps. At this level of textual negotiation, otherwise innocuous words can be scrapped over for weeks. 'The Irish paragraph had to fit into the sort of text we were preparing, which all the time tended to be very focused so as to avoid silly discussions about adjectives and qualifiers. It had to focus instead on the real essentials.'

Between January and the end of March, negotiations intensified. 'They came up with a wording,' says one Irish diplomat, 'which, frankly, didn't do it for us. We came up with a wording which was pretty much like the wording that was [eventually] approved.'

The discussions became rather Jesuitical. 'We had phrases in there and we were clear what they meant,' says one of the Irish negotiators, 'and they were *absolutely* non-contentious. But the wording led the Council to fear that they might mean something that we were pretending was innocent, but wasn't.'

One phrase, indeed one *word*, had European and Irish officials arguing for the best part of two weeks. The phrase talked about Ireland's 'unique circumstances', followed by the words 'including geographic, historical and economic'. 'They baulked at the word "including",' says the Irish negotiator. 'They said, "Clearly that means there's more, and we don't know what that *more* is." But we were not that clever! It was only meant to be illustrative, nothing more.'

The Council felt that the Irish paragraph should state that the EU had historically supported the achievements of the Good Friday Agreement. 'They wanted it in a backward, historical way,' says one Irish negotiator, 'but for us the key thing was to make it forward-looking.' This might open up the prospect, for example, of future EU funding for the North.

Tusk and his team were eager to help Ireland. But other member states suspected that by being too flexible on the Irish border, they were playing into the hands of the British. Concessions given to Ireland might just suit the British as well, who would put them in the bank. 'We had to make it clear to the Irish,' says a Council negotiator, 'that, while we wanted to do our utmost to help them, they had to understand there were fears elsewhere that we might be playing into the hands of the UK, who would like to split us.'

These fears revolved around another sequence of words that, to the untutored eye, seemed innocuous. The Irish text stated that the EU would protect the 'achievements, benefits and commitments' of the peace process. To Dublin, this was all about highlighting the various elements within the Good Friday Agreement, such as the creation of a zone of peace and prosperity, the protection of human rights, the unique situation of Northern Ireland and so on.

Council officials frowned at the word 'benefits'. Was this code for something that might blow up later? Could it give the UK a free pass on trade with the Republic of Ireland if it was outside the single market and customs union? In response, the Irish side sent the Council a list of what those 'benefits' were. A short time later, a senior Irish negotiator received a text message from his Council interlocutor. 'It was all fine,' he says.

The Council was also concerned by the rhetoric emerging from Dublin and London about no return to a hard border. 'We did notice a certain gap,' says a senior EU official, 'not a very big gap, but a certain gap between what our interlocutors understood and said to us, and what was sometimes said in public discourse in Ireland. This is a natural political instinct: you tell people what they'd like to hear, and what they'd like to hear is that the world is *not* going to change. Brexit is a bad thing, but we are going to protect you from it. It will not have any consequences. There will be no border.'

The official adds: 'To that we have to say, "Look, the Brits have told us that (1) they're leaving the European Union; (2) they're leaving the single market; and (3) they're leaving the customs union. That creates a border. That creates a border in a legal sense. A single market has a border. A customs union has a border, because there are different rules on two sides of that border." That has not been present in public discourse in Ireland. I'm not criticizing anybody, but for us it has been important to underline that there will be consequences. Why? Because if you promise people the moon and you're unable to deliver, then suddenly what is, and should be, seen *entirely* as the fault of the British, will suddenly be blamed on the bloody bureaucrats in Brussels and the European Union.'

While Irish and Council officials were continuing to labour over the Irish paragraph, Dublin was also working closely with London on another Irish paragraph, this time in Theresa May's Article 50 letter. This was a result of close coordination at official level, and also in the meetings between May and Kenny on 30 January, and on 9 March at the EU summit. In the event, Ireland's concerns were enshrined as the fourth out of seven principles May highlighted in the letter. 'In particular,' May wrote, 'we must pay attention to the UK's unique relationship with the Republic of Ireland and the importance of the peace process in Northern Ireland.' As far as Dublin was concerned, the rest of the paragraph hit all the right notes: no hard borders, the retention of the Common Travel Area, the need to make sure Brexit didn't harm the Republic or jeopardize the Good Friday Agreement.

Finally, the two documents were ready. May's letter was delivered on 29 March, and two days later the EU Draft Negotiating Guidelines were circulated to capitals. Following three months of excruciating drafting over words and phrases, the Irish concerns were there in Paragraph 11.

> The Union has consistently supported the goal of peace and reconciliation enshrined in the Good Friday Agreement, and continuing to support and protect the achievements, benefits and commitments of the Peace Process will remain of paramount importance. In view of the unique circumstances on the island of Ireland, flexible and imaginative solutions will be required, including with the aim of avoiding a hard border, while respecting the integrity of the Union legal order. In this context, the Union should also recognise existing bilateral agreements and arrangements between the United Kingdom and Ireland which are compatible with EU law.

To the naked eye, this looked like a considerable achievement for the Irish side. The Good Friday Agreement, the peace process, the idea of using 'flexible and imaginative solutions' to avoid a hard border, the reference to the

Common Travel Area ('existing bilateral agreements') – they were all there.

But the Irish had not had it all their own way. Senior European Council officials had pushed back on various points. While 'flexible and imaginative solutions' made the cut, the Council insisted on a key word in the same sentence: 'with the *aim* of avoiding a hard border'. It was an *aim*, no more. 'That was important for us,' says the Council source. 'I'm sure that we *will* find practical solutions, because it's an expression of a determination. But we don't at this stage *promise*. And we will not promise that the world will not change – because we cannot.'

During the months when the future of the Irish border was arguably the most prominent item on Ireland's Brexit agenda, a separate but related drama was brewing behind the scenes.

On 9 July 2016, just 16 days after the referendum, politicians from Ireland and the UK gathered at the Irish National War Memorial Gardens in Islandbridge to honour the thousands of Irish soldiers who had died at the Battle of the Somme 100 years previously. The Taoiseach, Enda Kenny, was present, as was President Michael D. Higgins and Theresa Villiers, Secretary of State for Northern Ireland, who was representing the British government.

Also present was Mark Durkan, the SDLP Foyle MP and a key negotiator during the Good Friday Agreement. Durkan took Kenny aside. He knew intimately the legalities and politics of the Good Friday Agreement and was worried that Brexit could unravel key parts of it.

Durkan was thinking about the Agreement's 'unity clause'. 'The Agreement states,' says Durkan, 'that it's for the people of Ireland alone, North and South by agreement and without *external impediment.* We couldn't afford a situation where people would say that Brexit had created an external impediment, in the sense that unity didn't necessarily mean EU membership. You could have a future proposal for a unity referendum in which people are saying, "Well, there's a complication about getting the North into the EU, or indeed that it creates complications for the South's *existing* membership because it ends up being treated as a new state."'

Durkan alerted Kenny to an intriguing parallel. At the moment of German reunification, East Germany automatically became a part of the European Union. This was by no means inevitable. Many questioned the haste with which the East was able to join the EU, since it was far from qualifying for the convergence criteria that accession normally demands. As it happened, East Germany's accession was agreed during the Irish presidency of the EU in April 1990. The manoeuvre used, which was supported by the Taoiseach, Charles Haughey, involved Article 23 of the West German Basic Law, which held that the Law extended to different parts of the country. It was agreed that the East German government would ask Bonn to invoke Article 23, saying it wished to be considered as part of German territory. The Bundestag would amend Article 23 to make that happen.

Articles 2 and 3 of the Irish Constitution, which asserted the Irish State's sovereignty over the whole island, might have played the same role as Germany's Article 23 in an Irish unification scenario. But those articles had been deleted as part of the Good Friday Agreement.

Durkan's analysis did not fall on deaf ears. Kenny himself was aware of the German parallel and had been alerted to it a couple of days after the referendum by Pat Cox, the former

Progressive Democrats MEP and one-time President of the European Parliament. Kenny was in regular contact with Cox in the run-up to the vote and in the days that followed.

Eight days after the Islandbridge conversation, Kenny raised the issue at the MacGill Summer School in Glenties. He had floated the East Germany idea, and the need, post-Brexit, to protect the unity clause in the Good Friday Agreement, with officials both in the Department of Foreign Affairs and in his own department. According to a source close to Kenny, he met considerable resistance on the grounds that it would go down very badly with unionists. His prepared speech to the summer school made no reference to the unity question. But the Taoiseach departed from the text, telling the audience that provision for a future unity referendum *should* be included in any final deal between the UK and the EU. He said he didn't think the time was right for such a referendum, but afterwards he told reporters that if ever it did happen, the East German model should be adopted, so that Northern Ireland would not 'have a tortuous and long process applying for membership of the European Union'.

The remarks were welcomed by Sinn Féin Leader Gerry Adams, but were dismissed as 'mischievous' by the DUP's Ian Paisley Junior. The issue then disappeared. But the German parallel was kept within the ether. A senior Irish official confirmed to the author the following December that it was still being looked at, but that the government didn't necessarily want to draw attention to it. 'The model is Germany after the fall of the Berlin Wall,' he said. 'The principle is that nothing is disturbed [in the event of Irish unity]. No one is contesting this. But there's no need to put it up in lights.' But it was being discussed at the highest level. A confidential memo, dated 26 October 2016, was circulated among senior officials in the Departments of the Taoiseach and Foreign Affairs, spelling out the German parallel and the key role Ireland had played in 1990. 'A point that we need to focus on,' the memo concluded, 'is the gratitude that Germany at the time felt it owed to Ireland for pushing German reunification within the EC. Kohl certainly had that sense of gratitude. It may well have dwindled greatly two chancellors later and with the passage of time, but the German precedent . . . is something that would be definitely worth exploring.'

Enda Kenny put the German precedent in lights on a second occasion. On 23 February 2017, after a meeting with Commission President Jean-Claude Juncker in Brussels, he told reporters that the unity provision in the Good Friday Agreement would have to be 'contained in the [Brexit] negotiation outcome'. Again, he referenced East Germany's 'seamless' accession to the EU after German reunification in 1990.

Some Irish officials were startled that he had been so explicit. Given the zero-sum mentality in the North, any gain for nationalism would be perceived as a loss for unionism. 'The Taoiseach was slightly stronger than we would have expected,' says one official. 'Perhaps it was for domestic consumption.'

The SDLP, meanwhile, were raising the issue with James Brokenshire, the Secretary of State for Northern Ireland. 'Brokenshire kept trying to ignore the issue,' says Durkan. 'Then he said that the German precedent would apply in its own right, and that it would automatically be there.' But Durkan wasn't convinced. A cross-party legal challenge by Stormont MLAs and a second challenge by the victims' rights campaigner Raymond McCord that Brexit undermined the Good Friday Agreement had been rejected by the UK Supreme Court on 17 January 2017, on the basis that the

Agreement covered Northern Ireland's place in the UK but not in the European Union. 'That was a clear warning to people. Don't just rely on assumption or precedent. You need to get things written in.'

Durkan and Kenny remained in touch. In Westminster, Durkan was a member of the House of Commons Select Committee on Exiting the EU. The Committee had spent months drawing up a report on Britain's negotiating mandate for Brexit. Durkan had worked assiduously to get language into the report that reflected Dublin's concerns about the North's prospects for EU membership in the event of a unity referendum. The DUP's Sammy Wilson was also on the Committee, watching Durkan's and, by extension, Dublin's, efforts with some disdain. 'We saw that as the Irish government simply pandering to the SDLP's interpretation of the Good Friday Agreement and trying to bring in a stronger Irish dimension,' Wilson says. 'It was a load of nonsense. Most of the people on the Brexit Committee hadn't had a clue what he was talking about. The House of Commons people had this glazed look over their eyes.'

However, when it was published on 29 March, the Select Committee report 'noted' Kenny's remarks in Brussels. It also quoted Brokenshire's belief that in the event of a unity referendum, as envisaged in the Belfast Agreement, 'Northern Ireland would be in a position of becoming part of an existing EU Member State, rather than seeking to join the EU as a new independent state.' A letter sent by David Davis to Durkan on 20 March repeated in writing what Brokenshire had told the Committee.

On the day the Committee reported, Durkan was unwittingly helped by the pro-Brexit members, including Wilson, Michael Gove, Dominic Raab and Peter Lilley, who walked out of proceedings saying the report was 'too gloomy' about life outside the EU. 'It actually worked in my favour,' says Durkan. 'It allowed me to get a bit more into the text at that time than I might have done, had they all been there in the usual mode.'

The moment the text was finalized, Durkan texted Kenny to let him know he had managed to reference the unity issues in the final report.

By now the clock was ticking. Article 50 had been triggered on 29 March. The Draft Negotiating Guidelines were circulated two days later. According to the choreography, the 27 remaining EU leaders would formally approve them at an extraordinary summit on 29 April. If Irish officials wanted to insert a unity clause into the guidelines, as the best way of giving the idea cast-iron legal certainty, they had only a few weeks to do it.

They decided the best option would be to spring the idea late in the day. 'These are gambles,' says a senior Irish negotiator, 'because sometimes you deploy something late and you just get blocked off. But we felt on this one it was better played quite late.'

The European Council was not itself blindsided by the Irish move. Dublin had already discussed the idea with senior officials. 'This was only something we discussed within the last month or so before we tabled the guidelines,' says one Council official. 'As far as we were concerned, this was stating the facts.'

Usually, three or four days before an EU summit, the sherpas meet in Brussels to work on the agenda. Irish officials decided to subtly raise the unity declaration at the meeting on Monday, 24 April. They let it be known that there was an issue Kenny wanted to have addressed, but the specifics were left vague.

According to sources on both sides, Dublin wanted the

unity clause to be inserted into the Irish paragraph in the Draft Negotiating Guidelines. But the Council resisted. 'We said no,' says a Council source. 'We can't do that. That would unnecessarily create tensions with the UK.'

This was not simply a case of diplomatic caution. The Council had a specific reason for fearing the UK's response, and it had nothing to do with Northern Ireland.

The reason was Gibraltar.

The Draft Negotiating Guidelines had included a paragraph relating to the status of Gibraltar, inserted at the last minute at Spain's insistence. The paragraph stated that no agreement between the EU and UK could apply to Gibraltar without separate agreement between the UK and Spain. To Madrid, this was perfectly reasonable. The Rock was disputed territory. (The key issue was Gibraltar Airport, which Spain has always argued is outside the territory ceded to the UK by the 1713 Treaty of Utrecht.) So long as both countries were in the EU, the dispute was managed within an EU framework. But if the EU and UK reached a deal that had an impact on Gibraltar, Spain felt entitled to have a say.

That was not how London saw it. The tabloid press screamed treachery, seeing the Spanish paragraph as a veto at best, or a land grab at worst. Within four days of Article 50 being triggered, Michael Howard, a former Tory Cabinet minister, suggested that Theresa May would send the Royal Navy to the Mediterranean in the same way that Margaret Thatcher had responded to Argentina's invasion of the Falklands.

Both Dublin and the Council were keenly aware of this context. Council officials, on orders from President Tusk, told their Irish counterparts that a Northern Ireland clause had to be seen to be coming from Dublin, and not the EU institutions. '[Tusk] was very clear on this,' says one source.

'We could not take this responsibility. You saw the row we had about Gibraltar.'

Dublin, mindful of how unionists would react, agreed. After the sherpa meeting, Irish officials presented a succinct text to the Council. The Council took the text to their legal services and, according to an Irish source, quickly confirmed that the text was 'absolutely solid legally'.

The next step was to present it to EU ambassadors at the COREPER meeting on Wednesday, 26 April. This would be the first time the other member states would see the detail of the Irish demand. By any measure, it was coming very late in the day. The summit was 72 hours away. Although Dublin was convinced it was legally sound, prime ministers do not like to be bounced into something unless they're sure they know exactly what it's about.

By now, both Dublin and the Council had agreed that the unity text would be written into the minutes of the summit as the best way of copper-fastening it legally. Yet even that option was carefully managed so as not to draw attention to it. Rather than have hard copies circulated to the 26 EU ambassadors, the declaration would be read out by a Council official at the COREPER meeting.

It was not the only addition going into the minutes. The Greeks had raised a problem with the Irish paragraph in the guidelines at the sherpa meeting on the Monday; the line about using 'flexible and imaginative solutions' to avoid a hard border in Ireland had particularly spooked Athens. The Greeks were worried that a fix for a sensitive border between an EU member state and a third country, using 'flexible and imaginative solutions', might somehow be seized upon by Turkey as a legal precedent, if there were ever issues over the border between Northern and Southern Cyprus.

That flare-up actually gave both Ireland and the Council some useful cover. As well as the Irish unity clause going into the minutes, there would be a second declaration, asserting that nothing in the guidelines could act as a precedent in any future negotiations on other issues. This additional declaration would give Ireland some shelter in case the unity clause drew unwelcome heat.

Sometime after the COREPER meeting that Wednesday morning, Irish officials contacted their counterparts in DexEU, letting them know that Enda Kenny would seek a declaration on Irish unity and Northern Irish EU membership at the summit on Saturday. European Council officials also contacted UK Rep.

On Thursday, Preben Aamann, President Tusk's spokesman, received a call from the *Financial Times*. Was Ireland seeking a unity declaration? On Friday morning, the day before the summit, the *Financial Times* splashed the headline on its front page: EU LEADERS BACK MEMBERSHIP PLAN FOR A POST-BREXIT UNITED IRELAND.

The story accurately portrayed Dublin's aspirations. But even before it hit the news-stands, there was a diplomatic onslaught from London to block the move.

The political backdrop to Brexit in the UK had suddenly shifted on 18 April, when Theresa May called a general election. 'Britain is leaving the European Union and there can be no turning back,' she declared. The will of the people was being frustrated by the Labour Party, the Liberal Democrats, the Scottish National Party and the unelected House of Lords. 'Every vote for the Conservatives,' she vowed, 'will make me stronger when I negotiate for Britain with the prime ministers, presidents and chancellors of the European Union.'

Now it seemed that, following the tabloid uproar over Gibraltar and the ongoing sniping that Brexit was undermining the United Kingdom, London was not prepared to tolerate a United Ireland story in the middle of a general election campaign.

'It was unambiguous,' says a senior Irish negotiator. 'Their biggest concern was that this was bang straight into the election. They went into a fairly full-on diplomatic offensive.'

Downing Street started calling senior officials in the European Council to get them to drop the unity clause. They were given short shrift. 'Our line was that this is for the Irish,' says a senior Council source. 'If the Irish request this, they will get it. It's as simple as that. We said upfront to the Brits, "If this is what the Irish want, we're going to do it. They are around the table. You are not around the table."'

An Irish Cabinet minister says, 'It was an example of the EU27 being the EU27, an example of where the British were *outside* the area of influence.'

Officials from the Northern Ireland Office also weighed in, with phone calls to Dublin. As the pressure continued, the DexEU officials contacted the Department of the Taoiseach to set up a phone call between Theresa May and Enda Kenny. By now, Downing Street wanted the unity clause to be delayed until the EU summit at the end of June, long after the general election. A blunt message went back to London. Kenny was sticking to his guns. The phone call was declined. An internal mail circulated within the Department of Foreign Affairs captures the moment.

The UK have got wind of it and are unhappy about the impact it may have in their domestic media. D/ExEU have been in touch with D/Taoiseach asking that such a statement is deferred until June European Council (post General

Election) and suggesting that the PM may call the Taoiseach tomorrow to make such a request.

However, the firm message has gone back, as directed by the Taoiseach, that he will be proceeding with seeking this statement at the EC this Saturday.

Dublin was adamant that the issue could not be postponed until after the general election. 'If you did it in June,' says one Irish diplomat, 'it wouldn't necessarily be in the [Negotiating Guidelines] framework. At that stage there wasn't any indication that Brexit would be discussed in the European Council in June at all. When would you do it? Would you do it when the UK is around the table? When Theresa May is around the table? Would she object or not object? For us it certainly wasn't appropriate to go to the June Council.'

In the event, the pressure tapered off. Irish sources believe that British civil servants were half-hearted in their objections: the pressure was entirely party-political. The British civil service was attempting to block a bid by a sovereign country to insert a clause into the legal process of a supra-national union that the UK was leaving, simply to help a political party avoid negative publicity during a general election campaign. It was highly questionable, to say the least.

On Saturday, 29 April, the remaining 27 EU leaders gathered at the extraordinary summit in Brussels. It was a solemn occasion. The EU was formally responding to Britain's request to leave the Union, and it was setting out its own principles and objectives as to how that departure would be managed. By now the unity text had been circulated.

The European Council acknowledges that the Good Friday Agreement expressly provides for an agreed mechanism whereby a united Ireland may be brought about by peaceful and democratic means; and, in this regard, the European Council acknowledges that, in accordance with international law, the entire territory of such a united Ireland would thus be part of the European Union.

Irish officials were quietly confident. The unity declaration appeared to be watertight. Dublin had circulated, both to the European Council and to the Commission, the 20 March letter from David Davis to Mark Durkan that essentially repeated the gist of the Irish text. Donald Tusk's people were standing over it. It had been shared with the other member states, and had been given prominence by the *Financial Times* front-page splash the day before.

Suddenly, however, on the morning of the meeting, Ireland's Ambassador to the EU, Declan Kelleher, received a phone call. It was from the French Ambassador, Pierre Sellal.

Sellal explained to Kelleher that French lawyers were concerned. Could this declaration create a dangerous precedent, since European Council declarations carry strong legal weight? What kind of united Ireland were we talking about?

A meeting involving Kelleher, Sellal and Jeppe Tranholm-Mikkelsen, the European Council Secretary General, was hastily scheduled in the Irish delegation room in the Europa Building, where the summit was due to take place within a matter of hours. The Irish side insisted that the only united Ireland scenario was one expressly catered for in the Good Friday Agreement. The excruciating care with which the text had been drafted was cited to convince the French Ambassador and his lawyers. The key word was 'such'. The European Council would be acknowledging that 'in accordance with international law, the entire territory of *such a united Ireland* would thus be part of the European Union.' The word 'such' related back to the 'agreed mechanism' in the Good Friday Agreement. Thus, the wording could not be applied to any other situation.

Sellal and the lawyers took the explanation to President François Hollande. The French dropped their objections immediately.

The summit got under way. Donald Tusk put the Draft Negotiating Guidelines, complete with the Irish paragraph and its 'flexible and imaginative solutions', to the 27 leaders. The entire document, including the Irish paragraph, was adopted in just four minutes. (It would have been two minutes, but two prime ministers had yet to enter the room.) The speed with which it was adopted was hailed by many as a rare moment of EU unity, one that had – ironically – been a side effect of Britain's decision to leave the EU.

A short time later, Enda Kenny made his pitch on the Irish-unity clause. Following the last-minute French bombshell, Irish officials were in a state of high anxiety. One official even texted Kenny, in mock seriousness, to tell him, 'Don't forget to ask for the unity text!'

One senior EU source who was present in the summit room recalls: 'President Tusk said, "As you know, we have two declarations. One [i.e. the precedent issue raised by the Greeks] is of interest to a number of you. One is specifically requested by the Taoiseach. We circulated the text so everyone had it, and there were no problems with it."'

The 26 EU leaders accepted Kenny's request without any objections.

It was a significant achievement by the Irish side. They had certainly used a number of diplomatic tricks to get such a sensitive issue over the line. There had been the French objections. Luxembourg had also wondered about a slight rephrasing (from 'in this regard' to 'on this basis' in order to reinforce the notion of a united Ireland happening *only* on a democratic basis), but Council officials effectively talked them out of it. 'We said,' says a Council source, 'is that *really* necessary? If we start drafting on it we'll create a lot of confusion, since everything is known.' The support of the Council's General Secretariat was vital in the end. It had acted as Ireland's advocate in the face of outright opposition from London, and some unease from a number of member states. Council officials insist, however, that no matter how late Ireland played it, the approach was all above board and within the normal limits of diplomatic endeavour.

This was Enda Kenny's last summit as Taoiseach. According to a source close to Kenny, he had invested a considerable amount of political capital in the unity issue, from his speech at the MacGill Summer School right up to the summit in Brussels, raising the issue with every EU prime minister he had met bilaterally in the nine intervening months. On several occasions, Kenny would produce an A4 sheet of paper and draw a map of Ireland, complete with border, in order to convey the complexity and importance, as he saw it, of the issue. Among those enlightened by Kenny's cartography skills were Theresa May, Angela Merkel and Jean-Claude Juncker.

As he left the European Council building around 5 p.m. that Saturday afternoon, the Council's audio-visual department's cameras, which are trained on all leaders as they enter and leave summits, captured Kenny punching the air.

15. Le Royaume Uni: Nul Points

Amid the anxiety over Brexit, the opportunities are often overlooked. 'The *risk* is what you see first,' says a senior Irish diplomat involved in the negotiations. 'You do the risk analysis, you negotiate to mitigate that risk, and then you look for the opportunity. The opportunities are downstream.'

But they do exist. Ireland is an English-speaking country, with a similar common-law system to the UK's. International companies serving the single market from a UK base could relocate to Ireland. European companies sourcing inputs from UK suppliers may look to Irish suppliers instead.

At its hi-tech facility in Craigavon, County Armagh, the Almac Group takes drugs on licence, manufactures them and distributes them to European, American and Asian markets. Every year, Almac ships 84,000 consignments of pharmaceutical goods from Craigavon to the EU single market via Dublin. These are 'cold-chain' products, despatched in highly regulated, refrigerated and sealed containers. Under EU rules, every time one of these products is released it must be done by a qualified individual, and the testing done in an EU-certified laboratory. Starting on the morning after Brexit, Almac started getting phone calls from customers wanting to know if this would still be the case, and if the seals would be broken at new customs posts on the Irish border.

'If there is a hard border,' Almac's Executive Director, Colin Hayburn, told the House of Commons Northern

Ireland Affairs Committee, 'any issues which cause those products to be delayed, to be opened, whether it's a refrigerated door on a lorry, or seals tampered with, will lead us into a non-competitive situation. Our customers will not really tolerate that.'

Almac could not afford to be vague. Its non-British rivals were already telling Almac's customers that *they* could provide compliance certainty. 'There was only one answer we could give there,' said Hayburn. 'It had to be "yes". They wouldn't listen to us saying we were confident that in two or three years' time equivalent [UK] legislation would be in place, so that our distribution and quality regimes would not be hindered.'

In January 2017, Almac opened a multimillion-euro facility employing 100 people in Dundalk. Further expansion across the border is likely. 'It's something we don't want to do,' Hayburn told MPs. 'It's something we'll fight hard not to do. But it will be very much driven by our customers. If our customers ask for that EU solution now, we have to address it or we'll lose out.'

In 2015, the UK still had the largest share of foreign direct investment (FDI) in Europe, holding 18.7 per cent of the entire FDI 'stock'. The Economic and Social Research Institute estimates that a hard Brexit could increase Ireland's FDI share by 7.3 per cent, or €23.4 billion over 10 years. The big targets are pharmaceuticals, information technology and financial services.

The City of London is the world's biggest and wealthiest financial hub. It represents 7 per cent of Britain's GDP. But Brexit poses an existential threat. According to the Brussels think-tank Bruegel, 35 per cent of the City's wholesale banks service EU27 clients, so as much as €1.8 trillion in assets might be on the move, including potentially 15 per cent of banking jobs. That would include 3,300 positions in five major US investment banks, 10,000 regular jobs, and up to 20,000 consultancy, legal and accounting positions. Frankfurt, Paris, Amsterdam, Luxembourg and Dublin are circling.

Brexiteers argue that a flight of assets and professionals will starve the eurozone of a vital source of funds and trades and threaten its stability. That remains to be seen, but financial institutions cannot wait around to find out. 'The regulatory lead time is so long that they have to start now,' says Martin Shanahan, Chief Executive Officer of IDA Ireland. 'Our expectation is that as other companies look at what impact is happening, we will see more mobile investment out of the UK.'

After the 2008 financial crash, the sector underwent deep reform both at EU and at global-governance level. A key reform was the EU single rulebook. In theory, a single rulebook will limit the kinds of destructive cross-border transmission of risk we saw during the crisis. Key to a single rulebook is the single passport. A financial institution acquires a 'passport' in the member state in which it is registered, and because that country complies with the harmonized rulebook, the institution can then trade its services across the EU without duplicate regulation or supervision.

It was partly because of this that international institutions established subsidiaries in the UK. A US derivatives firm, if it is UK-registered, has free access to the EU market. Britain may try to claim that the financial rules it applies post-Brexit will provide an 'equivalence', but it is not that simple. The single rulebook, according to Professor Niamh Moloney of the London School of Economics, is of 'massive scale and depth'. There are legislative and technical rules and soft guidelines. It is highly dynamic, meaning it is changing all the time. It may be impossible for the UK to keep up.

Could Britain's loss be Dublin's gain?

Even before the referendum, the Irish government was already targeting financial services with its IFS2020 Action Plan, aiming to boost growth by 10,000 jobs over five years. 'As a result of Brexit we anticipate that we're going to break that 10,000 job-creation target,' says Eoghan Murphy, who was the Minister of State with responsibility for the sector at the time of the referendum. 'We're already ahead of target as it is. Brexit is likely to bring that number higher.'

A large number of firms were expected to make a final decision by the summer of 2017 in order to be passport-compliant by March 2019. The battle to win them over has been ugly. 'It is extremely competitive,' says Martin Shanahan. 'All other jurisdictions are putting their best foot forward. I wouldn't expect anything less.'

The Central Bank of Ireland issues licences for any operator relocating to Dublin. In the autumn of 2016 there were rumours that it was resisting riskier categories of investment, and struggling to retain the staff needed to do the licensing. On 22 November, Reuters reported that Ireland had 'signalled to several large investment banks it would be reluctant to host large trading operations', quoting sources saying the bailout experience had left Ireland risk-averse. Both the Central Bank and the Minister for Finance, Michael Noonan, issued sharp denials.

In its February 2017 study, Bruegel estimated that Frankfurt would win 45 per cent of the wholesale banking market that might potentially leave the UK, Paris 20 per cent and Dublin 15 per cent. In May, it was reported that

J. P. Morgan had paid €125 million for an office block in Dublin Docklands that would accommodate up to 1,000 employees. Northern Trust, the wealth-management company, added 400 jobs to its Limerick facility. In one week in July, Barclays, Morgan Stanley, Citigroup and Bank of America Merrill Lynch all announced significant Brexit-related expansions in Dublin. In another boost, the EY Brexit Tracker reported that 19 out of 222 financial services companies monitored by the consultancy said they were moving operations and/or staff to Dublin as a result of Brexit, putting the Irish capital just ahead of Frankfurt, which had attracted the confirmed interest of 18 firms.

In June, the *Financial Times* reported that Dublin's ambition to become an insurance hub was dealt a blow when RSA and QBE, two leading insurers, opted for Luxembourg and Brussels. (Lloyds had already plumped for Brussels.) QBE's Richard Pryce said the Belgian regulator had been 'very pragmatic'. At an event in Dublin on 8 June, the Department of Finance's international finance division head Paul Ryan accused rival cities of spreading 'black propaganda' about housing and infrastructure shortages in Ireland.

Eoghan Murphy was quoted by the *Financial Times* as having lodged a complaint to the European Commission that Luxembourg had engaged in 'regulatory arbitrage' by offering inducements to AIG in order to lure it to the Grand Duchy. (The head of the Luxembourg Agency reportedly shot back that he 'didn't expect the Irish to be sore losers'.) Murphy insists it was not a formal complaint, but that he was hearing so many tales of regulatory inducement that he feared a systemic risk to the single market. Ken Thompson, the Chief Executive of Insurance Ireland, said there were rules to prevent this, telling the *Sunday Times* that there was no evidence that other cities were cutting regulatory corners. 'Solvency II [a 2009 directive that harmonizes insurance regulation] established a standard of regulation that prevents brass plating and ensures that any Brexit-related relocations are in line with Europe-wide standards,' he said.

The Paris-based European Securities and Markets Authority warned in May 2017 that companies wanting to keep access to the single market could not simply set up 'letterbox' operations elsewhere while keeping the bulk of their business in London. One of its nine relocation conditions required regulators, like the Central Bank of Ireland, to verify the 'objective reasons for relocation'. But determining how to do that has not been easy. Take a company with 300 staff doing insurance underwriting, risk management and operational risk assessment. How many staff would they need to transfer to Ireland to keep their passporting rights? Twenty? Thirty? And at what level: Chief executive? Chief financial officer? Chief risk officer? What if they outsourced most of their activities back to London, so the risk flowed from the Dublin books to the London books? Could authorization be granted quickly since these firms had already been authorized by the UK?

At a meeting of the government's Brexit stakeholders committee in November, several members reported that 'at all levels' Ireland was being briefed against by other member states on its supposed lack of commercial and residential space, and the weakness of its infrastructure. The government has been reassuring investors that there are 3.5 million square feet of new office space under construction in Dublin, one million under refurbishment and five million in the planning process. 'We have more than enough space to facilitate what might be coming across,' says Eoghan Murphy. 'There isn't going to be a big bang moment here. Thousands of bankers aren't going to jump on boats and come up the Liffey. People are going to move over time.'

The Central Bank's Macro-Financial Review in June 2017 indicated that Irish house prices had risen at an annual rate of 10.5 per cent as of April, the figures coinciding with a warning by the OECD that 'another bubble may be forming'. The Central Statistics Office showed that, while the numbers of residential properties had increased by more than 50 per cent since early 2013, the national index was still 31 per cent below the 2007 peak. In April 2017, the Dublin Regional Homeless Executive put the number of homeless families at 1,091, with 2,262 dependants in homeless accommodation.

Jeremy Godfrey, of the International School of Dublin, told the Joint Oireachtas Committee on Education and Skills that housing and education were the two most important issues for executives thinking of relocating to Ireland. 'We have heard anecdotal evidence,' he told the Committee, 'of people who had turned down posts in Ireland because of the lack of what they considered to be suitable education for their children.' The government has since announced one new International Baccalaureate school with 800 primary and secondary places off the M50, opening its doors in 2018, with the potential of a second in the city centre.

The state faced its stiffest challenge in its bid for the two EU agencies that have been based in the UK, the European Banking Authority (EBA) and the European Medicines Agency (EMA).

The medicines agency is the far bigger prize. The EMA approves any drug or medicine that the pharmaceutical industry wants to sell in the EU. Apart from 890 direct jobs, the agency brings with it an ecosystem of scientific expertise. It is extremely valuable both financially and reputationally. 'A lot of work gets subcontracted,' says one Irish diplomat. 'It would be a huge boost for the local pharma industry.'

Dublin argued that moving the agency from Canary Wharf to Ireland would cause minimum disruption, due to the similar legal system and language, and the fact that Ireland already hosted nine of the globe's top 10 pharmaceutical companies. While 18 member states placed bids, only a handful had a realistic chance: Germany, France, Ireland, Denmark, Sweden, Italy and Spain. Denmark and Ireland argued that the competition should be based on the Eurovision model, with each country allocating points to candidate member states in order of preference. France and Germany preferred the decision to be taken at an EU leaders' summit. 'This decodes as a smoke-filled room at 3 a.m.,' says an unimpressed Irish source, 'with the French taking the banking authority and the Germans taking the medicines agency.'

At the EU summit in Brussels on 22 June, leaders finally clarified and adopted an elaborate set of rules for the competition – culminating in a Eurovision-style vote. In the first round, each member state would have one vote consisting of six voting points, with three points allocated to the preferred offer, two to the second-choice country and one to the third choice. If there was no clear winner, the process would move to a second and, if necessary, a third round. In the event of a tie, lots would be drawn. The competition took place on 20 November 2017, at a meeting in Brussels of European Affairs ministers. In the event, Ireland did better than expected. Realizing at an early stage it was out of the running for the EMA, Irish officials joined in the horse-trading, offering to vote for candidate countries that were in with a chance on the EMA in return for support on the EBA. Ireland qualified for the second round, and then made it into a tie with France, only to cruelly lose out on the EBA when it fell to lots being drawn.

Could Brexit provide a bonanza for Irish universities?

Currently, EU students in England, Wales and Northern Ireland pay the same fees as 'home' students, and those studying in Scotland do not pay fees at all. Following the Brexit vote, the UK government has spelled out short-term commitments in terms of entitlements and access. In general, existing tuition-fee and student-loan arrangements will continue to apply to students seeking to start courses in the 2017/18 academic year in England, Wales and Northern Ireland, while Scotland will continue their own arrangements. Scotland has said it will extend those arrangements to students applying for courses starting in 2018/19, but the other parts of the UK have yet to show their hand. The assumption is, however, that EU students will most likely have to pay fees similar to those paid by 'international' students.

According to 2017 figures supplied by the Small Firms Association, there were 12,000 Irish students in the UK, 791 Northern Irish students in the Republic and 2,000 students from the South studying in Northern Ireland. When the UK applied tuition fees in 2012, there was a 38 per cent increase in the numbers of British students coming to Ireland. But Brexit immediately reversed that trend, with a 10 per cent fall in applications for the academic year 2017/18, and an 18 per cent decline in Irish applications in the other direction. So, while more EU students will turn to Ireland, fewer Irish students will choose the UK because they will most likely have to pay 'international' fees.

The prospect of more demand for Irish education from EU students comes with a price tag: higher and more flexible funding for third-level education, the need for more capacity and the risk of making access for Irish students more difficult.

For the research side of Irish universities, it is an altogether different scenario.

There are 2,330 Irish academics in the UK university system. A profound debate is under way over how Irish universities might benefit from the UK leaving the European Union's flagship research-and-innovation funding programme, Horizon 2020 – and its successor.

The funding period for Horizon 2020 runs from 2014 to 2020. It is worth €80 *billion*. The money goes to universities, companies and charities supporting medical research. The fundamental prerequisite is that research across the EU which avails of Horizon 2020 money must be done on a cross-border basis.

Ireland is currently targeting €1.25 billion of the overall Horizon 2020 fund, more than double the target of the previous seven-year programme. But the UK's Horizon 2020 footprint is the biggest of all. Britain's universities dominate the landscape, and their scientific excellence is unsurpassed. Under the EU structure, Britain contributes €5.4 billion to Horizon 2020 (and to research sources embedded in structural funds and the European Investment Bank), but wins back €8.8 billion in research grants. Five British universities – Oxford, Cambridge, University College London, Imperial College London and the University of Edinburgh – are among the top 10 in Europe in terms of winning EU funding. Much of Horizon 2020 funding will already have been allocated, and Britain will continue to avail of it until the day it leaves the EU. The question of what will replace it, and how Irish universities might position themselves to benefit from the next funding round, is now under discussion.

Currently, more than 90 per cent of UK researchers collaborate overseas, and 17 per cent of staff in British universities are EU citizens (including 12,000 PhD students). According to the *Lancet*, 80 per cent of UK research papers have a non-UK name attached. 'It has been estimated that [in future] many of these would not qualify for a UK visa under the current UK regulations,' says Professor Mark Ferguson, Director General of Science Foundation Ireland (SFI) and the government's chief science adviser.

Professor Ferguson believes Ireland can start leading more projects previously led by UK researchers, and, in so doing, attract those researchers to Irish universities. 'I want star researchers who are thinking of leaving the UK to come to Ireland. They attract funding, they attract bright students, they attract other people to work with them. Across the spectrum there are people who don't like the current Brexit atmosphere, who want to be part of Horizon 2020 programmes, who don't like immigration controls.'

Ireland need not be predatory in this regard. While SFI wants to deepen research links with other European centres of excellence, such as the Fraunhofer-Gesellschaft, the leading institute for applied research in Europe and based in Munich, it also wants to enhance existing links with UK universities. Irish universities already collaborate with the major UK funding agencies, such as the Engineering and Physical Sciences Research Council, the Biotechnology and Biological Sciences Research Council, the Royal Society and the Wellcome Trust.

'The positioning of Ireland in the past few years,' says a senior official in the European Commission's research directorate-general, which administers Horizon 2020, 'in the way Ireland understands how the knowledge economy works and then builds the structures and processes around it, has been more successful than people realize. They see the Intel labs. But they don't see the leadership in other areas. Not just in pharmaceutical and biotech, but even in the advanced-food business, where there's a whole new value chain. It's the intellectual engine room of the next economy. Because of this, the Germans are starting to look at Ireland and saying, "Well, maybe we could partner some of our top institutes in Ireland as well."'

Caution is required, however. Ireland will need to attract more funding, from more diverse places. As of May 2017, European Commission officials in the research directorate were instructed to assume a 15 per cent cut in budgets across the board as a worst-case baseline impact of Britain pulling its annual net EU budget contribution of €8.6 billion. The UK has long been Ireland's ally at EU level when it comes to research funding, driving policy on issues such as clinical trials and data protection. It will no longer be at the table.

There is also the question of Northern Ireland. Some 54 per cent of the North's EU research projects come via North–South collaboration. Post-Brexit, centres of excellence like Queen's University Belfast could lose their appeal. According to one senior academic source at Queen's, a number of researchers who are funded by the European Research Council, the high-end EU panel described as a factory for future Nobel Prize winners, have turned down positions at Queen's because they were convinced they would not be able to renew their ERC grants.

'It's hard to measure the effect of Brexit,' says Professor Mark Lawler, who runs the Centre for Cancer Research and Cell Biology at Queen's. 'If you haven't been invited to the party, you don't know what you've missed.'

The centre is the jewel in the crown of UK cancer research, leading expertise on colorectal cancer, immunotherapy, genomics, precision and personalized medicine. In January 2017, Professor Lawler was the architect of a 60-strong coalition of patient advocates, healthcare professionals and scientists from 20 EU countries that published a blueprint for increasing cancer survival rates to 70 per cent by 2035. It works closely with industry, and has scientists working in its research building from Almac, the company that announced it was moving part of its manufacturing and distribution operations to Dundalk from Craigavon.

Much of Queen's' success in cancer and other fields was based on the ease of cross-border collaboration.

'I think there will be more opportunities for the South,' says Professor Lawler, who has witnessed a high degree of cooperation in the fields of health, agri-food, nanotechnology and cyber-security. 'A lot of work that people did together was very favourable. It was a very easy collaboration, very close, very beneficial to both sides.'

Professor Lawler believes Queen's and its cancer research reputation are resilient. But the university will inevitably suffer because of Brexit. 'I think we'll probably be strong enough to survive, because we have the collaborations. Some other areas will be more affected if they're very reliant on European funding. Under the Framework Programme 7 [Horizon 2020's predecessor], there was a €6 million funding programme. Would we still be able to go in on that? It's unlikely. We were told right at the start there was a potential that the EU would feel they shouldn't be giving us €6 million if we aren't going to be there.'

The UK is expected, however, to want to retain its links to EU research. That will be an issue for the Brexit negotiations.

'It will be the last thing they solve because it is so

important to the British establishment,' says a senior European Commission official. 'If they do get access they'll pay for it. And they'll pay a lot. It's not just the money. Knowledge is the oil of the next economy and they know this. And it's done in a collaborative way.'

There has been much focus on Switzerland. The country is not an EU member, but it has access to the single market (and Horizon 2020) via 120 bilateral treaties. In 2014, the eurosceptic Swiss People's Party (SVP) lobbied for a referendum that would limit free movement of people from the EU. The referendum passed with 50.3 per cent of the vote. As a result, the EU immediately froze Horizon 2020 grants going to Swiss scientists. Access was restored only through a convoluted parliamentary process that sidestepped the referendum result. It was not until 16 December 2016, when the Swiss parliament voted to approve a protocol allowing Croatian citizens free movement in Switzerland, that funding was restored after a costly two-year hiatus. And few missed the clear signal from the EU to the UK about the linkage between access to the single market (and Horizon 2020) and the free movement of people.

Every morning, Klaus Heinrichs gets into his Audi A6 3.0 TDI Quattro and leaves his home in Esslingen for the daily 30-minute commute to a management job in Stuttgart. When the car is stopped at traffic lights, he'll check his Facebook account on the car's touchscreen display. He will laugh at the pictures his daughter has just posted from the family's weekend ski trip to Chamonix. Klaus remembers the six-hour journey back to Esslingen from the slopes, and is, once again, grateful that the kids could watch Netflix in the back on their way home.

At another red light, Klaus taps on a news app. Brexit is mentioned, but it doesn't interest him, so he swipes over to a sports report.

Thanks to Brexit, however, more Europeans like Klaus (who, it must be said, is an entirely fictional character) might be enjoying high-speed in-car connectivity thanks to an Irish company called Cubic Telecom, based in Sandyford in Dublin.

Cubic is a licensed mobile operator, but it doesn't own cellphone towers. So it partners with 100 mobile operators across Europe to provide connectivity to the not insignificant number of Audi and Volkswagen cars on European roads. The SIM card that Cubic manufactures is built into the vehicle. That facilitates the on-screen apps and turns the car into a wi-fi hotspot for up to eight mobile devices.

Because of that tiny SIM card, Cubic can amass a wealth of highly valuable data. They will be able to tell where Klaus goes every single day, what apps he checks and where, how long his journey takes, where he goes at weekends, what his children watch on Netflix and so on.

All of the other Audi and Volkswagen drivers in Europe (and, if the deals currently in negotiation are completed, the Skoda, Bentley and Porsche drivers of the future as well) will be generating similar troves of data. And if Cubic's big roll-outs in China and the US go according to plan, the data harvesting potential is boundless.

All of this is conditional on compliance with strict EU data-protection rules – and here is where Irish firms may gain a competitive advantage post-Brexit, when the UK is likely to end up outside that regulatory sphere.

For Irish companies operating in the UK, the anxiety created by the Brexit referendum and its aftermath was not entirely conducive to trying to break into the European market.

'Brexit is a burning platform,' says Marina Donohoe, Enterprise Ireland's Director for UK and Northern Europe. 'A lot of our client companies were very safe and secure doing business in a country with a known language, a known business culture. Unless there was a very serious scaling agenda, it kept them in the UK, and didn't encourage them into the eurozone.'

The UK is all but certain to remain Ireland's biggest export market (in fact, in the year since the referendum there were more entries into the UK market and acquisitions by Irish companies than withdrawals). But there is a shift. Before the referendum there were over 600 Irish companies doing business in the UK, but not elsewhere in Europe. Fewer than 20 Irish companies opened eurozone offices in the first half of 2016. For the first half of 2017, the figure more than doubled, to 46. 'There was a very definite increase in numbers looking to establish a presence in Germany,' says Donohoe. 'Companies were hiring people on the ground, doing partnerships. Irish companies are saying, "Okay, Germany is now of relevance. I see a market opportunity. I'm getting traction in terms of the business-development calls I'm doing. I'm now going to establish a presence in Berlin, or Munich or Frankfurt."'

Language, or *localization*, can be an issue. Products that have been sold into English-speaking markets will be more adaptable to markets like Belgium and the Netherlands rather than France and Germany. 'There's more of a require-ment to invest up front in localizing and having native speakers to work with you,' says Donohoe. 'If you're trying to get into the French market direct, but you don't have native language skills, there's only so far you can go . . . Aerospace and aviation are English-speaking. But trying to get small-to-medium enterprises into the French nuclear market will be more difficult.'

One Irish company that has been shaken from its dependence on the UK is Crowley Carbon, a software and energy company. Based in Powerscourt in Wicklow, the company approaches large firms – Google, Pfizer, GE, etc. – to help them reduce energy consumption by up to 30 per cent.

On 23 June 2016, some 70 per cent of Crowley Carbon's business was in the UK. 'We were comfortable,' says Norman Crowley, the CEO and founder. 'The UK market is 17 times bigger than the Irish market. It's an hour's flight away. They speak English. Why wouldn't we?'

However, the tone and outcome of the Brexit campaign prompted a sudden response.

'The second it happened we saw the writing on the wall,' says Crowley. 'We did a dramatic U-turn. We stopped investing completely in the UK and we started investing globally. Since then, the business has trebled in size. Now only 15 per cent of our business is based in the UK.'

None of this has been easy. 'It was a perfect nightmare,' recalls Crowley. 'Revenue in 2016 dropped by about 50 per cent. The year was very, very tough. We really had to knuckle down. We did a lot of fast research and decided that the future of the UK, in terms of international trade and expansion, wasn't good. Our view since then has only hardened.'

Half of the company's expansion has been in Europe. 'In the first quarter of 2017,' says Crowley, 'Poland was our biggest market. We have projects in Croatia, Italy, Germany, France and Ukraine.'

In the spring of 2017, the company signed a $160 million deal for projects in Argentina, Brazil, North America, India and China.

'For years,' reflects Crowley, 'how Irish companies grew is they just got on the boat. It was very easy. Now everybody has no choice but to wake up and see what is outside of that. We have the talent to do it now, which we didn't have 20 years ago. We have the financial expertise, the international experience. We're credible. Now is the time.'

Crowley adds: 'If you take a five-year or a 10-year view of this, then Brexit is very good for Ireland. It forces us, *finally*, to stop doing what we've always done. Which is just hop on a boat.

'Now we have to learn Spanish and Chinese. Because otherwise we're *screwed*.'

16. A Red, White and Blue Brexit

On 18 April 2017, when Theresa May announced a general election for 8 June, the Tories were riding high in the polls. An average of three opinion polls gave the Conservatives a 46 per cent share of the vote, with Labour at around 25 per cent and the Liberal Democrats at 11 per cent. May would be ruthlessly targeting former Labour voters in Northern constituencies who had migrated to UKIP and were now up for grabs since UKIP's Brexit dream had been delivered.

On Wednesday, 26 April, Theresa May and David Davis hosted Jean-Claude Juncker and Michel Barnier at a dinner in Downing Street. Afterwards, Downing Street described the dinner as 'constructive'. But an entirely alternative account was leaked to the *Frankfurter Allgemeine* newspaper. It spoke of disbelief on the Commission side at what they saw as astonishing misconceptions by Theresa May. May insisted the UK did not 'legally' owe any money to Brussels on leaving, that the rights of EU citizens in Britain could be sorted out at the EU summit in June, and that a free-trade deal could be negotiated within two years. Juncker immediately phoned Angela Merkel describing May, according to the paper, as being 'in a different galaxy'.

An Irish Cabinet minister confirmed the Commission's growing unease. 'Most of the frustration is that the British side is not displaying the same clarity that we are,' he said. 'The EU side want them to be clear and organized and businesslike. The main motivation now is to get this bloody thing dealt with. It's going to become adversarial from now on.'

Over seven weeks, May's lead was whittled down by a poor campaign, a robotic style and a surprisingly good performance by the Labour Leader, Jeremy Corbyn. By the morning of 9 June, it was clear that her gamble had spectacularly backfired. Rather than extending her majority of 17, the Conservatives had lost 13 seats, and Labour gained 30.

Britain was once again in turmoil. Facing a hung parliament with just 318 seats, the Tories turned to a party at the very centre of Ireland's Brexit concerns. Like much of the Tory Party, the DUP were pro-Brexit. 'There was not much of a debate in the party ahead of the referendum,' says the DUP's Sammy Wilson, MP, who had served as both finance and environment ministers in the Executive. 'From day one we knew which side we were going to be on.'

It was impossible to gauge to what extent Theresa May's hard-Brexit rhetoric had turned British voters off. The Liberal Democrats, the only party campaigning for a second EU referendum, gained only four seats. The pro-EU Scottish National Party (SNP) *lost* 21 seats. Nonetheless, as the result was seen as a defeat for the Tories' Brexit stance, a clamour for a softer Brexit emerged. Ruth Davidson, the leader of the Scottish Conservatives, whose party had won 13 seats (their best since 1983), called for an 'open Brexit', prioritizing access to the single market over restricting immigration. Business groups made similar calls. A Survation poll found that 53 per cent of people supported a second referendum on the terms of the final Brexit agreement. Theresa May's threat to walk away from the negotiations was supported by only 35 per cent of people, while 69 per cent of voters opposed Britain leaving the customs union.

Dublin saw signs of a shift. 'If you look at the ingredients,' said a senior Irish diplomat, 'Britain wanted out of the customs union, out of the single market, no jurisdiction of the European Court of Justice, and control over immigration. Of all of those things, the one area where tectonic plates are likely to move is the customs union.'

Those hopes took a blow within days. Theresa May brought arch-Brexiteer Michael Gove back into the Cabinet, and appointed Steve Baker, MP, a prominent Leave campaigner opposed to membership of the customs union, as junior minister in the DexEU. (Shortly after Baker's appointment, footage surfaced of comments he made in 2010 to the right-wing Libertarian Alliance think-tank that the EU should be 'wholly torn down' and that it was an 'obstacle' to world peace and incompatible with a free society.) On the BBC's *Andrew Marr Show*, Philip Hammond, the great hope of soft Brexiteers, said categorically that Britain would be leaving the single market *and* the customs union.

What was happening? Brexit Britain was becoming a confederacy of angry, confused and fickle tribes. 'It's impossible to say what is going on,' said a senior Irish official. 'In terms of the official British position and the approach to the negotiations, it's almost as if the election hasn't happened. They're sticking to Plan A. On the other hand, it's clear there's huge pressure on May from within her own party and the business community and from others for more debate about what sort of Brexit it should be. But that hasn't translated yet into any meaningful change of position.'

The DUP was on record as favouring a soft border. But on 18 June, the DUP's North Antrim MP, Ian Paisley

Junior, was quoted as saying they wanted out of the customs union. 'You can't be half pregnant,' he said. 'We are either in or out of the EU.'

Throughout the post-election discussions, the DUP insisted they were fully in favour of Brexit, and of leaving the customs union, but would qualify that by saying they wanted a soft border. Such sentiments confirmed to Dublin that the DUP were in cake-and-eat-it mode.

In early February 2017, a three-part memo entitled 'Brexit and the Border between Ireland and the UK' was produced in the Cabinet of Jean-Claude Juncker. It was circulated to a number of departments and then passed to Charlie Flanagan, the Minister for Foreign Affairs, through the Cabinet of Phil Hogan, Ireland's EU Commissioner for Agriculture.

The first part covered the issue of the Common Travel Area, while the second dealt with the importance of trade between the Republic and the North. The note acknowledged the work that Irish customs officials put into 'designing a solution which aims to minimize the risk to the peace process', based on the creation of 'a near invisible border, with a very limited number of visible customs checkpoints, and which would predominantly rely on the pre-recording of relevant information'.

But it was the third part of the memo that was the most interesting.

It suggested that normal goods could not be given special treatment. However, it proposed that the agri-food trade should be done on an all-Ireland basis. The memo states: 'This note does not envisage an all-Ireland solution on trade in goods, *other than agri-food goods*.'

The memo continued: 'What is required to make this

work? By Ireland, with substantive investment in customs infrastructure (for general goods), and by the EU, by endorsement of the anticipated implementation of the Union Customs Code by Ireland.'

In other words, so long as Ireland invested heavily in customs infrastructure for general goods, the EU would acknowledge that Ireland is in full compliance with customs rules. All-Ireland treatment of agri-food would assume that all 32 counties would come under EU sanitary and phytosanitary rules, whereas the rest of the UK would remain outside those rules. If this were the case, there would be two options. Great Britain could continue to comply with European food-safety standards, including a scenario whereby the EU could certify that the British regulatory system was 'equivalent' and whereby the UK would have to *keep* complying into the future, probably under the jurisdiction of the ECJ. Or there would have to be the creation of 'a distinct all-Ireland solution based on the distinct devolution of competence to NI of agriculture and animal health. This would *require controls by the UK between NI and GB.*'

This was a politically explosive scenario. The only way to keep the border soft would be a combination of the hi-tech solution explored by the Revenue Commissioners, and an all-Ireland trade in agri-food that would place a sanitary and phyto-sanitary border on the Irish Sea, rather than on the land border. Any food or animal products crossing between Northern Ireland and the UK or vice versa would be subject to EU controls.

The memo acknowledges the sensitivity of this idea. 'As the Commission's Irish interlocutors have indicated,' it says, 'insisting on such a solution could harm the peace process.' In other words, unionists would automatically see it as weakening the Union. 'The note was good,' says an Irish source. 'It was well intentioned, but too premature. We're not yet at that stage.'

But the idea is still in the mix. On 4 May 2017, one month before he was elected leader of Fine Gael and five weeks before he succeeded Enda Kenny as Taoiseach, Leo Varadkar discussed the note at a meeting in Brussels organized by Phil Hogan and attended by other European Commission officials.

According to one source present, Varadkar felt that the Commission memo was a political proposition that could be addressed directly with the DUP.

On 19 June 2017, in sweltering sunshine, David Davis and a team of nine officials arrived in Brussels to start the long-awaited Brexit negotiations. It had been a tumultuous fortnight: first the election on 8 June; then, on 14 June, the cataclysmic fire at Grenfell Tower in West London, which was mishandled by Theresa May; and then, just hours before the talks began, a terror attack near Finsbury Park Mosque. The charred stump of Grenfell Tower stood as a macabre totem of a country that seemed to be losing its grip, right before the most challenging negotiations in its history. A withering editorial in *The Times* put it thus: 'The ruins of Grenfell Tower are seen abroad as symbolic of a country that wants to bestride the world of international trade but cannot keep poor tenants safe.'

Davis put a brave face on it with a statement before he arrived. 'While there is a long road ahead,' the statement read, 'our destination is clear – a deep and special partnership between the UK and the EU. A deal like no other in history.' On day one, the British team was forced into a concession: the negotiations on future trading arrangements would not be happening in parallel with the exit negotiations. Only if the EU was satisfied with Britain's bona fides on its exit bill and safeguards for the rights of EU citizens in the UK would talks on trade begin, but no earlier than October 2017.

In a news conference, both Davis and Barnier said that matters relating to Ireland had dominated the talks. The border issue would have its own dedicated structure within the negotiations, due to its complexity and political sensitivity. Two teams of officials would have an ongoing 'dialogue': with Olly Robbins and Simon Case on the British side, and Sabine Weyand and Nina Obermaier on the EU side. 'There will be a lot of days with damp towels around heads and a lot of ideas being exchanged,' says one senior British source.

Davis also conceded that the Irish question would be in play all the way to the end, as it involved trade and customs issues. And after all the toing and froing about the customs union, in the end the British would definitely be leaving. 'There is a problematic shorthand relating to the customs union,' says the British source. 'People aim for the simplistic in or out. It isn't like that. The customs union is so intertwined with the single market and the European Union that there was never any *question* of us staying in. The debate will be about what kind of new customs arrangements we are putting in place to connect us to the EU. It's about how tight or loose it is.'

London believes, however, that in the heat of the talks things will start to give, on Northern Ireland and on trade between Ireland and the UK. (One member of the British negotiating team brought a copy of the Good Friday Agreement into the first day of the negotiations, as if to challenge the EU side to abide by all of its commitments.) The other member states, the British source says, will simply start to put pressure on the Commission to do a deal. 'On Northern Ireland the political objective is clear,' the source says. 'No matter what we do elsewhere, we are committed to as seamless and as frictionless a border as possible. Pressure will come on the Commission to balance the wishes of the UK and Ireland and the political wishes of the other 26 leaders around the Council table.'

On 21 June, Elizabeth II delivered the Queen's Speech to the British parliament, setting out the new government's agenda. The Queen's Speech was bereft of most of the Conservative manifesto, because May would most likely lose Commons votes on any of its contentious issues. It also signalled that the Great Repeal Bill, which will have to transpose 43 years of EU legislation into British law, would dominate the life of the parliament, with eight hugely complex parliamentary bills needed. Most observers regarded this as an all but impossible task for a party with no majority.

At that point, the Conservatives still had no deal with the DUP. The talks had begun on Friday, 9 June, the day after the election, and would not conclude until Monday, 26 June (five days after the Queen's Speech), when a three-page 'Confidence and Supply' agreement was signed by the two parties' chief whips at a ceremony in Downing Street. In exchange for supporting May's government on any budget, finance or confidence votes, and on the Great Repeal Bill, the DUP was granted a number of promises: no change to the pensions triple lock, a 2011 measure that guarantees that the basic state pension will rise by 2.5 per cent, the rate of inflation or average earnings growth, whichever is largest; a continuation of the winter fuel allowance; and an extra

£1 billion for infrastructure, health and education spending for Northern Ireland. There was also a 'commitment' that London would match the EU cash payments to Northern Irish farmers under the CAP for the lifetime of the parliament.

Both parties made it clear the agreement would *not* be subject to the Barnett Formula, a convention that held that any funding increases in one part of the UK would be matched in other parts. Jeremy Corbyn said it was 'not in the national interest but in May's party's interest to help her cling to power', while the outgoing Leader of the Liberal Democrats, Tim Farron, described it as a 'shoddy little deal' and added: 'While our schools are crumbling and our NHS is in crisis, Theresa May chooses to throw cash at 10 MPs in a grubby attempt to keep her Cabinet squatting in Number 10.' The Welsh First Minister, Carwyn Jones, called it an 'outrageous straight bung to keep a weak prime minister and a faltering government in office'.

Dublin had been watching the DUP–Conservative talks anxiously, in terms of the impact they would have on the Brexit negotiations and on the talks to finally restore the Northern Ireland Executive, which had collapsed in January. Ireland was naturally excluded from the process, with no back-channel tic-tacking between Dublin and London, or between Dublin and the DUP. 'There was a lot of nervousness around the impartiality of the British government in those talks, if they were relying on the DUP at Westminster,' says one Irish diplomat. At his first meeting with Theresa May in Downing Street on 19 June, Leo Varadkar sought – and was given – 'robust' (according to one source present) assurances that the Conservative government would remain neutral in the Executive negotiations. The new Minister for Foreign Affairs, Simon Coveney, was given the same message in numerous phone conversations and meetings with the Secretary of State for Northern Ireland, James Brokenshire. As the Executive negotiations dragged on, Sinn Féin blamed the DUP–Tory deal for the hold-up.

Regarding Brexit, the fact that the Confidence and Supply deal gave the DUP an explicit involvement in the passage of the Great Repeal Bill provided some comfort for Dublin. The bill would convert EU law into British domestic legislation, some of it in areas that would impact on Northern Ireland. 'Given the DUP's views in terms of avoiding a hard border,' says an Irish diplomat, 'in terms of looking out for the interests of Northern Ireland in terms of agriculture and so on, they could be a softening influence in some of that legislation.'

Indeed, Dublin needed a functioning Executive with a clear, cross-party line on Brexit if Northern Ireland was going to have any purchase on the EU–UK negotiations now officially under way in Brussels. A single page of broad principles that all sides on the island of Ireland could sign up to had been agreed at the North South Ministerial Council in Armagh back in November 2016. It was very general, and had been gathering dust while the Executive was in hiatus.

One year on from the Brexit referendum, the Irish government was *still* looking for the UK's direction of travel. The two advisers who dominated Theresa May's thinking and policy on Brexit, Nick Timothy and Fiona Hill, were forced to resign after the debacle of the election, and in their absence a turf war appeared to have broken out across the Treasury, the Department of Exiting the EU and the Department of International Trade over the rightful ownership of the Brexit mantle. Philip Hammond wanted a long transitional period, even within the customs union; Liam Fox announced the start of UK–US trade negotiations.

On 2 July, Michael Gove, the new Minister for the Environment, announced that Britain was pulling out of the London Convention, a 1964 fisheries agreement among coastal states that gave a number of European fleets access to the UK's inshore waters between six and twelve miles from the coast. Gove described the move as a 'historic first step towards building a new domestic fishing policy as we leave the European Union'. The head of the Scottish Fishermen's Federation, Bertie Armstrong, said he was 'extremely pleased' with the news. The London Convention had been superseded by the EU's Common Fisheries Policy, so the move would make no difference as long as the UK remained a member state, and even post-Brexit its absence will affect only a small slice of UK territorial waters; but the *Daily Telegraph*'s take on it – 'a major boost to UK fishermen' – reflected a widespread view.

Meanwhile, a report by the Nursing and Midwifery Council in the UK that there had been a 96 per cent drop in the number of EU healthcare workers registering with the NHS was seized upon by Remainers as evidence that Brexit was going to have hard, tangible consequences.

Theresa May's acceptance that the trade talks would *not* be starting at the same time as the divorce negotiations was thought by some officials in Dublin to be a convenient way for her government to buy time and figure out what it wanted.

But the starting gun had been fired on 19 June and the clock was ticking.

An elaborate structure had been set up with groups of British and EU officials working on three key issues: Britain's financial commitment on exiting (the divorce bill); EU citizens' rights; and what were termed 'separation issues' – the role of the European Court of Justice, judicial cooperation, the Euratom Nuclear Treaty and so on. A working party had been set up involving senior officials from the EU27, chaired by the European Council General Secretariat, with regular inputs by Michel Barnier and his Article 50 Task Force. The group would give member states regular updates on how the negotiations were going, and would allow capitals to provide guidance on key issues as the talks evolved.

Within the talks themselves, the Irish border issue was, as noted, given a separate structure. 'That is a reflection of the complexity and sensitivity around those issues,' says a senior Irish diplomat.

The expectation was that early progress would be reported on the Common Travel Area and safeguards for the Good Friday Agreement to give the process momentum. But getting to grips with the border issue was going to be a tough balancing act, made even tougher by the political fluidity in London.

'We want to get this border issue resolved,' says a senior Irish diplomat, 'because there is the risk that there won't be a future-relationship agreement between the EU and UK. That would be a worst-case scenario for us generally and economically. But it would be particularly bad for the border. We need to look at the border in isolation and to look for bespoke solutions. We're not expecting those solutions to be fed in by October [2017], but at least we could make some progress in scoping out where the problems arise with a view to progressing possible solutions.'

Again, that would mean pushing the UK to show what it was willing to commit to, how flexible it was going to be and how politically daring it would be, even if that meant upsetting its new best friends in the Democratic Unionist Party.

However, the sensitivity around the Irish border issue was graphically exposed at the end of July. Following a report by the London *Times* that Ireland would propose moving a future customs border into the Irish Sea in order to get around the border dilemma, Leo Varadkar launched a scathing critique of Britain's attitude to the Irish problem. 'What we're not going to do,' he told reporters at a briefing in Government Buildings on 28 July, 'is to design a border for the Brexiteers, because they're the ones who want a border. It's up to them to say what it is, say how it would work, and first of all convince their own people, their own voters, that this is actually a good idea . . . We're not going to be doing that work for them because we don't think there should be an economic border at all. That is our position. It is our position in negotiations with the British government and it's the very clear position that we have when we engage with the [Barnier] Task Force that is negotiating on our behalf with the UK.'

A senior Irish diplomat insisted Varadkar was simply echoing Enda Kenny's policy articulated in his Institute for International and European Affairs speech in March, albeit in a more robust way. Certainly, Varadkar was saying out loud what officials had been saying in private for months: Britain would have to solve the hard border conundrum, and not Ireland. Although Simon Coveney, the Minister for Foreign Affairs, later clarified that there was 'no proposal' for a border on the Irish Sea, it was clear the new leadership of Fine Gael was prepared to assert a preference for a soft sea border between the island of Ireland and Great Britain over a hard land border. As Varadkar stated in the same briefing: 'If [the British] want to put forward smart solutions, technological solutions for borders of the future and all of that, that's up to them.'

Unionists were predictably furious. The DUP's Nigel Dodds threatened to use his party's newfound influence with Theresa May to scotch such talk outright. 'The DUP,' he told reporters, 'will not tolerate a border on the Irish Sea after Brexit that makes it more difficult to live, work and travel between different parts of the United Kingdom. The Prime Minister has already reiterated this. At Westminster we will continue to use the influence of our 10 MPs to ensure that respect for the integrity of the UK remains at the core of the negotiations process.' Ian Paisley Junior tweeted: 'One of two things will now happen: a very hard border, or Ireland will wise up and leave the EU.' The British government also weighed in. 'As we have always been clear,' said a statement from DexEU, 'our guiding principle will be to ensure that – as we leave the EU – no new barriers to living and doing business within the UK are created. Therefore we cannot create a border between Northern Ireland and Great Britain.'

The spat was instructive of the toxic impact Brexit will have on the delicate political relations between Dublin and Belfast, and between Dublin and London. Yet, with the Irish government's concerns enshrined in both the EU's Negotiating Guidelines and the European Commission's Negotiating Directives, Dublin was confident that its interests and the EU's interests were now indivisible. Given that level of confidence, the Irish government appeared emboldened to assert that what is at stake is not simply a trade or economic issue. 'There's been a sort of flavour from the British,' said one senior diplomat in the immediate aftermath of the row, 'that this is a technical, trade-related thing. The border and the whole peace process are about communities, about societal change, political stability. All those factors are woven into the Good Friday Agreement. And it is something which the European Commission Task Force and the Barnier team understand *extremely* clearly.'

On 15 and 16 August, the British government published two position papers. The first was on future EU–UK customs arrangements, the second on the Irish question, but both were linked. In the customs paper, London recommended a temporary customs union between both the EU and the UK for up to three years, during which time Britain would be free to negotiate and sign, but not necessarily implement, free-trade agreements with third countries. The paper then posed two alternative scenarios for the future: a new 'highly streamlined customs arrangement', in which technology, entry/exit declaration waivers and other innovations would deliver 'as frictionless a customs border as possible' between the EU and the UK; or, a new 'customs partnership' that would involve the UK 'mirroring' the EU's treatment of imports from third countries for goods that will be consumed in the EU, so that tariffs (and therefore customs checks) would not apply between the EU and the UK. The paper admitted it would be 'unprecedented' and 'challenging to implement' (a European Commission statement issued hours later said bluntly that 'frictionless trade is not possible outside the single market and customs union').

The Northern Ireland paper ran to 25 pages and set out the UK's proposals for protecting the Good Friday Agreement and Common Travel Area, avoiding a hard border for the movement of goods, and preserving North–South and East–West cooperation, especially in energy. Many of the solutions for avoiding any physical border infrastructure related back to the previous day's customs paper. London was recommending a blend of waivers, fast-track access for large 'trusted traders' and a 'cross-border trade exemption' from customs forms for cross-border goods by SMEs. A senior Irish diplomat was cool on the paper. 'It's clear the British would like this whole thing just to go away,' he said. 'The British have been asked, "Stop messing around, you've created the mess, let's see what you've got." They've produced what they've got on the two areas. You can see the customs one almost crashed, it's been not well received. The Irish paper will require extremely rigorous analysis.'

As the Brexit negotiations moved into a more critical phase in the autumn of 2017, the Irish government was banking on the EU's determination that talks on Britain's future trading relationship with the EU would not begin until Michel Barnier, and the EU27, were convinced that London was willing to address three key issues: its continuing contributions to the budget, the rights of EU citizens living in the UK and the Irish border. Senior Irish officials say the three issues hold equal weight both within the Task Force and across European capitals. If Britain wants to move quickly to a settlement of how it will trade with the EU in the future, according to Dublin's thinking, then it will have to grasp a difficult Irish nettle.

It could be a long time before we know the outline of Britain's future trading relationships. The most recent EU trade agreement signed with Canada gives an indication of what is likely to be involved. Known as the Comprehensive and Economic Trade Agreement (CETA), it took seven years to negotiate. While CETA provides for the lowering of tariffs on goods, it covers very little by way of services. The UK will be desperate to include financial services in its trade agreement with the EU, but it is virtually unimaginable that the City would enjoy the same access it currently does. 'There's a real sense on the British side that they are going to lose out,' says one Irish diplomat, 'even if they manage to maintain reasonable access. They're not at the table to change regulations. All the other services too – the non-financial services, advertising, legal services, broadcasting, culture – they will lose out on.'

What the Irish government will be pressing for is strong transitional arrangements so that Irish exporters, especially in the agri-food sector, can adapt until a comprehensive trade agreement is reached. Exporters called for Brussels to relax the rules on state aid, so that vulnerable sectors can be supported financially by the government in the event of a hard Brexit. Such a demand would be frowned upon by the European Commission's competition arm, which is notoriously strict on state aid. But there may be flexibility. 'I suspect the Irish authorities will be looking at transitional arrangements,' says Phil Hogan, 'which will include some element of flexibility on funding, whether in the form of flexibility in state aid, or on loans from the EIB, or some other relaxation of the deficit ceilings which we've had since the Troika in order to allow for more capital investments. These are all possibilities. There's an openness there to help Ireland.'

If there is no trade deal, then the hardest of hard-Brexit scenarios is the default to World Trade Organization rules. The UK is a WTO member, but only because it is a member of the EU, which imposes a single schedule of external tariffs for the outside world. If the UK were to join in its own right, it would have to agree its own schedule of all the tariffs it would impose on imports coming in from countries with which it does not have a free-trade agreement.

The day after doing this, the UK would switch from the EU external tariff to the UK external tariff, whatever that may be. In December 2016, the UK announced that it could simply adopt the EU's schedule of tariffs, the so-called cut-and-paste option. The problem with that, however, is that it would have to be agreed by all the other WTO members. And since the EU and the UK would have to work out what to do with quotas from countries that currently enjoy a free-trade agreement with the EU (remember the New Zealand lamb issue?), it could take the UK a very long time before it can start striking new trade agreements.

The UK could say to the EU that it was not imposing tariffs on EU products, and effectively dare the EU not to do the same. But if the UK offers zero tariffs to the EU, it also has to offer them to every other WTO member.

If the UK stuck to the WTO model, it would find that EU tariffs on many goods are not that high. But on key goods, such as agriculture and the automotive sector, they are much more punitive. Production chains snake across several EU member states when a car is assembled, and each time a component crosses a border it attracts a tariff. That is also why Irish farmers are so worried: in beef production some of the tariffs for certain cuts are around 12.8 per cent plus €300 per 100 kilo. That makes those cuts 40 per cent more expensive when going into the UK.

If the UK wanted to trade its financial services under WTO rules, it would face many more restrictions. 'People go to the WTO,' says an Irish official, 'and list their service concessions, which is one page. Then they bring out the tele-phone book, which is the service areas which they're exempting from competition.'

But the real crunch would be on what are called non-tariff barriers.

Access to markets is now more likely to depend on

compliance with the regulatory systems of those markets. It means UK products will have to comply with EU rules. Even if most products in the UK already conform on the day of Brexit, they may not conform over time. And if those products require independent testing, the agencies in the UK that carried out the testing are no longer EU-certified.

'UK service suppliers seeking to trade in, or into, the EU27,' writes Michael Johnson, a former UK trade negotiator, in a paper for the London School of Economics, 'could be subject to new checking and authorisation procedures which could become more burdensome over time as EU and UK regulatory procedures develop and possibly diverge.'

A study by Edgar Morgenroth of the ESRI indicates that when economic and political blocs break up, trade between the former constituent parts declines. Examining the cases of France and Algeria, Greenland and the EU, the two constituent parts of Czechoslovakia and the states of the former Yugoslavia, Morgenroth concludes that trade inevitably declines. The same is likely to happen between the UK and the EU.

These, then, are the complexities of Brexit. They are for the sovereign government of the UK to resolve, but are profoundly important for Ireland's economic and political destiny.

At every turn, there are surprises and complications. The Law Society of Ireland reported in July 2017 that 803 solicitors from England and Wales had registered to join the Roll of Irish Solicitors in 2016, and a further 300 had registered in the first half of 2017, availing of an EU directive that allows lawyers from common-law jurisdictions to easily adapt their qualifications to work in either system. (Previously, between 50 and 100 English and Welsh solicitors would have made the application in a normal year.) Although not all have sought practising certificates, by registering in the Irish system ahead of Brexit, they will be able to practise throughout the EU. The departure of the UK from the EU Audio-Visual and Media Services Directive means that British broadcasters may not be able to operate freely in another member state (Sky alone carries 43 British channels into the Irish market and in the process takes 80 per cent of a €50 million advertising spend for content that is not Irish). Angela Merkel had her own take when she addressed a G20 summit event in Berlin on 17 May 2017. 'Currently, the 250,000 pets, cats and dogs that travel from Britain to the Continent or the other way around each year are managed within an EU framework,' she said. 'Now they'll need hygiene certificates – things we don't even remember.'

Under a series of liberalizing 'freedoms', any airline certified by one member state can operate out of another; Ryanair, for example, can fly from Stansted to Barcelona without having to connect back to its home state of Ireland. Britain will fall out of this system, and its airlines will no longer be regarded as 'community carriers'. That will have a major implication for Easyjet, which regularly runs services between non-UK cities.

In 2007, the EU and US concluded the Open Skies Agreement, which gives airlines from either side the right to operate air services between any point in the US and any point in the EU. Britain will fall out of this agreement too. Furthermore, Britain will exit the European Aviation Safety Agency, which issues airlines with air-safety authorization certificates that verify compliance with all the EU's safety standards. Britain will have to set up its own national agency; as UK airlines replace their planes, their air-worthy certificates won't be recognized unless they have an agency with which the EU has a bilateral arrangement. 'This authorization stuff is extremely technically complex,' says one Irish diplomat. 'There aren't hundreds of people they can call upon to set something up.'

On the morning after the Brexit referendum, the European Council General Secretariat hit 'send' on an email intended for 27 EU governments.

It was a statement by Donald Tusk, the European Council President. Forty-eight hours before the vote, Tusk phoned 27 leaders, telling them, 'If Brexit happens, this is more or less what I'm going to say.'

There were three points: respect for the UK vote; determination that the EU continue; and the need for a future relationship between the EU and the UK. The most important line was in Paragraph 3: 'Any agreement, which will be concluded with the UK as a third country, will have to reflect the interests of both sides and be balanced in terms of *rights and obligations.*'

High in the ozone of the EU's response, this is the key. As far as Brussels is concerned, those rights and obligations will determine and constrain the process. The EU is an historic political project whose future is at stake. The Brexit and Trump victories threatened a populist wave that would engulf the EU.

'We have been going through a sense of existential crisis,' says one Council source, 'and a realization that we need to get this right. If we just add up all interests, whether individual member state interests or sectoral interests, then we will end up allowing the UK to have their cake and eat it.

'And that would destroy the European Union.'

More than any other country, Ireland's individual and sectoral interests *are* at stake. Other member states know Ireland is potentially the weakest link in the EU chain. 'There are 22 different controls that happen on an EU–third country border to ensure normal controls,' says one EU ambassador. 'The Brits have 350 million annual goods declarations, so there will have to be commercial and physical checks on the Irish border. You can't negotiate that away. Ireland hopes you can negotiate it away. But you can't.'

There is undoubtedly an awareness that Ireland has a special case. 'Ireland is a good EU citizen,' says a former senior Commission figure. 'They went through the crisis and agony of the [bailout] programme and came out as the poster boy for resilience and toughing it out. So, what is at stake is absolutely enormous.'

The weight of Ireland's biggest concerns – trade and the North – has led the Irish government to fuse the two in its negotiating strategy. 'The logic of the peace process,' says a senior Irish diplomat, 'is based on a method to depoliticize the underlying constitutional problems, and to create a zone of peace and prosperity. That peace and prosperity is underlined by the free movement of goods and services.'

'I came in before the Nordics joined, when this was a francophone organization,' says a senior Irish staff member in the European Commission. 'I feel it again. It's subtle. The Brits will be gone. The Irish . . .'

The Irish heyday in the EU institutions is passing. Catherine Day, an Irishwoman, was Secretary General in the Commission – its most senior civil servant – between 2005 and 2015. She took over from another Irish official, David O'Sullivan (now the EU Ambassador in Washington). While there are many able Irish officials working their way up through the system, there is a natural cycle in the ascent of officials from different member states within the institutions. The rise of people like Day and O'Sullivan was a result of the Irish intake after Ireland joined in 1973; likewise, the prominence of Eastern European officials from the 'big bang' accession of 2004, when 10 mostly Central and Eastern European countries joined, will become apparent in due course. The departure of Ireland's natural ally, with whom it shared strong views, particularly on taxation and the single market, will inevitably result in a dimming of Ireland's influence. 'This will be the first time we have to stand up for ourselves diplomatically, since we became a Republic,' says the Irish Commission official. 'We've been hiding behind the British skirts institutionally for donkey's years. The Brits have done a lot of heavy lifting for us for so long. I don't think we're psychologically ready for it.'

The importance of the UK went beyond the bilateral relationship. The UK also took a leading role on issues of concern to a wider group of economically liberal member states: Denmark, the Netherlands, the Baltics, the Czechs and Slovaks, and Ireland. 'The UK was always a key figure in these issues,' says one Irish diplomat. 'There is a lot of single-market and digital-single-market stuff in the pipeline. The UK used to be the intellectual powerhouse on these issues. They would draft letters for ministers to feed to the Commission. We're very keen on this and we want to play a bigger role.'

Meanwhile, the victory of Emmanuel Macron in France has restored punch to the Franco-German engine, a development that Ireland will (nervously) welcome. The spectre of a common consolidated corporate tax base has never gone away, even though each country maintains a veto. Dublin will be watching carefully so that, when the tectonic plates shift as the second largest European economy wrenches itself out, Ireland doesn't lose its balance.

'Brexit is the process,' says the Irish Commission official. 'It's about us as well. We are changing. It's like taking a huge part of your brain and putting it aside. What are the consequences 10 years down the line if this goes badly wrong for Ireland? We need to be lucky twice. We need to be lucky in that the Brits *don't* go for a hard Brexit. And we need to be lucky in that the final settlement allows us to *breathe* inside whatever the EU is going to look like.'

17. The Bullet Point

At 12.15 on Monday, 4 December 2017, Theresa May's fleet of limousines swept down Rue Stevin and into the European Commission's headquarters. The world's media watched. Inside, the British Prime Minister would hold a working lunch with Jean-Claude Juncker, the European Commission President. This was the deadline for May to meet the EU's demands on the three key issues of the first phase of Brexit negotiations: the financial settlement; EU citizens' rights; and the Irish border. Unless Britain showed 'sufficient progress' on all three, the talks would not proceed to Phase II, in which the future trade relationship was to be resolved.

A deal was on the cards. Diplomats had worked on the Irish issue all weekend. As dawn broke that Monday morning, agreement was within reach. An extraordinary Cabinet meeting had got under way in Dublin. May and Juncker would seal the deal over lunch. Leo Varadkar would make a statement at 2.30 p.m. Irish time in Government Buildings.

But, just as she was entering the Commission, Theresa May's Chief Europe Adviser, Olly Robbins, took her aside.

'There is a problem,' he told her.

The origins of that problem can be traced back to the opening day of the Brexit negotiations: 19 June.

The Irish border issue had been mandated at the highest level as a priority that Britain would have to address if it were to get to Phase II. On the night before negotiations began,

Irish officials told their British counterparts that Dublin wanted the border to be treated as a political problem, not a technical exercise; they didn't want teams of officials tinkering around with technical solutions. So it was agreed that there would be a high-level political 'dialogue', led by Sabine Weyand on the EU side and Olly Robbins on the British side.

In July, Irish officials asked Michel Barnier's Task Force to push the British team harder on its understanding of the Good Friday Agreement, in particular the North–South element. Britain had been saying it wanted to protect the Good Friday Agreement. But what did that mean?

British officials admitted they hadn't fully explored the risk that Brexit posed to North–South cooperation. It was something, after all, that was managed between Dublin and Belfast. London agreed to look at the issue more deeply. By September, British officials returned to say that, according to their analysis, there were 142 different dimensions to North–South cooperation. It was at that point that the so-called 'mapping' exercise got under way. Its impact would prove decisive.

From September, weekly meetings were held in Brussels to forensically explore how each of the 142 areas related to EU law. These were gruelling sessions, involving civil servants from Dublin and London, and later the Northern Ireland Office and the Northern Ireland Executive, all under the supervision of the European Commission.

Both governments accepted the extent of North–South cooperation under the Good Friday Agreement. 'The only question,' says a senior Irish official, 'was to what extent did it rely on the EU? That was where the debate was: whether you needed the underpinning of EU law to make that cooperation meaningful.'

The EU Task Force swiftly concluded that EU law *was* essential: across the board, the various aspects of North–South cooperation relied upon it. 'We realized how all-encroaching the single market is,' says a senior Task Force official. 'One bit is linked to another . . . Without an agreement on how to manage that, it cannot continue to work.'

On Friday, 22 September, Theresa May delivered a major speech in Florence. Its key messages related to the financial settlement and the need for a transition period. London was formally requesting a two-year extension beyond the exit date of 29 March 2019. On the divorce bill, May promised that member states would not 'need to pay more or receive less over the remainder of the current budget plan as a result of our decision to leave'.

The speech was well received. Michel Barnier said it had 'created a new dynamic in our negotiations'. But Brexit Britain was still convulsed by political division and rancour. Every time Theresa May inched towards accepting European demands, there was a backlash from Brexiteers and she inched back. With the Tory Party Conference approaching, Boris Johnson set out his own 'red lines' in an article for the *Daily Telegraph* in which he dismissed the idea of Britain paying large sums in order to access the single market. Amber Rudd, the Home Secretary and a leading Tory Remainer, accused Johnson of 'back-seat driving'. Instead of preparing for her party conference speech, Theresa May was fending off calls to sack her Foreign Secretary.

As the October European Council meeting approached, it was clear that on all three issues the British government had simply *not* shown 'sufficient progress'. On Tuesday,

3 October, Barnier confirmed to the European Parliament that 'serious divergences' remained.

That meant the conclusion of Phase I of the negotiations would have to wait until the next EU summit in December. One EU Commissioner looked on with alarm. 'There will be a big effort now for the next phase,' he said, 'but there will have to be movement from the British side. She'll have to do things that are unpalatable for herself. If she doesn't do them, she'll run into quite a difficult situation in December.'

On Wednesday, 8 November, a senior member of Michel Barnier's Task Force phoned her interlocutor on the British side. 'I've something to show you. Can you pop over?' she asked. 'That's great,' came the response. 'I've something to show you too.'

The British negotiator was in an upbeat mood. There was a stiffening of purpose now that December was the deadline. He had been working on a new draft of a paper on Ireland that he wanted to run by the Task Force.

When he arrived on the fifth floor of the European Commission building, he was shown an internal Task Force working document, entitled 'Dialogue on Ireland/Northern Ireland'.

There were six bullet points. The first noted that agreement in principle had been reached on how the Common Travel Area would function post-Brexit. The second, third, fourth and fifth points related to the ongoing mapping work.

But when the British official came to the sixth bullet point, he was stunned.

'It consequently seems *essential*,' the bullet point read, 'for the UK to commit to ensuring that a hard border on the island of Ireland is avoided, including by ensuring no emergence of regulatory divergence from those rules of the internal market and the customs union which are (or may be in the future) necessary for meaningful North–South cooperation, the all-island economy and the protection of the Good Friday Agreement.'

This, the British negotiator said, would be a *major* problem for Theresa May. The EU was suggesting that, in order to avoid a hard border, Northern Ireland would have to remain *de facto* inside the single market and the customs union.

When the paper was leaked the next day, there was uproar among Conservatives and the DUP. The Irish border had for months been eclipsed in importance by the financial settlement and citizens' rights. This was now a major escalation. Downing Street suspected Dublin had deliberately leaked the paper. An internal British enquiry got under way. The British side established that the Irish had *not* leaked the working paper. But the mood darkened considerably nonetheless.

Even before the leak, there were suspicions that Dublin was hardening its position now that Leo Varadkar had taken over from Enda Kenny. One senior British official spoke about how in the spring he had travelled to Dublin on two occasions to shoot the breeze with his Irish counterparts. Now, with Varadkar, 'the shutters went up.' The official says: 'It was a completely different atmosphere. It took us by surprise. The instructions that he'd given to John [Callinan] and company were that the dialogue was not to be conducted any more.'

Was the Irish position hardening under Varadkar? The new Taoiseach, as we have seen, had expressed an unwillingness 'to design a border for the Brexiteers'. But senior Irish figures in Dublin and Brussels dispute the notion that Varadkar was taking a harder line. His remarks followed a logic that went back at least as far as Enda Kenny's IIEA speech on 15 February. The decision to stand down the Revenue Commissioners from their explorations of technical solutions had been taken by Kenny, not Varadkar, despite a popular perception to the contrary. Varadkar's assumption of the premiership coincided almost exactly with the start of the Brexit negotiations. 'The reason he's been more vocal,' says one Irish diplomat, 'is that there is a negotiation that he has had to respond to.'

When Varadkar and May met in Downing Street on 25 September, Irish frustration was mounting. 'At the start of that meeting,' recalls one Irish official, 'there was this tête-à-tête situation, and the cameras were on. Literally, in sixty seconds she managed to repeat every one of the clichés that had been doing the rounds for months. She used them all: seamless borders, no borders of the past, close relationship, etc. For months those conversations didn't really advance.'

London had, meanwhile, been briefing against Varadkar in European capitals. A senior government adviser says: 'The British felt that it would be to their advantage to say, "You have a new Taoiseach, he's just trying to find his feet, so he's taking these very unreasonable and extreme positions, and we're sure sensible people in the end will realize that it isn't the appropriate thing to do, that it's kind of ridiculous that Ireland would hold back progress on this vital issue for everybody. In the end they're going to back down on this."'

The briefing was noticed in Brussels. 'Everybody knows what is happening,' says one senior EU official. 'The Brits have been briefing all the time, trying to undermine the position of the European Union. But so far they have failed miserably.'

Now, with the leak of the Task Force internal working paper, tensions between Dublin and London were blown wide open.

The key bullet point on 'no regulatory divergence' in Northern Ireland had been worked on by Irish and Task Force officials over the previous ten days. The text was finalized on Monday, 6 November. It was a deliberate attempt by Dublin to push London into turning platitudes about avoiding hard borders into actionable proposals.

'It was clear the UK was stuck,' says a senior Irish diplomat. 'The note was to put in plain language the central dialectic that needed to be dealt with. We were surprised that they were surprised, because they would have known that.'

There had been an intense discussion in Dublin throughout October involving Leo Varadkar, Simon Coveney, and key officials in the departments of the Taoiseach and Foreign Affairs over how Ireland should define 'sufficient progress' on the border question. How would a hard border be avoided? How much progress would have to be made on the Common Travel Area and the EU citizenship rights enjoyed by Irish-passport holders in Northern Ireland?

Now the EU was effectively telling the UK that the only way to avoid a hard border in Ireland was to keep Northern Ireland in, or as close as possible to, the EU's single market and customs union. How did that come about?

The key is in the mapping exercise.

The Good Friday Agreement created six North–South Implementation Bodies: Waterways Ireland, the Food Safety Promotion Board, the Trade and Business Development Body (InterTradeIreland), the Special European Union Programmes Body (which disburses EU funding), the Language Body, and the Foyle, Carlingford and Irish Lights Commission Body.

The Good Friday Agreement also established the North South Ministerial Council, which prioritized the first seven cross-border areas that should be looked at in the wake of the Brexit referendum from a list of areas which included environment, health, agriculture, transport, education/higher education, tourism, energy, telecommunications/broadcasting, inland fisheries, justice and security, and sport.

When teams of officials from Dublin, London and Brussels started the mapping exercise in September, they first went through the North–South Implementation Bodies, and then the seven priority areas.

'For each policy area we looked at,' says one Task Force official, 'we went through the relevant body of EU law. We then looked at what happens if this law no longer applies on one side of the border.'

It soon became clear. 'From day one of this mapping exercise, we identified that regulatory divergence [between Northern Ireland and the Republic] was the *biggest* single risk to its continuation. It's barn-door obvious once you start looking at it.'

Another EU official explains: 'North–South cooperation mostly covers things like health, waterways, and so on. The mapping meant combing through every single possible example that you can think of: child cancer, heart surgery, waterways management, education. If you take the health area alone, it's easy to explain the single-market dimension. Not only do you have all the equality of rights, but things like single standards for medical devices, the approval of medicines, mutual recognition of qualifications, ambulance services, etc. All of this is completely aligned at the moment.'

The mapping exercise brought clarity to the Task Force and the Irish government. There was no piecemeal, sector-by-sector way of preserving the cross-border arrangements in a situation where the UK no longer played by the rules of the single market and the customs union. Hence the necessity of 'no regulatory divergence'.

To Dublin, there was now an irresistible logic. Britain had been happy to promise no hard border. On 6 September, the Task Force had published its so-called 'Guiding Principles' paper as a direct response to the UK's August papers on Ireland. The principles spelled out that the border was more than just an economic and trade issue, and that it was up to the British government to show how, exactly, they were going to avoid a hard border, thereby protecting the Good Friday Agreement in its totality. Britain said, in response, that it could support those principles. Dublin, however, wanted more than that. 'This was a way of saying,' says one Irish diplomat, 'the Guiding Principles have an *ask*. So this was the first articulation of the ask.'

British officials insist they *were* coming up with solutions. One negotiator produced three papers between early October and late November. But a senior Irish diplomat dismissed them as 'muzak'. According to another diplomat: 'What they came up with was just, "Here is a load of problems," but absolutely *no* solutions. Zero. Not a thing. They were meaningless. There was nothing in it.'

On Thursday, 9 November, the Task Force paper was circulated to officials from the 27 member states. The same day there was a negotiating round involving Michel Barnier and David Davis. It was a stormy session. Davis accused the EU of trying to interfere in the constitutional order of the UK by suggesting Northern Ireland be treated differently. The following day the Brexit Secretary told a news conference: 'We recognize the need for specific solutions for the unique circumstances of Northern Ireland. But it cannot amount to creating a new border inside the UK.'

Irish officials were furious. Dublin believed there was no way that London could not have seen that this was the logical outcome of the mapping exercise, in which the UK had willingly participated. 'We were furious with British officials that they had let that happen,' says a senior Irish diplomat. 'From then on things got really difficult.'

A meeting was called to clear the air. On Wednesday, 15 November, Irish, British and EU officials gathered on the fifth floor of the Commission building. Until then, according to Article 50 rules, the negotiations were strictly between Task Force and UK teams. But things had got so difficult that the rules were bent to allow a trilateral meeting. On the Irish side were John Callinan, Declan Kelleher and Émer Deane. On the UK side, Olly Robbins, Simon Case, and Kay Withers from the British Cabinet Office. The EU team was made up of Sabine Weyand, Nina Obermaier and an official from the European Council General Secretariat. The British side brought along a paper, but the Irish were not interested in discussing it: they felt it introduced nothing new. It was, according to one participant, a very frank discussion.

As well as British anger over the bullet point, there were irreconcilable differences over when and how the Irish problem should be fixed. Although the UK had agreed to the principle of addressing the Irish issue in Phase I, Theresa May did not want to make commitments on the Irish border in Phase I that would make it more difficult for her to deliver what she was promising in Phase II: a free-trade deal between the UK and the EU. At the meeting, Robbins told Irish officials that May was not willing to sign up to 'no regulatory divergence' until she had had time to test her own grand

Brexit vision. 'The central problem,' said Robbins, 'is that we can't sign up to *anything*. We have to leave that path fully clear and clean and ready for the *future* relationship to solve this.' The EU accepted that there could be no comprehensive resolution of the Irish border issue in Phase I; but it was demanding 'sufficient progress'. In the end, the crucial question would be how stringently the EU defined that term.

Robbins's Irish counterparts responded: 'That doesn't work because this is a Withdrawal issue, and we need to deal with this *now*. We all know where this is going, so let's just spit it out.' The Commission Task Force agreed.

Two days later, EU leaders were gathering for an informal summit in Gothenburg. Varadkar and May met in an awkwardly small room for thirty minutes. It was, by all accounts, a difficult meeting. 'The Taoiseach talked about needing assurances,' says one British negotiator. 'But it did not register with us *in any way* that what he was talking about was that [Task Force] bullet point.' According to the British view, Theresa May left the meeting with a clear impression that Varadkar had agreed to find some language other than 'no regulatory divergence'. 'We'd come back to talking about *outcomes*, not methodology,' recalls a senior British source. 'We don't need to be prescriptive about "divergence" or "convergence" as per the Task Force bullet point. It's about the *outcomes*. Maybe we can just go back to stating "no hard border"?'

But this was not Dublin's understanding of the meeting. 'I think the British had a sense prior to that meeting,' says a senior Irish source, 'that May would come and say, "We want to work with you, and we're anxious to move on," and that we would cave in.'

Another senior Irish diplomat is even more frank. 'It was *very* difficult. It was essentially May saying, "Trust us." This is where the Taoiseach said, "You don't expect me to take a leap in the dark." He said, "It was *your* decision, it was Her Majesty's Government's decision, to take the single market and customs union off the table. So we want you to take the *hard border* off the table."

'Then she said, "We didn't decide to take the single market and customs union off the table: that was simply our decision to leave the EU." She was effectively saying, if it weren't for the European Union being so pesky about the four freedoms and things like that, then we wouldn't have this problem. In other words, we'll give you what you want but let us have our cake. They pushed this idea that we're all on the same page. They hyped it very publicly. We were *not* on the same page. Again, it was this tendency to minimize the force of our concerns. The Irish will roll over.'

The prospect of Ireland derailing the Brexit negotiations was now real. On 20 November, Theresa May's Brexit Subcommittee approved the doubling of Britain's potential exit bill to £40 billion. The next day Simon Coveney told the *Evening Standard*: 'Anybody who thinks that just because the financial settlement issue gets resolved . . . that somehow Ireland will have a hand put on the shoulder and be told, "Look, it's time to move on." Well, we're not going to move on.'

Twenty-four hours later, Anglo-Irish relations suffered yet another body blow.

In any political context with stakes as high as those of Brexit, the protagonists sometimes talk to journalists in real time; documents sometimes get leaked to the media; and journalists can get stories online in a matter of minutes. Journalists are thus liable to become a part, however small, of the story they're reporting. It happened to the present author a couple of times as the Phase I negotiations reached their climax in November and December, and so I beg the reader's indulgence for my use of the first-person pronoun.

On the evening of 22 November, I obtained a highly sensitive Irish government document. Entitled 'EU–UK Digest: Reporting from Missions, 6–10 November 2017', it was a confidential compendium of political insights gathered by Irish Embassy staff through their contacts with government departments in Japan, Portugal, France, Cyprus, Greece, Czech Republic, Latvia, Sweden, Germany, Italy and Luxembourg.

The digest focused exclusively on Brexit. The portrait that emerged of Britain's handling of the negotiations, as seen through the eyes of foreign and European governments, was not flattering. There was 'chaos' within the British system, incompetence among ministers and a hapless foreign service trying to explain Britain's muddled policy. Alongside references to Boris Johnson's 'gaffes' and concerns about the rights of Eastern European citizens in the UK, the digest highlighted French incredulity over a meeting between David Davis and two French ministers in Paris. 'Despite having billed this in the media in advance as a meeting to "unblock" French resistance, Davis hardly mentioned Brexit at all during the meeting, much to French surprise, focusing instead on foreign policy issues.' The British judge in the European Court of Justice bemoaned 'the quality of politicians in Westminster' and wondered if the British public might view Brexit as 'a great mistake' when they realized what leaving the EU entailed.

There was understandable fury within the Department of Foreign Affairs at the leak. But the reaction in Downing Street was worse. 'When that story came out I was in London,' recalls one British negotiator. 'My successor in Number 10 called up and said, "I hear you're in London. Could you come in?"'

'I said, "Sure."'

'He said, "You need to see the boss."'

The Prime Minister was livid. She ordered the official 'to phone everybody you know in Dublin and tell them how serious this leak is and what damage this is doing'.

The negotiator had, in fact, already made contact with the Department of Foreign Affairs. 'I told the Prime Minister, "It isn't what it looks like. It wasn't a paper that was written that was designed to leak. It's the same as we do, embassies producing weekly digests, things that other people are saying about Brexit to our embassies. Yes, it's obviously a politically timed leak, but it's not a grand conspiracy."'

The negotiator contacted his Irish counterparts. He could not, he said, complain in strong enough terms. 'They were apologizing,' he recalls, 'saying what kind of document it was, saying they hadn't done it, and that it was politically motivated.'

Irish officials convinced the official (correctly) that the paper had not been leaked by Dublin. But antagonism towards Ireland was deepening. The *Sun* had already run a front-page lead with unnamed Conservative ministers saying that 'Sinn Féin/IRA' had leaned on Varadkar to ambush the UK. In the *Daily Telegraph*, Theresa May's former adviser Nick Timothy wrote: 'Having taken a bold stance, Varadkar may find it difficult to back down. Some believe he is bluffing, and trying to force Britain into concessions, but it is more likely that a young and inexperienced leader, under domestic political pressure, is miscalculating.' To complicate things even further, the domestic crisis over Frances Fitzgerald's handling of the Maurice McCabe affair had brought the Fine Gael minority government to the brink of collapse. Downing Street now wondered if, in the teeth of a bruising election against Fianna Fáil and Sinn Féin, Varadkar might harden his position on the border even further.

A senior British source says that, as 'no regulatory divergence' had crystallized into a hard Irish demand towards the end of November, a view that Dublin had been playing a devious game took root in Theresa May's Cabinet. While negotiators who had worked with their Irish counterparts since the referendum did not necessarily share this view, there was a belief at the highest level that Dublin had, through the 8 November bullet point, deliberately ambushed Britain at a time of maximum leverage.

At 4.30 p.m., on Friday, 24 November, Donald Tusk, the European Council President, met Theresa May in Brussels. According to two reliable sources, Tusk repeatedly asked May how she was going to solve the Irish question, warning that Ireland was now the hardest issue. When the Prime Minister responded with stock answers about creative solutions, Tusk politely but firmly said: 'You must sort out your problem with Ireland. When Ireland is satisfied, they will tell Barnier. And then Barnier will tell me there has been sufficient progress.' He warned that the EU27 would back Ireland and the whole process would be delayed, if necessary, until February 2018.

May responded to the effect that 'one country cannot hold up progress.' The UK, she said, was a 'much bigger and much more important country than Ireland'.

Tusk set a deadline of Monday, 4 December – ten days hence – for the UK to deliver 'sufficient progress'. Eurosceptic anger in London was reaching boiling point. Jacob

Rees-Mogg, a leading Tory backbench Brexiteer, said: 'The EU cannot expect the UK to continue to give into its absurd demands. The integrity of the United Kingdom is not up for negotiation.'

At 10 a.m., on Thursday, 30 November, British negotiators received a draft text drawn up by Irish and EU Task Force officials. It was a synthesis of the Guiding Principles and the 8 November bullet-point paper: 'no regulatory divergence' for Northern Ireland was its most prominent element. The teams were due to meet at 1 p.m. in the Commission headquarters. For the second time, a trilateral meeting was agreed. The personnel were the same as at the 15 November meeting, with the exception of Tim Barrow, the UK Ambassador to the EU, who took the place of Kay Withers.

The negotiations opened with a key concession. Rather than insisting on 'no regulatory divergence' as the sole way in which to avoid a hard border, Ireland was allowing the UK scope to propose additional solutions that related to the future trading relationship, and to Phase II.

'We basically found a fix for them,' says one Irish official. 'It was to cast the text in a way that gave them the political space to continue to say, in the future we – the UK – will solve this. We had been saying, you're *not* going to be able to solve this in the future relationship. Now we had absolutely *stopped* saying that. We said, okay, maybe you are. We will now give you the political space to try. The solution was to leave *both* in there.'

But British officials were still adamant that 'no regulatory divergence' had to go. The teams worked through four separate drafts until 9 p.m., when the meeting broke up. Olly Robbins returned to London to brief the Prime Minister, who was appalled by the latest draft, according to one British negotiator. 'We got totally and utterly raspberried. "This is totally unacceptable," she said.'

John Callinan and Declan Kelleher, meanwhile, flew to Dublin to update the Taoiseach. Irish negotiators were unyielding. 'Leo Varadkar would have been very involved in the preparation of the line we were going to take, before John went [to the 30 November meeting],' says one senior Irish government figure. 'There would have been regular reporting back, and there would have been discussions between the Taoiseach and us, and Simon Coveney. But the position the government had reached was very clear. And John was reflecting that.'

Ireland, of course, knew it had the support of the EU27. Donald Tusk had hoped to meet Varadkar at the EU–Africa Summit in Côte d'Ivoire on 29 November, but because of the political crisis in Dublin the trip was cancelled. Tusk then decided to travel to Dublin on Friday, 1 December, the day after the marathon negotiating round, to meet the Taoiseach. Irish officials were struck by the degree of support. 'I remember thinking during the meeting with Tusk,' says one official, 'he is so clear in what he is saying. I wondered what he would say when he went down to the press conference.'

At the press conference, Tusk was even stronger. Quoting the Irish proverb that there was no strength without unity (*Ní neart go cur le chéile*), Tusk said: 'Let me say very clearly: if the UK's offer is unacceptable for Ireland, it will also be unacceptable for the EU. I realize that for some British politicians this may be hard to understand. But such is the logic behind the fact that Ireland is an EU member, while the UK is leaving. This is why the key to the UK's future lies – in some ways – in Dublin, at least as long as Brexit negotiations continue.'

The statement had been carefully discussed by Tusk's Cabinet, with as many as ten officials having an input. According to one senior British official, Theresa May was furious. (The source claims that May confronted Tusk about it later and sought, and was given, an apology, a claim flatly contradicted by two senior EU officials.)

Phone calls and text messages between John Callinan and Olly Robbins continued throughout the Saturday. The British side was pushing for a phone call between the Taoiseach and the Prime Minister, but Dublin was reluctant. 'It was felt that if it got to the point of the need for a discussion to iron out a couple of final points, then absolutely, a call could be set up,' says one Irish official. 'The British looked for it early in the weekend, but the Taoiseach wanted things to move on a bit further. The sense was this was best done when we got down to the final wire, rather than having another conversation about "seamless borders" and "no borders of the past". It would need to be worthwhile.'

On Sunday, 3 December, some 24 hours before the deadline, there was a phone call between Martin Fraser, the Irish government Secretary General, and Sir Jeremy Heywood, the British Cabinet Secretary. That was followed by another call between John Callinan and Olly Robbins. Callinan suggested that a phone call between May and Varadkar was still not on the cards, but that Dublin was willing to consider an alternative phrasing to 'no regulatory divergence'. Eventually, Dublin agreed a key change. Instead of forbidding regulatory *divergence*, the document would require the UK to maintain regulatory *alignment*.

What was the difference?

According to the British interpretation, 'aligning' is more voluntary than 'not diverging'. It will be for the UK to 'align' with the EU rulebook where Northern Ireland is concerned. That is, it will, by its own actions, come close to the way the EU operates the single market and customs union. Some have likened it to train tracks – parallel, but not identical.

A senior EU official puts it this way: 'They want to be able to say, "We've regained our freedom. We decide which of our laws to align of our own accord." But the meanings are fuzzy.'

For its part, Dublin was comfortable with 'alignment'. Since alignment was to be 'maintained', there was reassurance that, as far as Northern Ireland is concerned, the status quo would remain. Furthermore, 'align' is a robust legal term found in association agreements between countries seeking to join the EU: they must 'align' their rules with EU rules.

London believed the text was not fully agreed, but that an outline agreement was more or less in place. Theresa May would come to Brussels on Monday, 4 December, for a working lunch with Jean-Claude Juncker to seal the deal. Michel Barnier would then recommend to the European Council that 'sufficient progress' had been achieved, and at the summit on 15 December, EU leaders would finally give the green light for Phase II.

As dawn broke that Monday morning, the deal was still not done. Simon Coveney went on RTÉ's *Morning Ireland* programme at 8 a.m. He was circumspect, saying, 'These discussions are in a sensitive place right now.'

When the Cabinet met an hour later, there was a powerful sense of the historic moment. All ministers were asked to leave their phones and tablets outside the Cabinet Room. 'The real confidential nature of this wasn't lost on anybody,' says one minister. 'You got the sense that something very significant was going on. Nobody wanted to scupper it.'

The Taoiseach was the first to make a presentation. He made it clear that a text had not been agreed, but that he was asking the Cabinet to give him their imprimatur for what would be finalized. Varadkar explained what 'no regulatory divergence' and 'continued regulatory alignment' meant. The government had taken detailed legal advice on both phrases, and would be content with either of them.

Around 11 a.m. Irish time, the meeting was interrupted. Jean-Claude Juncker was on the line. Varadkar left the Cabinet Room. Martin Fraser, who had stepped out when Juncker called, returned to suggest that Coveney join the Taoiseach.

'There was a general presumption that it was a good sign,' says one minister. 'Leo was very clear – it wasn't yet a text. But Juncker was telling the Taoiseach, "We're good to go here. We're waiting for your agreement."'

Varadkar returned to the Cabinet Room. He told his colleagues that the UK had agreed the text. There had been a second phone call from Donald Tusk. Minutes later the European Council President quoted the Boomtown Rats on Twitter: 'Tell me why I like Mondays! Encouraged after my phone call with Taoiseach @campaignforleo on progress on #Brexit issue of Ireland. Getting closer to sufficient progress at December #EUCO.'

While the Cabinet meeting was under way in Dublin that Monday morning, I was in Brussels talking to sources, trying to work out what was happening. With the clock ticking towards the May–Juncker lunch, I managed to get hold of one reliable source. After several minutes of conversation, the source said that they had seen the text as it had stood on Saturday, and read out the key paragraph on Ireland:

> In the absence of agreed solutions the UK will ensure that there continues to be no divergence from those rules of the internal market and the customs union which, now or in the future, support North–South cooperation and the protection of the Good Friday Agreement.

In the view of the source, this was a major concession by the UK. I agreed: the language was startling, given London's public hostility to the idea in early November. I then ran the paragraph past a second source, who confirmed the accuracy of the paragraph but told me that the phrase 'no divergence' had been changed to 'continued alignment'. It was the view of my first source that the commitment represented by 'no divergence' could not be fulfilled unless Northern Ireland remained in the single market and the customs union; and it was my view at that point that there was no clear substantive difference between 'no divergence' and 'continued alignment'. Clearly, the text was still in flux and agreement was not guaranteed. But the fact that eleventh-hour versions of the text contained such language was very big news.

With two reliable and well-placed sources, RTÉ decided to run the story on its website.

The story read:

> The UK has conceded that there will be no divergence of the rules covering the EU single market and customs union on the island of Ireland post-Brexit, according to a draft negotiating text seen by RTÉ News.
>
> The concession, if accepted by the Irish government, would have far-reaching implications for how closely Northern Ireland remains bound to EU structures.
>
> But it remains an open question if the final text will be agreeable to both the Irish and British governments.

The discussions are still ongoing amid signs that the British government are having difficulties with the latest version of the text on Ireland …

It's understood the text on Ireland was updated to refer to 'continued regulatory alignment' on the island of Ireland.

After I filed the story, I composed a pair of tweets. The first, at 11.16 Brussels time, read: 'BREAKING: UK will concede that there will be no "regulatory divergence" on the island of Ireland on the single market and customs union, acc to a draft text seen by @rtenews.'

The second, four minutes later, read: 'The draft text on Ireland has since been updated to include the phrase "continued regulatory alignment" rather than "no regulatory divergence", acc to well-placed sources.'

At that very moment, a DUP delegation was being briefed on the EU–UK text by the Conservative government's Chief Whip, Julian Smith, at his office in Number 9 Downing Street. Within minutes, the RTÉ story came to the attention of Number 9 and the DUP delegation. The DUP immediately suspected that the story was the result of briefing by Irish officials – which it categorically wasn't. 'The DUP read it,' says a British source, 'and saw it as the Irish government briefing you in a triumphalist display and that the PM had caved.'

Julian Smith contacted Theresa May's Chief of Staff, Gavin Barwell, and told him to get to the meeting. Barwell arrived and tried to talk down the DUP, without success. Theresa May and her team were in the air, en route to the lunch in Brussels with Jean-Claude Juncker. Frantic text messages went back and forth between Downing Street and UKRep in Brussels. One senior figure in UKRep recalls: 'I got a text message from the people who were in the room with the DUP. They said, "There's a problem here. There's a really big problem."'

At 12.15, May arrived at the Commission. It was at that point that Olly Robbins took her aside to tell her that the DUP were unhappy. 'It looks like the Irish are leaking,' he told her.

The lunch got under way on the thirteenth floor of the European Commission. On the EU side were Juncker, Barnier, and Martin Selmayr, Juncker's Chief of Staff; on the British side were May, Davis and Robbins. In Dublin, Varadkar had already announced a statement for 2.30 Irish time. He had begun briefing opposition leaders, clear in his mind that the deal was done. Simon Coveney went on RTÉ's *News at One* to say: 'We hope to be in a place, in just over an hour's time, where the Taoiseach will be able to make a positive statement.'

A source close to Juncker recalls: 'You never take anything for granted. But there was no evidence, no reason for us to be particularly wary. But during the course of the lunch phones started ringing. Then it became obvious there was a problem. We knew it was a DUP issue.'

Juncker, Barnier and Selmayr left the room. May, Davis and Robbins stayed to continue their calls. May then took a call from the Leader of the DUP, Arlene Foster, who was in Belfast. A short time later, Juncker went back into the room. May told him, 'We need to give this a bit more time.'

Irish officials had been waiting anxiously. They had seen RTÉ's reports, but were still in the dark as to what was happening at the lunch. Olly Robbins phoned John Callinan, but Callinan missed the call. The UK Ambassador, Tim Barrow, called his Irish counterpart, Declan Kelleher, saying:

'You guys don't go off talking to the press. It wouldn't be quite fair to say that things are done and dusted.'

A senior Irish official texted a contact on the Task Force to check if the lunch was still under way. A text message came back to say that there was a 'pause'. When the Irish official asked why, she was told that May was 'taking a phone call'. Her heart sank. Then her Task Force contact called her to say it 'had all gone wrong'. The Irish official immediately started calling Dublin. The news conference was postponed.

At Stormont, Arlene Foster led a delegation of MPs to the front lobby, where she read a statement: 'We have been very clear. Northern Ireland must leave the European Union on the same terms as the rest of the United Kingdom, and we will not accept any form of regulatory divergence which separates Northern Ireland economically or politically from the rest of the UK, and the economic and constitutional integrity of the United Kingdom must not be compromised in any way.'

In London, the DUP's Sammy Wilson told the Press Association that Dublin was responsible. 'I think that this is emanating from the Irish government, obviously, trying to push the UK government into a corner in the negotiations.'

Had the UK negotiators really gone to the last minute without telling the DUP what they were about to do? Had my report on the draft agreement really sunk a deal that would otherwise have gone through?

Several sources in Brussels, Dublin and London suggest that the situation on that fateful Monday was a lot more precarious than had appeared.

First, the British government did *not* at any point believe that the deal was done. That morning, the European Council

General Secretariat circulated an email to British and Task Force officials saying that the text was 'closed'. But British officials replied that, as far as they were concerned, it *wasn't* closed. However, both Dublin and Brussels regarded the text as 'stable' when the lunch got under way. Yet, according to EU sources closely involved, UK officials were trying to make changes to key phrases on alignment and divergence right up to the very last minute, and were of the view that Theresa May and Jean-Claude Juncker would be able to deal with any minor issues the UK side had.

British sources also say that the DUP were not happy with the text. A senior British source says, 'When they saw the text they said, "This is totally unacceptable."'

The DUP was in a confidence-and-supply arrangement to support the Conservative Party in government. Because it was not a formal coalition, it was decided that it wasn't strictly necessary to keep the DUP in the loop on the negotiations. If they had been briefed, the other Westminster parties would have wanted to be briefed as well. According to a DexEU source, the DUP were sore that they hadn't been given privileged access. DUP figures like Diane Dodds, MEP, and others had been seeking information from civil servants for at least six weeks, but the messages had not been getting through because everything was being done 'on political channels'. In other words, if the DUP were to be kept in the loop, it would be done via the Cabinet and not by civil servants.

Another factor that antagonized the DUP was that they felt that Dublin had had too much influence over the entire EU–UK negotiation process. This, combined with what they regarded as 'aggressive' rhetoric from Leo Varadkar and Simon Coveney (in particular Coveney's comments to a Dáil committee in late November that he wanted to see a United

Ireland in his 'political lifetime'), meant the party was in a state of high anxiety as the deadline approached. During the weekend before the Brussels lunch, some DUP figures were briefed 'on generalities'. Party officials said they would not sign off on something they hadn't seen in writing. By the time they *did* see the joint EU–UK text in writing – and were taken through it line by line by Julian Smith that morning – their frustrations were at boiling point. When they saw the RTÉ story, they assumed it was the result of briefing by a triumphant Irish government (which I can confirm was not the case) and those frustrations boiled over.

'Your tweet,' a British source told me, 'was the straw that broke the camel's back. It fitted a pattern.'

That afternoon, May and Juncker confirmed that the deal had not been completed. In Dublin, a deflated Leo Varadkar told a rescheduled news conference he was 'surprised and disappointed' at the turn of events.

All sides realized things would have to be salvaged quickly. Juncker said that May had until Friday to retrieve the situation.

'It became clear quite quickly that the British were keen to do a deal,' says a senior Irish government adviser. 'The question was, could something be found that would put things back together?'

Within 24 hours, there were phone calls between John Callinan and Olly Robbins, and between Callinan and Sabine Weyand. Dublin insisted that regulatory alignment was not going to be reopened. 'The British wanted to look at the language there,' says a senior Irish source. 'It was made absolutely clear that there could be no change to that paragraph. It was closed. They felt it would have been helpful if we'd reopen it.

But we said, "This has been negotiated and agreed, and we're not going to move on it.'"

On Tuesday, 5 December, a senior British negotiator spent the entire day with a DUP delegation in Chief Whip Julian Smith's office at Number 9. They worked through all the party's concerns regarding the substance of the text, word by word. They were joined by the Secretary of State for Northern Ireland, James Brokenshire. 'I worked overnight on the Tuesday to add some additions to the text that I thought might deal with those concerns,' says a British source. 'I played them back to them on Wednesday morning and said, here are some drafting suggestions that might meet your concerns. They said, okay. They'll do.'

The changes were passed on to Olly Robbins at lunchtime on Wednesday. He in turn talked to Sabine Weyand and John Callinan, pointing out what was acceptable to the DUP, and what was unacceptable.

On the Wednesday night, the Taoiseach addressed a scheduled Fine Gael Parliamentary Party meeting. Ministers had been fearful that the solidarity between the EU and Ireland might start to crumble. 'We'd always wondered,' says one senior Cabinet minister, 'at what point does some EU leader tap the Taoiseach and say, "Listen, Ireland is important but . . . help us out here."'

According to people present, Varadkar dispelled such doubts. He said: 'This is a test for the European Union that we support each other, and that the European Union can support smaller countries. Ireland will be fine with clarifying things. But we can't change the substance.'

Late on Thursday morning, British officials told the DUP what they had managed to secure from the Irish and European sides. The DUP were still not happy.

On Thursday afternoon, May phoned Varadkar. According to a British version of events, the Prime Minister pressed the Taoiseach to change 'a few words on what had been agreed', but the Taoiseach had said it was too late.

A senior Irish official says: 'The conversation moved on to look and see could they add material elsewhere, about the east–west relationship. The view in Dublin was, we don't want any border between Northern Ireland and Ireland, and equally we don't want a border between the North of Ireland and the rest of the UK. If they're happy to commit to that, then we're very happy.'

This proved a crucial opening. It would be impossible to amend the language regarding North–South regulatory alignment in such a way as to rule out the thing the DUP most feared: the creation, in effect, of a border between Northern Ireland and the rest of the UK. But perhaps the agreement could incorporate separate language ruling out a new east–west barrier.

After the phone call, May stepped into the meeting in Number 9 Downing Street. 'The PM drops into the conversation to explain *herself* what difference they'd made,' says a British official who was present. 'The DUP then left to fly back to Belfast to brief Arlene.'

At that moment, Varadkar was attending a prearranged dinner with Cabinet colleagues. 'By the end of it,' says one minister present, 'the feeling was there was a decent chance of a breakthrough. There were a few calls going back and forth. It was highly likely we'd have something early in the morning.'

May phoned Arlene Foster at 9.30 p.m., and later at 11 p.m. 'The 11 p.m. phone call with Arlene was finished,' says a British source. 'Arlene was not saying she could support it.

What she said was, "I need more time and I need more changes."

'The Prime Minister said to her, "You haven't got any more time, and I can't get any more changes."'

At 2.30 a.m., the DUP called the Chief Whip and the official to say they had agreed. 'They patently didn't like the text,' says the official, 'but they wouldn't bring down the government over it.'

Theresa May left Downing Street at 3.44 a.m. and was driven to RAF Northolt, where in the dark chill she boarded the Royal Flight to Brussels.

The *Joint Report from the Negotiators of the European Union and the United Kingdom Government*, published on 8 December, contained sixteen paragraphs on Ireland and Northern Ireland. There was language confirming how the Common Travel Area would work, and on how the EU rights of Irish citizens in Northern Ireland would be protected.

Paragraph 49 read as follows:

The United Kingdom remains committed to protecting North–South cooperation and to its guarantee of avoiding a hard border. Any future arrangements must be compatible with these overarching requirements. The United Kingdom's intention is to achieve these objectives through the overall EU–UK relationship. Should this not be possible, the United Kingdom will propose specific solutions to address the unique circumstances of the island of Ireland. In the absence of agreed solutions, the United Kingdom will maintain full alignment with those rules of the Internal Market and the Customs Union which, now or in the future, support North–South cooperation, the all-island economy and the protection of the 1998 Agreement.

Paragraph 49 offered three possible paths to the desired destination. The first path, which, as we have seen, represented a concession by Dublin, allows the UK to pursue a solution 'through the overall relationship' – in other words, through the trade deal to be negotiated in Phase II. The second path is that if a hard border cannot be avoided through the terms of a trade deal, then the UK 'will propose specific solutions' to achieve the same end.

Unless and until the aims of Paragraph 49 can be achieved via one of these two paths, the default would apply: 'full alignment'.

Paragraph 50 reads:

In the absence of agreed solutions, as set out in the previous paragraph, the United Kingdom will ensure that no new regulatory barriers develop between Northern Ireland and the rest of the United Kingdom, unless, consistent with the 1998 Agreement, the Northern Ireland Executive and Assembly agree that distinct arrangements are appropriate for Northern Ireland. In all circumstances, the United Kingdom will continue to ensure the same unfettered access for Northern Ireland's businesses to the whole of the United Kingdom internal market.

This was to reassure the DUP there would be 'no new regulatory barriers' between the North and the rest of the UK if the default option in Paragraph 49 applied. In other words, no border along the Irish Sea to check goods coming from Great Britain into Northern Ireland, which would be 'aligned' with the EU's single market and customs union.

The Irish government put a positive spin on this new complication. If Northern Ireland was 'aligned' with EU rules, and London decided that the North was not going to be treated differently from the rest of the UK, then that was an unexpected bonus: the net effect would be to bind the *entire* UK closer to the EU, something that would obviate the need for tariff- and non-tariff barriers that might devastate €65 billion in two-way Ireland–UK trade. 'It significantly revives the chance that the single market and customs union are going to come back into play for the Brits,' says one senior Irish Cabinet minister. 'If anything, the DUP have inadvertently made Theresa May's life more difficult down the road, but Ireland's chance of getting a more favourable outcome quite positive.'

There was, of course, another way of reading Paragraph 50: that it could lead to a Brexit so soft as to be, perhaps, politically unattainable. The logic of paragraphs 49 and 50 could yet see the Irish border prove the undoing of an orderly Brexit deal.

On 15 December, EU leaders formally declared that the Brexit negotiations could move into Phase II. It was seen as a formidable achievement by Theresa May, given the weakness of her political position since her election gamble in June. But was it built on an unsustainable fudge?

An hour after the December summit closed, a senior EU official told the author: 'This is and will remain one of the very difficult issues – both because of the issue itself, on its own merits, but also because it exposes the contradictions in the UK position. That is that you can't at the same time have frictionless trade and be outside the customs union and the single market. The way to have frictionless trade is to be *in* those constructions.'

The Irish reading of Paragraph 49 was that it provided, in Leo Varadkar's words, a 'bullet-proof' guarantee that there would be no hard border in Ireland. The British reading was different. David Davis told the BBC's Andrew Marr the deal was 'not legally binding'. Michael Gove then said it could 'all be reversed at the next general election'.

The Brexiteers' backsliding was met with a warning from the EU. When the 27 leaders approved the move into Phase II, they had to update the Negotiating Guidelines that were originally adopted in April. The new Negotiating Guidelines stressed that 'negotiations in the second phase can only progress as long as *all commitments* undertaken during the first phase are respected in full and translated faithfully into legal terms as quickly as possible.'

On 13 December, Michel Barnier told Simon Coveney that Ireland would be given a 'distinct strand' in Phase II of the negotiations. Beyond that, Ireland would have to give its consent every time the Negotiating Guidelines were updated. If anything in those negotiations threatened the border guarantee, then Ireland could veto it. 'In Phase II the EU will decide by consensus,' says a senior EU official. 'At every step of the way the Irish can hold the process hostage.'

It did not take long for Ireland to face its first challenge. As 2018 dawned, the October deadline to finalize the Withdrawal Treaty felt closer than ever. In mid January, EU Task Force officials began drafting an outline. The December deal, contradictions and all, would have to be converted into a watertight legal document and folded into the treaty.

Over the next six weeks, intense drafting work was done by the Task Force and teams from the European Commission and European Council's legal services. There was also significant input from Dublin. There was regular contact between Sabine Weyand and Olly Robbins, but, while the British were given the general direction of travel, they were not shown drafts.

It was decided early on that the Irish question would be handled in a separate protocol. Fianna Fáil's Brexit spokesman Stephen Donnelly claimed that this would weaken the force of the deal. But Irish and EU officials insisted the protocol *would* be legally binding, and that special arrangements for individual member states in key EU treaties historically tended to be handled through protocols (protocols 19 and 20 of the Lisbon Treaty, which relate to the Common Travel Area, are good examples).

The December *Joint Report* had spoken of three ways to avoid a hard border. These now became known as Option A (avoiding the need for border checks through a deep and comprehensive trade deal); Option B (London making specific proposals for ways of avoiding border checks); and Option C, the 'backstop' of 'maintaining full alignment' with EU regulations in North–South trade. Dublin's priority in the draft treaty was for the backstop to be 'operationalized' in clear language. London's priority was to keep the idea of alignment out of the treaty as much as possible. They insisted options A and B should be contained within the main chapters of the treaty text, with the backstop shunted into a protocol.

British officials urged the Task Force to be mindful of events in Belfast. On 17 January, the latest attempt to restore the Northern Ireland Executive and Assembly collapsed. In Brussels, British negotiators argued that Northern tensions would be inflamed if the forthcoming legal text contained any sensitive detail on the Irish border.

British pro-Brexit politicians took a very different tack: former Northern Ireland Secretary Owen Patterson, the hardline

Daniel Hannan MEP and Labour Party MP Kate Hoey all called into question the continued relevance of the Good Friday Agreement, which they saw as a worrying obstacle to Brexit.

Against this backdrop, the drafting continued. One EU official closely involved says: 'The text was moving around a lot. The British were putting up taboos, and the Irish were resisting these taboos. It was slipping and sliding all over the place.'

Eventually the text was completed on Thursday, 22 February. The following Wednesday, it was formally adopted by the College of 27 EU Commissioners, then published on the Task Force website and circulated among officials from the other member states. The 118-page *Draft Withdrawal Agreement* contained 15 articles on Ireland. EU officials had wanted to lead with the material regarding the movement of goods, but Dublin insisted the Common Travel Area should be at the top ('You have to put people before goods,' observed one EU official). While the Task Force had worked hard to keep the tone neutral and technocratic, a few key phrases immediately jumped out.

The treaty would 'establish . . . [a] common regulatory area' between the EU and Northern Ireland. 'The common regulatory area shall constitute an area without internal borders in which the free movement of goods is ensured and North–South cooperation protected . . .'

It continued: 'The territory of Northern Ireland . . . shall be considered to be part of the customs territory of the [European] Union.' Customs duties 'shall be prohibited between the [European] Union and . . . Northern Ireland'.

The draft envisaged a Joint Committee, involving the EU and Northern Ireland stakeholders, that would meet to discuss any issues relating to North–South cooperation that might be drawn into the new common regulatory area system.

The European Court of Justice would have jurisdiction over those EU rules that continued to apply in Northern Ireland.

To the Task Force, the text was faithful to the December deal, spelling out its logical implications. But it met with a thunderous response from the DUP and eurosceptics. Arlene Foster said it would be 'catastrophic' for Northern Ireland. Jeffrey Donaldson, the DUP MP, said: 'This fundamentally breaches the understanding reached in December and would undermine the constitutional status of Northern Ireland in the Belfast Agreement. If the EU or Dublin believes the UK government will be signing up to a border in the Irish Sea, they are deluded.' In the House of Commons, Theresa May was equally emphatic: 'The draft legal text that the Commission has published would, if implemented, undermine the UK common market and threaten the constitutional integrity of the UK by creating a customs and regulatory border down the Irish Sea, and no UK Prime Minister could ever agree to it.'

The Prime Minister was suggesting that the EU had moved the goalposts. But at a news conference, Michel Barnier insisted that the 'common regulatory area' was entirely consistent with Option C – the backstop – as agreed in December. If and when Option A or B was brought into effect, the need for Option C would fall away. Theresa May was right, of course, to note that Option C would effectively create the need for 'border' checks between Great Britain and Northern Ireland, but there was nothing new about that. 'As the *Joint Report* says,' a senior EU official explained, 'the commitments to no hard border, North–South cooperation, the Good Friday Agreement have to be upheld in *all* circumstances – *independently* of the nature of the future relationship. The UK signed up to it.' There was no reference in the *Draft Withdrawal Agreement* to Paragraph 50 in the *Joint Report*, which referred to avoiding a barrier between Northern Ireland and Great Britain. This silence was not an accident; and in the EU's eyes it was entirely appropriate, because the presence or absence of such a barrier was an internal matter for the UK. 'Any legal instrument to give effect to this,' observed a senior Irish official, 'is seen as *absolutely* a matter for the British to deal with themselves. They're not happy that it's been presented that narrowly. But the EU position has been so clear from the get-go, even as far back as the December text, that we never got to the point of even *considering* what that might look like.'

Leo Varadkar was sharply critical of the backlash from London and the DUP. 'It's not okay for people,' he said, 'whether pro-Brexit politicians in Britain or parties in Northern Ireland, to just say no now.' Dublin would be perfectly happy to explore options A and B – thereby avoiding the necessity of Option C – *if* the UK would come forward with detailed, legally sound proposals: something it had not yet done. 'We're really messaging this out very strongly,' said a senior Irish negotiator, 'that our absolute preference is to find a solution under Option A and we will continue to work with the Task Force and the British to that end.'

This was scant comfort for a Prime Minister in the throes of an existential struggle within her Cabinet and party. Britain's efforts to influence the drafting process had come to little.

The *Draft Withdrawal Agreement* did not so much change the dynamics of Brexit as remove the ambiguity that shrouded the process for nearly 20 months. The narrowing of options for the British government has sharpened the prospects for a calamitous outcome. The Negotiating Guidelines are clear that the UK cannot nail down a transition period if there is backsliding on the December guarantee. Even though the February text was a draft (and will have been negotiated further by the time this edition goes to print), it left Theresa May precious few options. Either she faces down the DUP and Tory hardliners and accepts the legal outworking of the *Joint Report*; or she plays hardball and refuses to acquiesce, gambling on the prospect that, as the cliff-edge approaches, Ireland's EU partners will put unbearable pressure on Dublin to soften its position on the border.

A 'no deal' scenario would be highly damaging. According to Department of Foreign Affairs officials, all government departments have been working on a Mitigation Plan to limit the effects of such an outcome. Reports from the ESRI and others indicate that it could reduce Ireland's GDP by between 5 and 7 per cent, causing some 40,000 job losses.

In the meantime, Anglo-Irish relations are at their lowest point in decades; and the DUP's trust in the Irish government has evaporated. 'There is a real danger here,' muses a senior British negotiator, 'that we had started to take for granted that Anglo-Irish relations were becoming freer and easier and that politics in Northern Ireland were moving in the right direction. My Irish counterparts were warning about how dangerous Brexit was, right back at the start. We've taken it for granted that we all speak the same language. But what this last month in particular has shown us is that it's all much more fragile.

'The border is back in Irish politics.'

Acknowledgements

This book was written during an extremely busy news period in European affairs – so busy, the joke went, it was hard to see how journalists could get any work done. I would like to thank RTÉ News for giving me leeway to complete the project, especially Jon Williams, the Managing Director of News and Current Affairs, Hilary McGouran, Managing Editor News (Television), and Eimear Lowe, Deputy Foreign Editor.

I would also like to thank Michael McLoughlin and Brendan Barrington of Penguin Ireland for getting the project off the ground, and helping me to stick to deadline.

Telling the story of Ireland's collision with Brexit has required an enormous amount of help. I have had immeasurable levels of support from across a range of Irish government departments and agencies, from dozens of officials, ministers and diplomats in Dublin, Brussels, London and other parts of the EU. Their perspectives, technical expertise and insights into a complex, unfolding and sometimes chaotic situation were necessarily provided on a background basis. I would like to thank them all for being so gracious in their help and generous with their time.

I would especially like to thank Liam MacHale, Kevin Kinsella and Catherine Lascurettes of the Irish Farmers' Association, Tara McCarthy of Bord Bia, T. J. Flanagan of the Irish Co-operative Organisation Society (ICOS), Sean O'Donoghue from the Killybegs Fishermen's Organisation (KFO) and Niall Duffy, Editor of the *Skipper*.

I would also like to acknowledge the help of IBEC, the Small Firms Association, the Irish Exporters Association, Enterprise Ireland, Science Foundation Ireland and IDA Ireland in providing statistics, insights and examples, often at short notice. Thanks are also due to Chartered Accountants Ireland, Cooperation and Working Together (CAWT), the Institute for International and European Affairs (IIEA), and the Centre for Cross Border Studies (CCBS).

I would also like to extend a special thanks to Liam O'Brien from the Oireachtas Press Office, Edgar Morgenroth from the ESRI and Noelle O'Connell from European Movement Ireland (EMI) for their repeated help and signposting of the issues.

I would like to thank James Crisp of the *Daily Telegraph*, and formerly of EURACTIV, for supplying details of the UK Rep playlist on referendum night.

Index

Aamann, Preben 297
Abbott 102, 231
Adams, Gerry 291
Adams Foods 108
agriculture/farming: animal
  diseases and health scandals
  42, 90–91, 92, 177, 180, 207 *see
  also* foot and mouth disease;
  and 'Brexit and the border
  between Ireland and the UK'
  memo 324–6; Brexit's impact
  on agri-food sector 21–2, 38–9,
  84–6, 92–100, 102–7, 117–29,
  324–6; dairy farming *see* dairy
  industry; EU Common
  Agriculture Policy *see* Common
  Agriculture Policy (CAP); EU
  subsidies 44, 89–91, 113, 126;
  food production 83–100 *see also*
  beef industry; dairy industry;
  meat industry; sheep/lamb;
  food standards *see* food
  standards; Irish Department of
  Agriculture, Food and the
  Marine 42; livestock exports
  86–7, 197; mushrooms 21–2,
  37–9; New Zealand 96–9;
  sanitary and phyto-sanitary
  checks/rules 42, 176–80, 197,
  205–6, 325; Teagasc farm
  management survey 95, 97
Ahern, Bertie 78, 79
AIG 307
Aiken, Frank 238, 241–2
airlines 340–41
airports 202, 243, 295
Aliens Order 236
All-Island Civic Dialogue 74–6, 277
Allister, Jim 276
Almac Group 303–4, 314–15
Altnagelvin 255
Amsterdam, Treaty of 237
Anderson, Martina 172
Andorra 41
Anglo-Irish Beef Producers
  (AIBP/ABP) 89–90, 92
Anglo-Irish Free Trade
  Agreement 104
Anglo-Irish Treaty negotiations
  (1921) 233
Apple 54–5
Armstrong, Bertie 140, 331
Article 50 of the EU Treaty 25,
  31, 48, 162, 187, 188; Article 50
  Task Force *see* Task Force
  (TF50); Irish paragraph in
  May's letter 287–8; May's
  triggering principles 236, 288

ATA Carnets 200–201
Aurivo 103–4, 105
Authorised Economic Operator
    (AEO) certificates 199
Automated Number Plate
    Recognition (ANPR) 196,
    200, 203–5
Avonmore 118

Baileys Irish Cream 121–3
Baker, Steve 323
Baltics 232, 343
banks: and Brexit 304–5, 306;
    and the City of London 304–5;
    European Central Bank 27,
    30, 279; European Investment
    Bank 212, 213, 312; Frankfurt
    and the wholesale banking
    market 306; Irish 26 see also
    Central Bank of Ireland
Barker, Alex 66
Barnes, Richard 145
Barnier, Michel 60–62, 65, 66–7,
    68, 73, 144, 170, 171, 174, 175,
    182, 185, 246, 327, 332, 335, 336,
    346, 347, 348, 353, 367, 376, 379;
    Downing Street dinner 321
Barroso, José Manuel 270
Barrow, Sir Tim 283, 360, 367–8
Barry, Linda 219
Barwell, Gavin 366
beef industry 84–96, 99; Beef
    Tribunal 91; BSE crisis 90–91;
    and foot and mouth disease
    42, 92, 177, 180; tariffs 335

beer industry 123–5
Belfast 236; Agreement see Good
    Friday Agreement; Queen's
    University 314–15; Skainos
    Project 269
Belgium 41, 94, 96, 209, 228, 318
Bergin, Jer 84–5, 86, 93, 100
Biden, Joe 16
Billington, Declan 275
biopharmaceuticals sector 229–30
Biotechnology and Biological
    Sciences Research Council 313
Bord Bia 27, 118, 120, 171
border, Irish 7, 31–2, 52–3, 74, 79,
    101–2, 165, 166, 174–8, 186,
    197–208, 250–51, 287, 332, 333–6;
    'Brexit and the border between
    Ireland and the UK' 324–6;
    cross-border commuting 257;
    cross-border healthcare 252–6;
    cross-border social welfare
    258–60; and customs see
    customs control; and customs
    union 348–56, 360–81; and
    double peripherality 253; Irish
    Central Border Area Network
    257; phyto-sanitary checks/
    rules 42, 176–80, 197,
    205–6, 325
Border People 259–60
Boswell, Timothy Eric, Lord
    Boswell of Aynho 77, 79
Bovine Spongiform
    Encephalopathy (BSE) 42,
    90–91, 207

Bradley, Denis 271–2
Bradley, John 273–4
Bratislava 65
Brehon Brewhouse 123–4
Brexit 92–100; and the agri-food
    sector *see* agriculture/farming;
    beef industry; beer industry;
    dairy industry; meat industry;
    attitude changes with and after
    2017 election 322–3; and the
    CTA *see* Common Travel Area;
    and the customs union *see*
    customs union; 'divorce bill'
    66, 331; and the EAW network
    58, 261–3; and energy *see*
    energy; and EU 'associative'
    relationship 168–9; and the
    EU Commission/Council
    debate 49; and financial
    services 305–7; and fishing *see*
    fishing industry; and the four
    freedoms 34, 161; and the
    Great Repeal Bill 216, 224,
    328, 330; 'hard' 49, 112; House
    of Commons Select
    Committee on Exiting the EU
    292–3; Ireland's exposure to
    economic/trade effects of
    40–45, 69, 84–6, 92–100, 102–7,
    117–29, 199–206, 337–9; Irish
    anxiety over 5, 21–2, 36–7, 76,
    78, 93–6, 119–20, 125, 137–9,
    188, 216, 258, 272–3, 317–18;
    Irish Brexit Cabinet
    Committee 53; and the
Locarno Suite meetings
    70–72, 76, 180; May's Lancaster
    House speech 164–6, 236;
    May's letter to European
    Council 283, 287–8; 'means
    Brexit' 46, 69, 161; and the
    mushroom trade 21–2, 38–9;
    negotiations 66, 73–4, 158, 159,
    326–7, 331–2; and new trade
    deals 42, 46, 94, 98–9; no deal
    better than bad deal 165–6;
    and the North/South border
    see border, Irish; and North–
    South trade 44, 99–100, 102–7,
    115–17, 122–3, 177; 'open' 322;
    opportunities for Ireland
    303–20; pre-negotiation refusal
    63–4; punitive deal impulse
    34, 58–9; referendum *see*
    referendum on EU
    membership; rights and
    obligations balance 341–2; and
    the Singapore model 225–6;
    and the single market *see* single
    market; 'soft' 49, 173; Task
    Force *see* Task Force (TF50);
    Toolkit 120; transitional
    period 163, 330–31; and a
    United Ireland 289–302;
    White Paper 167–8
British–Irish Visa Scheme 242
British Nationality Act (1948)
    238–9
Brokenshire, James 167, 281, 292,
    293, 330, 371

Brown, Gordon 19, 47
Bruegel 304–5, 306
Brussels NI 274
Bruton, John 45, 78–9
BSE (mad cow disease) 42,
    90–91, 207
Bulgarians 38, 193, 244, 245, 247
Butler, R. A. (Rab) 250
Byrne Nason, Geraldine 7

C&C Group 124–5
Callinan, John 27, 33, 47, 53, 67, 72,
    184, 354, 361, 362, 367, 370, 371
Cameron, David 5–6, 8, 9, 33,
    166–7, 217; attempts to get EU
    concessions 10, 33–4; and
    Kenny 9–10, 12, 13, 33–4, 51;
    and the referendum 5–6, 12,
    13, 23–4; resignation 24
Campbell, Shane 257
Canada, Comprehensive and
    Economic Trade Agreement
    41, 336
cancer research 314–15
capital gains tax 222–3
Carbery Group 109–10
Carlsson, Carolin Blanco 191–2
Carney, Mark 26
Case, Simon 327, 354
Castletownbere Co-Op 153
cattle 84–5, 207; beef industry see
    beef industry; BSE 42, 90–91,
    207; dairy cows 88, 113, 122–3;
    foot and mouth disease 42, 92,
    177, 180, 207

Cavan 40
Celtic Interconnector 212
Central Bank of Ireland 27, 30,
    306, 308; Macro-Financial
    Review 309
Centre for Cross Border Studies
    256, 257
Chartered Accountants Ireland
    222, 223
Cheddar 107–8, 109, 110–11,
    112, 119
cheese 107–12, 119
Cheltenham Festival 2017 213
child benefit payments 10
China 102, 103, 128
Chinatown, London 114
citizenship 233–4; 1935 Irish
    Nationality and Citizenship
    Act 238, 240–41; 1956
    Nationality and Citizenship
    Act 241; rights 162, 241,
    245–6, 249–50, 345, 349, 351,
    357, 373; 'Safeguarding the
    Position of EU Citizens
    Living in the UK and UK
    Nationals Living in the EU'
    249; and special status for
    Northern Ireland 279–82
civil law 263
Cooperation and Working
    Together (CAWT) 253–5
Coakley, John 272
Colmcille Heritage Centre,
    Letterkenny 5
Colmcille Winter School 5

Combilift 217–18, 229

Common Agriculture Policy (CAP) 89; and Norway 41; payments 44, 113, 275; reforms 90

Common Fisheries Policy (CFP) 44–5, 138, 140, 142, 146, 149, 154–5, 156, 331

Common Transit Convention 201

Common Travel Area (CTA) 30, 58, 67, 72, 165, 236–8, 242–51, 332, 335, 348, 351, 373, 378; and the EAW network 261–3; and social welfare/pension entitlement 245–6, 258–60

Commonwealth Immigrants Act (1962) 240, 241

Community Plant Variety Office 226

Comprehensive and Economic Trade Agreement (CETA) 336

Confederation of British Industry (CBI) 9

Conservative Party 34, 51, 328; 2017 general election 297, 321, 322; 2017 Manifesto 275–6, 328; Conference, Birmingham 69–70; DUP Confidence and Supply deal 328–30

Contingency Plan 28–31

Corbyn, Jeremy 34, 322, 329

COREPER meeting 296

Cork 44, 111, 202, 255; University Hospital 134

corporate tax 54–5

Corrib Gas 210

Costello, Roisin 211

Council of the European Union 48

Country Crest 126

Coveney, Simon 281–2, 329–30, 333, 351, 355, 361, 363, 364, 367, 369

Cox, Jo 15

Cox, Pat 290–91

Crabb, Stephen 34

Creed, Michael 74, 99, 118, 120, 141, 155, 156

Creutzfeldt Jakob disease (CJD) 91

Cronin, Donie 252

Crowley, Norman 319–20

Crowley Carbon 319–20

Crumlin, Our Lady's Hospital 255

Cubic Telecom 317

Cullen, Barry 114, 115–16

Cunliffe, Jon 7

Curran, Dermot 27

currency hedging 21–2

Curtice, John 14

customs control 7, 79, 195–208; at airports 202; and ANPR technology 196, 200, 203–5; and ATA Carnets 200–201; Norway–Sweden border model 79, 190, 191–3, 195, 202; officers 202; Union Customs Code 199, 205, 206

customs union 40, 41, 46, 72, 159, 163–4, 167–9, 177, 185, 323, 327; and border 348–56, 360–81

Daily Express 62
Daily Mail 158
Daily Telegraph 61, 139, 331, 358
dairy industry: cheese 107–12,
    119; dairy cows 88, 113, 122–3;
    milk *see* milk; United Dairy
    Farmers (UDF) 105
Dairygold 110
Daly, Edward 265
Daly, Tom 253, 256
D'Arcy, Gabriel 101–3, 107
data protection 224, 314
Davidson, Ruth 322
Davis, David 47, 51, 56–9, 66,
    273, 293, 300, 321, 326–7, 353–4,
    357, 367, 376
Davos 166
Dawn Farms 126–8
Dawn Meats 92
Day, Catherine 173, 342
de Freitas, Geoffrey 236
Deane, Émer 170, 354
Democratic Unionist Party
    (DUP) 36, 75, 177–8, 277–8,
    281, 291, 323–4, 326, 333, 379,
    380, 381; Confidence and
    Supply deal with Tories
    328–30; and Sinn Féin 60, 273,
    277; and 'Dialogue on Ireland/
    Northern Ireland', Task Force
    working document 349;
    reaction to the 'No
    Divergence' draft text of
    2 December 366–73
Denmark 9, 112, 141, 232, 310, 343
Derry Journal 203

Dervla 136–7
DexEU (Department for Exiting
    the European Union) 46–7,
    297, 298, 334
Diageo 122
'Dialogue on Ireland/Northern
    Ireland', Task Force working
    document 348–53; sixth bullet
    point 348–51, 354, 355, 359
diplomatic service 27
DNA records 262
Dodds, Diane 369
Dodds, Nigel 281, 334
Doherty, Enda 155
Doherty, Frank 144–5
Donaldson, Jeffrey 379
Donegal Creameries 105
Donnelly, Stephen 377
Donohoe, Marina 318
Dorrell, Stephen 91
Doyle, Andrew 74
Doyle, Kevin 31
Draft Negotiating Guidelines
    283, 288, 294; and Gibraltar
    295; Irish paragraph and unity
    clause 283–7, 288–9, 294–302
    see also Negotiating Guidelines
Draft Withdrawal Agreement 378,
    379, 380; Option A 377, 379,
    380; Option B 377, 379, 380;
    Option C 377, 379, 380
Dublin: Cattle Market 86–7, 88;
    Docklands 307; Government
    Buildings 2–3; paediatric
    hospital 255; South 44; transit
    through 201, 202

Dublin Corporation 86
Dubliner cheese 110
duck 114–17
Duffy, Niall 144, 153–4, 157
Duncan Smith, Iain 10
Dungiven 203
Durkan, Mark 289–90, 292–4, 300

East Germany 290, 291, 292
Economic and Social Research Institute (ESRI) 304, 381
Economic Community of West African States (ECOWAS) 103
Economist 34–5
economy: and foreign direct investment in Europe 304; FTSE 100 Index 26; interdependency of the British and Irish economies 9; Ireland's exposure to economic/trade effects of Brexit 40–45, 69, 84–6, 92–100, 102–7, 117–29, 199–206, 342–3; Irish economic boom 83; Irish economic recovery from property crash and EU–IMF bailout 20; Irish share prices 26, 32; the pound see sterling; and tax see tax
education 309; higher 311–12 see also universities
electricity 45, 210, 212
Elizabeth II, Queen's Speech 328

Emmental cheese 110
employment rights 225, 226, 260
energy: EU Energy Union rules 211; interconnections 211–12; Irish ties to UK in 40, 45, 209, 210–13; natural gas see gas, natural; single electricity market 45, 210, 211
Engineering and Physical Sciences Research Council 313
Enterprise Ireland 27, 29, 228, 318
European and Mediterranean Horse Racing Federation 213
European Arrest Warrant (EAW) 58, 261–3
European Aviation Safety Agency (EASA) 340
European Banking Authority (EBA) 309, 310–11
European Central Bank (ECB) 27, 30, 279
European Chemical Agency (ECHA) 226–7, 230
European Commission 48–9, 54–5, 61, 73, 74, 88, 90, 95, 168, 172, 177, 179, 180–82, 183–4, 212, 231, 246, 248, 284, 328, 334–5; 'Brexit and the border between Ireland and the UK' 324–6; Brexit Task Force see Task Force (TF50); and the Common Travel Area 244–5, 246, 248; and the fishing industry 141–2, 147–8, 149, 150; Northern Ireland Task

European Commission – *cont.*
Force 270; research directorate
313–14; room 201, Brussels
169–70, 172, 175, 178, 180, 246,
283; SECEM software 63
European Council 48, 61, 283–7,
295–6, 297, 299–301
European Court of Justice (ECJ)
70, 164, 212, 225, 249, 262, 263,
279, 332, 379
European Economic Area
(EEA) 40
European Economic Community
(EEC) 40, 88–9, 141, 142, 153,
242; and New Zealand 97
European Financial Stabilisation
Mechanism (EFSM) 66
European Fisheries Alliance
(EFA) 155, 171
European Free Trade Association
(EFTA) 40
European Investment Bank
(EIB) 212, 213, 312
European Maritime Safety
Agency (EMSA) 226
European Medicines Agency
(EMA) 309–10
European Movement Ireland
(EMI) 4, 171
European Parliament 48, 149
European Peoples Party (EPP) 5
European Research Council 314
European Securities and Markets
Authority (ESMA) 308
European Union: agencies 226;
Article 50 *see* Article 50 of the

EU Treaty; 'associative'
relationship with 168–9;
Audio-Visual and Media
Services Directive 340; Balance
of Payments facility 66;
Canada's trade agreement with
41, 336; citizens' rights in UK
162; cohesion policy 252–3;
Common Agriculture Policy *see*
Common Agriculture Policy;
common external tariff 167–8,
338–9; Common Fisheries
Policy 44–5, 138, 140, 142, 146,
149, 154–5, 156; cross-border
health project funding 252–6;
customs union *see* customs
union; Draft Negotiating
Guidelines *see* Draft
Negotiating Guidelines;
Energy Union rules 211;
'ever-closer union' 10; Fiscal
Compact 6; and the four
freedoms 9, 34, 41, 161;
freedom of establishment rules
222; healthcare workers
registering with NHS 331; Irish
funding/loans 30, 61, 66, 67,
252–6, 257, 315 *see also* Interreg
funds; Irish presidency 7;
membership referendum *see*
referendum on EU
membership; migrants to UK
9, 33, 38; and the Northern
Ireland peace process 45, 79,
174, 182, 325–6, 342–3 *see also*
Good Friday Agreement;

Northern Ireland 'win-win' involvement 268; and Norway 40–41, 190; PEACE programmes *see* PEACE programmes; refugee crisis 8; reputation 8; Security of Gas Supply Regulation 210; sherpa meetings 32–3; single market *see* single market; Special EU Programmes Body 268–9; subsidies 44, 89–91, 113, 126; summit, 9 March 2017, Brussels 186–8; summit, 22 June 2017, Brussels 310; summit of EU leaders following referendum 32–3; trade agreements 41; Unitary Patent 225

'EU–UK Digest: Reporting from Missions, 6–10 November 2017', leaking of 357–9

Eustice, George 139–40, 141, 146, 151

Exclusive Economic Zone (EEZ) 151–2

Export Trade Council 74

exports: beef 87, 88, 89–90; biopharmaceutical 229–30; British fish exports to EU 152; customs clearance *see* customs control; German 40; growth of food and drink exports 117; Irish Exporters Association 219, 220, 222; and Irish exposure to effects of Brexit 40–44, 93–4, 117–29, 199–206, 342–3; Irish GDP proportion of 40; livestock 86–7, 197; mushroom 21; refunds/ subsidies 89–91; by SMEs 7; and sterling 32, 117; and the Task Force 172

Express Dairies 109

Farage, Nigel 16, 55, 158–9

farming *see* agriculture/farming

Farming Independent 86

Faroe Islands 147, 148

Farron, Tim 329

Faull, Jonathan 28

Ferguson, Mark 313

Fianna Fáil 12, 171

financial services 305–7 *see also* banks

Financial Times 151, 193, 297, 300, 307

fingerprint records 262

Finland 228, 232

Finsbury Park Mosque terror attack 326

Fishing for Leave 140, 146

fishing industry 130–57; EU Common Fisheries Policy 44–5, 138, 140, 142, 146, 149, 154–5, 156, 331; and European Commission negotiations with Coastal States 147–8; European Fisheries Alliance 155, 171; exports to EU 152; fish stocks 135–6, 148–9, 157; fishing quotas *see* fishing quotas; and identity of fish in British waters 145–6; Ireland's

fishing industry – *cont.*
fishing fleet 44–5; Ireland's
post-Brexit priorities 149–50;
London Convention 331;
Maximum Sustainable Yield
(MSY) 149; and the NEAFC
147–8; prawn sector 130–31,
135–6, 137, 150, 153; pro-Leave
fishermen 140, 147
fishing quotas 138, 142, 150, 152;
Hague Preferences 143,
149–50; Relative Stability
142–3, 152–5; Total Allowable
Catch (TAC) 142
Fitzgerald, Frances 50, 57, 58, 66,
358–9
FitzGerald, Garret 143
Flanagan, Charlie 9, 12, 24, 53,
66, 74, 75, 81, 161–2, 167, 185,
324
Flanagan, T. J. 107, 112
food and drinks sector: and
animal diseases and health
scandals 42, 90–91, 92, 177,
180, 207 *see also* foot and mouth
disease; export growth 117;
farming *see* agriculture/
farming; food production
83–100; geographical spread of
SME food producers 121;
industries *see* beef industry;
beer industry; dairy industry;
fishing industry; meat
industry; Ireland's exposure to
effects of Brexit 21–2, 38–9,
44–5, 84–6, 92–100, 102–7,

117–29, 324–6; mushrooms
21–2, 37–9; standards *see* food
standards
Food Drink Ireland (FDI) 120
Food Safety Authority of Ireland
(FSAI) 197
food standards 42, 100, 120, 175,
197; Origin Green label 93;
Red Tractor label 93
food supplements 231–2
foot and mouth disease 42, 92,
177, 180, 207
Foreign and Commonwealth
Office (FCO) 25–6; Locarno
Suite meetings 70–72, 76, 180
forklift trucks 217–18, 229
Foster, Arlene 32, 36, 276, 277,
278, 367, 368, 372, 379
Fox, Liam 46, 51, 57, 161
Foy, John 36–7
Framework Programme 7
funding 315
France 33, 91, 96, 112, 124, 142,
145, 150, 151, 153, 155, 175, 211,
212, 214, 216, 228, 231, 232, 310,
319, 339, 344
Frankfurter Allgemeine 321
Fraser, Martin 16, 23, 70, 71–2,
362, 364
Fraunhofer-Gesellschaft 313
FTSE 100 Index 26
Funston, Ken 271
Funston, Ronnie 271

Gage, Conolly Hugh 235
Garda Síochána 262

Garry, John 272
gas, natural 209, 210; LNG 213
Gas Networks Ireland 210
General Affairs Council
    (GAC) 15
Germany 40, 71, 94, 95, 111, 112,
    228, 231, 232, 310, 318, 319; East
    Germany 290, 291, 292
Gibraltar 295–6
Gillespie, Kathleen 265, 267–8,
    270–71
Gillespie, Patsy 265, 267
Glanbia 103–4, 108, 110, 118–19,
    121–3
Glaslough 113
Godfrey, Jeremy 309
Good Friday Agreement 36, 45,
    67–9, 75, 79, 100, 183, 272, 279,
    286, 289, 327–8, 332, 335, 346, 378,
    379; Belfast Agreement 379; and
    Contingency Plan 30; and
    'Dialogue on Ireland/Northern
    Ireland', Task Force working
    document 348, 351–2; and
    'Guiding Principles' 353; SDLP
    interpretation 292, 293; and
    SEUPB 268–9; and a United
    Ireland 289–302; unity clause
    and German reunification
    parallel 290–92
Goodman, Larry 89–90
Gouldsbury, Conor 67
Gove, Michael 10, 24, 34, 293,
    323, 331, 376, 377
Grassick, Michael 214
Grayling, Chris 10

Great Repeal Bill 216, 224, 328, 330
Greece 8, 245
Grenfell Tower fire 326
'Guiding Principles', September
    response to UK's August
    Ireland papers 353
Gull, Operation 243–4
Gundersen, Maritha 190

Hague Preferences 143, 149–50
Hahn, Johannes 269
Hallinan, P. J. 207–8
Hammond, Philip 9, 12–13, 225,
    323, 330–31
Hannan, Daniel 378
Harris, Simon 35–6
Haughey, Charles 90, 290
Hayburn, Colin 303–4
Hayes, Caitlin (Caitlín Ní Aodha)
    136–7, 139, 143, 157
Hayes, Michael 130–32, 133–4,
    135, 136
Hayward, Katy 274–5
healthcare 252–6; Cooperation
    and Working Together 253–5;
    EU workers registering with
    NHS 331
Healy, Cormac 85, 92
Heatrick, Nigel 112–13
Heinrichs, Klaus 316–17
Heywood, Sir Jeremy 47, 70,
    71–2, 362
Higgins, Michael D. 289
Higgins, Paula 211
Hill, Fiona 51, 330
Hill, James 96–7, 98

Hoey, Kate 378
Hoey, Michael 126
Hogan, Phil 28, 62, 82, 176, 178, 183, 184–5, 324, 326, 337
Høiberget, Kristen 193, 194
Hollande, François 212
homelessness 309
Horizon 2020 programme 29, 311–12, 313, 316
horse racing 213–16
Horse Racing Ireland (HRI) 213, 214, 216
House of Commons Select Committee on Exiting the EU 292–3
House of Lords Select Committee on the European Union 76–80, 125, 140, 145, 151, 244, 257, 261, 275
house prices 308–9
Howard, Michael 295
Hume, Hugh 261
Hume, John 268, 272–3

I Once Knew a Girl 267
IBEC 4, 22–3, 171, 176
Iceland 147, 148
ICES (the International Council for the Exploration of the Sea) 148
IDA Ireland 27
IFS 2020 Action Plan 306
immigration/migration 233–51; and the 1935 Irish Aliens Act 241; and citizenship 233–4, 245–6; and the Common

Travel Area *see* Common Travel Area (CTA); Commonwealth Immigrants Act (1962) 240, 241; EU migrants to UK 9, 33, 38; illegal immigrants 243; immigration controls 238–42, 244, 247–51; migrant labourers 38, 276
Immigration Law Practitioners Association (ILPA) 244
imports 40, 42–3, 93, 151, 218, 221, 334; with ATA Carnets 200–201; Temporary Importation Procedures 200–201; VAT on 227
intellectual property 225
Industrial Development Authority 89
International Road Transport Union 201
Interreg funds 30, 252–3, 254, 257, 270, 273
InterTradeIreland 275
Ireland: 1916 Proclamation 186; Act of Union 233; All-Island Civic Dialogue 74–6, 277; Brexit and a United Ireland 289–302; Brexit Cabinet Committee 53; citizenship *see* citizenship; civil service 74, 180; Common Travel Area *see* Common Travel Area (CTA); Constitution of (1937) 290; Contingency Plan 28–31; demographics of Irish

community in Britain 11; Department of Agriculture, Food and the Marine 42, 118, 176; Department of Foreign Affairs 4, 23, 27, 30, 53–4, 291, 298–9; Department of Social Protection 258; diplomatic service 27; economy *see* economy; EEC membership 40, 88, 141, 153; energy *see* energy; EU funding/loans 30, 61, 66, 67, 252–6, 257, 315 *see also* Interreg funds; EU presidency 7; European Council engagement over Brexit 283–7; exports *see* exports; food and drinks sector *see* food and drinks sector; Free State of *see* Irish Free State; Good Friday Agreement *see* Good Friday Agreement; IFS 2020 Action Plan 306; immigration *see* immigration/migration; imports 42–3; North–South border *see* border, Irish; North–South trade 44, 99–100, 102–7, 115–17, 122–3, 177; Northern peace process 7, 45, 72, 79, 174, 182, 325–6, 342–3; opportunities with Brexit 303–20; PEACE programme *see* PEACE programmes; pharmaceutical/chemicals sector *see* pharmaceutical and chemicals sector; Revenue Commissioners *see* Revenue Commissioners; services sector 43; status quo with UK 80, 85–6, 176, 179, 198, 233, 239, 271; Taoiseach's Department 8, 26–7, 53, 298; tax *see* tax; trade with UK 7, 40, 42–3, 69, 79, 84, 93–4, 116, 117, 194–5, 199, 318; as weak link in EU chain 342

Ireland Act (1949) 240
Irish Aliens Act (1935) 241
Irish Central Border Area Network (ICBAN) 257
Irish Congress of Trade Unions (ICTU) 4, 226
Irish Cooperative Organisation Society (ICOS) 103–4, 107, 171, 176
Irish Embassy, London 50
Irish Exporters Association 219, 220, 222
Irish Farmers Association (IFA) 36, 39, 63, 95, 98, 107, 171; Position Paper (March 2017) 85
Irish Feed and Grain Association 171
Irish Free State 233–4, 235, 236, 238; 1925 Constitution 238
Irish Independent 31, 76
Irish Nationality and Citizenship Act 238, 240–41
Irish Post 11
Irish Republican Army (IRA) 60, 263–5
Irish Times 32, 56, 82, 90, 173, 184

Irish World 11
Italy 91, 94, 136, 137, 228, 310, 319

Jay, Michael Hastings, Lord Jay
    of Ewelme 76, 77, 80–81
Johnson, Boris 16, 24, 34, 46, 51,
    57, 161, 347, 357
Johnson, Michael 339
Joint Report from the Negotiators of
    the European Union and the
    United Kingdom Government
    373–6, 377, 379, 381; Paragraph
    49 373–6; Paragraph 50
    374–5, 379
Jones, Carwyn 329
J. P. Morgan 306–7
Juncker, Jean-Claude 19, 49,
    61, 183–4, 302, 345, 363, 364,
    367, 370; Downing Street
    dinner 321

Kavanagh, Brian 213, 215, 216
Keegan, Brian 222
Kelleher, Declan 8, 19, 33, 64,
    170, 184, 300, 354, 361, 367
Kennelly, Mark 16
Kenny, Enda 4, 8–9, 14, 15–16,
    20, 30, 31, 75, 80, 174, 184–5,
    190, 277, 289, 350; at Bratislava
    65; and Cameron 9–10, 12, 13,
    33–4, 51; and corporate tax
    54–5; and Davis 56–9; at EU
    summit following referendum
    32–3; and the fishing industry
    138, 155; and Foster/the DUP
    36; and freedom of movement

34; IIEA address 186; and
    May 50, 51–3, 166–7, 186–8,
    287–8, 298–9; statement
    following Leave vote 23, 26;
    and unity clause of Good
    Friday Agreement and Draft
    Negotiating Guidelines
    290–91, 292, 293–4, 298–9,
    301–2
Kepak 92, 93
Kerr, John 48
Kerry Group 119
Kerrygold 108, 111–12
Kershaw, Anthony 251
Kershaw, Kevin 131, 132–4, 135
Kilkenny 43
Killashandra 104
Killybegs Fishermen's
    Organisation (KFO) 148,
    155, 171
Kinsale gas fields 210
Kinsella, Kevin 86, 88, 98–9, 100
Kohl, Helmut 292
Kuenssberg, Laura 158–60
Kuster, Matthias 189, 190, 191

Labour Party 14
LacPatrick 102–4, 105, 107, 113
Laffan, Brigid 141
Lakeland Dairies 103–4, 105,
    110, 171
lamb *see* sheep/lamb
Lammy, David 14
Lancet 313
language 318, 319
Laois 43

Lascurettes, Catherine 106, 108, 109
Law Society of Ireland 339
Lawler, Mark 314–15
Leadsom, Andrea 141
Leave campaign 15, 33, 184
Leheny, Seamus 203–4, 205
Leprêtre, Olivier 151
Leprino Foods 119
Leyland, Andy 220–22, 226–7, 231–2
Liberal Democrats 7, 322
Libertarian Alliance 323
Lidington, David 15, 31
Lifes2Good 220–22, 226–7, 231–2
Lilley, Peter 293
Limerick 43
Lisbon Treaty 8, 12, 237, 242, 279, 377; Article 50 *see* Article 50 of the EU Treaty
Lithuanians 38, 189, 260
livestock exports 86–7, 197
Lloyds 307
localization 318
London, the City 304–5
London Convention 331
Longford 43
Lough Egish 171
Luxembourg 15, 16, 31, 124, 141, 242, 302, 305, 307; Court *see* European Court of Justice
Lynch, Kevin 203

McCabe, Maurice 358–9
McCarthy, Tara 118

McCord, Raymond 292
McCoy, Danny 22–3
McCullough, Elizabeth 67
McDaid, Michael 264
McDonald, Mary Lou 74
McDonald's 92
McDowell, Andrew 212–13
McGuinness, Martin 32, 75, 265, 276; resignation 278
McKay, Susan 256–7
McKeever, Simon 219–20, 222
mackerel 148
McMahon, Seamus 123–4
Macron, Emmanuel 340
MacSharry, Ray 90–91
MacSweeney, Dan 110–12
McVicar, Martin 217–18, 229
Mair, Thomas 15
Mallon, Seamus 60
Mallusk, Baileys plant 121–3
Mandelson, Peter 17–18, 60
Manorhamilton 256–7
mapping exercise, assessment of risk to North–South cooperation 346, 351–3, 354
Marr, Andrew 162, 376
Martin, Micheál 12, 173
Martin, Stephen 208, 261
Matthews, Alan 96, 100
May, Theresa 46, 47, 50–51, 56, 58, 59, 158, 162–3, 174, 181, 190, 225, 276, 302, 321, 323, 379, 381; 2017 general election 297, 321, 322; Article 50 letter to European Council 283, 287–8; Article 50 triggering principles

May, Theresa – *cont.*
236, 288; Birmingham speech
69–70, 71; at Brussels 9 March
2017 Summit 186–8; caution
51–2; Juncker on 321; and
Kenny 50, 51–3, 166–7, 186–8,
287–8, 298–9; Lancaster House
speech 164–6, 236; and
negotiations leading to the *Joint
Report from the Negotiations of the
European Union and the United
Kingdom Government* 345, 346,
349, 350, 354, 355, 358, 359, 362,
363, 367, 370, 372, 373, 375; and
the Queen's Speech 328; and
Rogers 158, 160; 22 September
Florence speech 347; and
Varadkar 329; White Paper on
Brexit 167–8; World Economic
Forum speech 166
meat industry: beef *see* beef
industry; duck 114–17; lamb
96–100; New Zealand 96–9;
pork 86, 100
Meat Industry Ireland 171
medical technologies sector
230–31
Merkel, Angela 9, 31, 34, 67, 302,
321, 340; and Northern
Ireland 54
Messina, Jim 17
Middletown 113
migration *see* immigration/
migration
milk 102–7, 113, 118–19; and
Baileys 121–3; liquid milk

production 105–6, 122–3;
Northern Ireland milk 102–7,
122–3; powdered 103, 107, 108,
118; quota regulations 105, 110;
Republic's liquid milk 106
Milk Marketing Board 104
mobile-phone roaming charges
35, 257–8
Moffat 209, 210
Mohamed, Abdelbaky 130–35
Mohamed, Wael 130, 131, 133, 135
Molloy, Eamonn 53
Moloney, Niamh 305–6
Monaghan 40; General
Hospital 255
Montgomery, Rory 4, 6–8,
53, 67
Moran, Matt 230
Morgan, Shan 2, 25
Morgenroth, Edgar 5, 6, 339
Mulhall, Dan 8, 10–11, 17, 70, 78
Murphy, Dara 13–14, 15–16, 18,
31, 35–6, 46, 57, 66, 67, 80, 187
Murphy, Eoghan 306, 307, 308
Murphy, Patrick 138
Murrin, Larry 126–9
mushrooms 21–2, 37–9

National Ploughing
Championships 200–201
Naughten, Denis 212
NEAFC (North East Atlantic
Fisheries Commission) 147–8
Negotiating Guidelines 234, 301,
376, 380 *see also* Draft
Negotiating Guidelines

Netherlands 9, 23, 112, 187, 209, 228, 232, 318, 343
New Zealand 96–9; and the EEC 97; lamb 96–9
Newcastle 16, 18
Nice, Treaty of 8
Nicholson, Jim 268, 281
'No Divergence' draft text of 2 December, 364–73
Nolan, John 145, 153
non-tariff barriers 174, 228, 338–9 see also customs control
Noonan, Michael 32, 55, 80, 306
Nordby 191, 192
North Derry Republican Group 203
North East Atlantic Fisheries Commission (NEAFC) 147–8
North South Ministerial Council 36, 74, 277, 330, 352
North–South Implementation Bodies 351–2
Northern Ireland 272–82; and the All-Island Civic Dialogue 74–6, 277; Confederation of British Industry 275; EU special status proposals 278–82; Executive 28, 52, 59–60, 187, 270, 273, 274, 278, 279, 329, 330, 346, 377; and Merkel 54; milk 102–7, 122–3; money under Tory–DUP deal for 328–9; North–South border see border, Irish; North–South trade 44, 99–100, 102–7, 115–17, 122–3, 177; peace process 7, 45, 72, 79, 174, 182, 325–6, 342–3 see also Good Friday Agreement; PEACE programme see PEACE programmes; referendum turnout and vote 272, 273; SDLP 279, 292, 293; vulnerability following Leave vote 272–6
Northern Ireland Assembly 60, 187, 273, 276, 278, 279, 377
Northern Ireland Food and Drink Association (NIFDA) 44, 275
Northern Ireland Law Centre 243
Northern Ireland Task Force (European Commission) 270
Northern Trust 307
Norway 40–41, 79, 141, 147, 148, 157, 189–92, 209; Norway–Sweden border 79, 190, 191–3, 195
Nursing and Midwifery Council 331

Obermaier, Nina 170, 182, 185, 327, 354
O'Briain, Tadhg 173–4
O'Brien, Declan 86–7
Ó Cinnéide, Lorcán 139, 141, 144, 156
O'Donnell, Jack 16, 20
O'Donoghue, Sean 148
Offaly 43
Office of Public Works (OPW) 206

O'Kane, Annemarie 259–60
O'Kelly, Brendan 142
O'Mahony, Jane 141
Open Skies agreement 340
Operation Gull 243–4
O'Reilly, Gerry 21–2, 37–8, 39
O'Reilly, Mary 38
Origin Green label 93
Ornua Foods 108, 171
Osborne, George 17
O'Sullivan, David 342
O'Toole, Fintan 90

Paisley, Ian 268
Paisley, Ian, Jr 291, 323–4, 334
Patel, Priti 10
patenting 225
Patterson, Owen 377
Peace Bridge 269
PEACE programmes 268–70;
    funding 30, 61, 254, 257;
    PEACE I 268; PEACE II
    61; PEACE IV 268
pensions 245, 258, 259, 260; triple
    lock 328
pharmaceutical and chemicals
    sector 43, 44, 309–10;
    biopharmaceuticals 229–30
pigs 86, 100
Poland/Poles 38, 155, 190, 195,
    232, 244, 319
police cooperation 72
Police Service of Northern
    Ireland (PSNI) 203–4, 208,
    243, 260–62
polls 1, 15, 16

Portugal 91
powdered milk 103, 107,
    108, 118
prawns 130–31, 135–6, 137, 150, 153
product standards 41–2, 93, 100;
    food see food standards
Prüm Convention 262
Pryce, Richard 307
Punch, Eddie 93–4
Purcell, Feargal 16, 24
PwC Ireland 120

QBE 307
Queen's Speech 328
Queen's University Belfast 314–15

Raab, Dominic 158, 293
racehorses 213–16
radiotherapy 254–5
REACH directive 226–7, 230
Red Tractor label 93
Rees-Mogg, Jacob 10, 359–60
referendum on EU membership
    1–6, 10–18, 19–20, 21–3; and
    Cameron 5–6, 12, 13, 23–4;
    Irish government
    communications plan for a
    Leave vote 23; Leave
    campaign 15, 33, 184;
    Northern Ireland turnout and
    vote 272, 273; polls 1, 15, 16;
    Remain campaign 2, 10,
    13–14; and UK Rep 1–2, 24–6
refugee crisis 8
Relative Stability 142–3, 152–5
Remain campaign 2, 10, 13–14

research 311–15
Revenue Commissioners 167,
    194, 197–8, 205, 206; 'Brexit
    and the Consequences for
    Irish Customs' report 198–203
Riekeles, Georg 67
Riso, Stéphanie 67
Robbins, Olly 47, 72, 327, 345,
    346, 354–5, 360–61, 362, 367,
    370, 371, 377
Rogers, Sir Ivan 2, 8, 18–19, 20,
    24–5, 47, 64, 158–61; and
    Kuenssberg's report 158–60;
    resignation 160, 161, 164
Roll of Irish Solicitors 339
Romanians 38, 244
Rooker, Lord Jeffrey William 145
Roscommon 43, 44
Rosslare 201
Royal Society 313
RSA 307
Rudd, Amber 17, 347
Rudd, Roland 17
Ryan, Bernard 233, 240, 241, 250
Ryan, Paul 307
Ryanair 340

'Safeguarding the Position of EU
    Citizens Living in the UK
    and UK Nationals Living in
    the EU' 249
St Andrew's Agreement 75, 270
salmon 152, 190
San Marino 41
sanitary and phyto-sanitary rules
    42, 176–80, 197, 205–6, 325

Sarkozy, Nicolas 55
Scandinavia 91, 191
Schengen Area 237, 242, 244–5
Schengen Information System
    (SIS II) 262
Scholar, Tom 7–8
Science Foundation Ireland
    (SFI) 313
Scottish Fishermen's Federation
    (SFF) 140
Scottish National Party (SNP)
    322
SDLP 279, 292, 293
SECEM (software) 63
security cooperation 72
Sedwill, Mark 51
Seeuws, Didier 48, 68
Sellal, Pierre 300
Selmayr, Martin 19, 367
Sepinuck, Teya 266–7, 268, 269
services sector 43
Shaban, Attiy Ahmed 132–3, 135
Shanahan, Martin 305, 306
Shannon, LNG terminal 213
Shawcross, H. W. 239
sheep/lamb: live exports 86;
    meat production 96–100
Silver Hill Farm 114–17
Simms, Nicholas 104
Singapore model 225–6
single electricity market (SEM)
    45, 210, 211
single market 9, 20, 40–42, 100,
    159, 163, 232, 323, 327;
    conditions for membership 34,
    41; and product standards 41–2

Sinn Féin 60, 172, 208, 276, 278, 279–80, 291; 'The Case for the North to Achieve Designated Special Status in the EU' 278; and the DUP 60, 273, 277; 'Securing Special Status for the North Within the EU' 279

Sinnamon, Julie 228

Skainos Project 269

Small Firms Association (SFA) 125, 218–19, 225

SMEs (small- and medium-sized enterprises) 7, 121, 126–7, 218, 336

Smith, Julian 366, 371

social welfare: and the Common Travel Area 245–6, 258–60; cross-border 258–60; restrictions 9–10

solicitors 339–40

Solvency II 307

Spain 91, 142, 144, 190, 228, 310; and Gibraltar 295

Special EU Programmes Body (SEUPB) 268–9

sterling: and exports 32, 117; fall after Leave vote/Brexit 22, 26, 32, 84–5, 93, 117, 120, 124, 224; and the mushroom trade 21–2, 38–9

stock market 4; Irish share prices 26, 32

straddle carrier machines 217

students 311

Sun, the 358

Sunday Times 307

Sunderland 16, 18, 22

supply chains 7, 83–4, 85, 99, 102, 104, 219–20

Sweden 190, 193, 310; Norway–Sweden border 79, 190, 191–3, 195

Switzerland 316

Taillon, Ruth 256

tariffs 97, 120, 152, 168, 229; common external tariff 167–8, 334–5; WTO 111, 211, 214, 217–18, 221

Task Force (TF50) 28, 65, 107, 167, 170–80, 182, 246, 283, 332, 346, 348, 352, 353, 354, 355, 376, 377, 378, 379, 380

tax: capital gains 222–3; and company relocations 222–3; corporate 54–5; VAT 218, 227

Teagasc farm management survey 95, 97

textiles 43

Thatcher, Margaret 104

Theatre of Witness 266–8, 269, 270–71

'30 November draft text', ensuing negotiations on 'no regulatory divergence' verus 'continued regulatory alignment' 360–66

Thompson, Ken 307

Tim Parry Johnathan Ball Foundation for Peace 271

Times, The 326, 333

Timmermans, Frans 28, 61

Timothy, Nick 330, 358

Tipperary 43

Tipperary Co-Op 110
TIR convention 201
Tit Bonhomme, MFV 130–35, 136
Tory Party *see* Conservative Party
Town of Monaghan Co-op 105
trade: agricultural *see* agriculture/
    farming; Anglo-Irish Free
    Trade Agreement 104; Brexit
    and new agreements 42, 46, 94,
    98–9; Brexit and North–South
    trade 44, 99–100, 102–7, 115–17,
    122–3, 177; customs control *see*
    customs control; and the
    customs union *see* customs
    control; EU trade agreements
    41; Export Trade Council 74;
    exports *see* exports; imports *see*
    imports; between Ireland and
    UK 7, 40, 42–3, 69, 79, 84,
    93–4, 116, 117, 194–5, 199, 318;
    Ireland's exposure to
    economic/trade effects of Brexit
    40–45, 69, 84–6, 92–100, 102–7,
    117–29, 199–206, 342–3; and
    localization 318; with New
    Zealand 96–9; non-tariff
    barriers 174, 228, 338–9 *see also*
    customs control; and the single
    market *see* single market; supply
    chains 7, 83–4, 85, 99, 102, 104,
    219–20; tariffs *see* tariffs; transit
    201–3, 218
Tranholm-Mikkelsen, Jeppe 48,
    68, 300
transit 201–3, 218
Trimble, David 60

Tripartite Agreement (TPA) on
    racehorses 214–15
Turkey 41, 193, 296
Tusk, Donald 283, 286, 295, 301,
    341, 359, 361, 364

UK Independence Party
    (UKIP) 5, 8, 140, 321
UKRep (UK Representation to
    the European Union) 1–2,
    24–6, 35, 47
Ulaanbaatar 54
Ulster Farmers Union 75, 275
Ulster Unionist Party (UUP)
    75, 281
Unified Patent Court 225
Union Customs Code (UCC)
    199, 205, 206, 325
Unitary Patent 225
United Dairy Farmers
    (UDF) 105
universities 311; research 312–16

Varadkar, Leo 281–2, 326, 329,
    333, 345, 349–50, 351, 355,
    359, 361, 364, 367, 369, 371,
    372, 380
VAT 218, 227
vehicle registration records 262
Villiers, Theresa 10, 274, 275,
    278–9, 289

Walker, Anne 263–6, 267–8,
    270–71
Walker, Robin 57
Ward, Tanya 263

Waterford 43, 44
Waterford Foods 118
We Carried Your Secrets 267
Wellcome Trust 313
Western Viking 144–5
Wethal, Tor 189–90
Weyand, Sabine 67, 327, 346, 354, 370, 371, 377
Whelan, Noel 173
Whittingdale, John 10
Wicklow 43, 44
Wilson, Sammy 281, 293, 322, 368

winter fuel allowance 328
Withers, Kay 354, 360
workers' rights 225, 226, 260
World Customs Organisation 199
World in Action 89–90
World Trade Organization (WTO): rules 41, 98, 107, 176, 334–5; tariffs 111, 211, 214, 217–18, 221

YouGov poll 16
Younger, Kenneth 235